The Sixth Man

The Sixth Man

A History of the NBA's Best Off the Bench

Łukasz Muniowski

McFarland & Company, Inc., Publishers
Jefferson, North Carolina

All photographs are from Steve Lipofsky, Lipofskyphoto.com

ISBN (print) 978-1-4766-8538-0
ISBN (ebook) 978-1-4766-4394-6

LIBRARY OF CONGRESS AND BRITISH LIBRARY
CATALOGUING DATA ARE AVAILABLE

Library of Congress Control Number 2021052799

Printed in the United States of America

*McFarland & Company, Inc., Publishers
Box 611, Jefferson, North Carolina 28640
www.mcfarlandpub.com*

For A.

Table of Contents

Preface

The idea for this book came to me when I was finishing up my previous one, also published by McFarland, about the history of the three-point shot in the NBA. Having surrounded myself with career narratives of professional basketball players for the last seven years, first for my PhD thesis, and then for the aforementioned book, I found myself torn between taking some time off from writing about the NBA (and basketball altogether) and producing one more book, about the league's unsung heroes, as it would require much less preparation but could turn out to be much more exhausting.

In fact, it did, as I have suffered mental fatigue somewhere along the way, but as much as I wanted to take some time off, I found being on the other side of sports writing too addictive. While in my PhD thesis I have attempted to deconstruct the career narratives of NBA superstars, trying to show how they were marketed in accordance with rather common heroic archetypes, here I have decided to do the same from an historical perspective and show "how things were" as accurately as possible. However, despite knowing about the narrative constraints imposed by the centrality of characters in these stories, I knew I eventually would succumb to certain forms of stereotypical thinking about how a sports book should be written, as well as how such stories are usually told. In order to free myself from this type of thinking, I have decided to narrow my focus and simply organize players into groups. There were obviously Streaky Shooters, but also Tough Guys, Redemption Stories or Career Sixth Men. The names kept piling up and the potential content was expanding, as almost every day a new name would pop into my head. Instead of allowing for a fuller picture, the ever-growing number of players started to create doubt that I was ever going to produce such a book.

This is where the deep understanding of the sixth man role came in handy, as I was able to convince myself that in this case less is more. A limited rotation is a natural thing for every team entering the postseason, so it was mandatory for me to sacrifice some players in the name of the greater

Philly's Bobby Jones was the first player in league history to win the Sixth Man of the Year Award (1985).

good. While I do not consider the players omitted from the book as mere footnotes and am truly in awe of anyone who has made an NBA team, let alone set foot on the court during an NBA game, there was just no avoiding relying on lineups that simply worked better together.

All that was left to do was collect the information about the players selected and use them as basis for a cohesive and, hopefully, interesting narrative. My greatest wish is that this book does not feel simply like a retelling of the same story, precisely by primarily placing the focus on the time the players have spent coming off the bench. For some of them it was just a few games, for others almost whole careers. Instead of focusing on what distinguished these stories from one another, I have decided to look for common ground, so that they could form a championship lineup. The result is this nine-chapter rotation that will hopefully enrich basketball scholarship and serve as a vital contribution, shedding light on something neglected, and often even feared, in professional and amateur sports alike: the bench.

Introduction

A regulated basketball game occurs when two teams, consisting of five players each, face each other on the court. It is good to have some reserves, but they are not always necessary for a game to take place. And in fact, in the early days of organized basketball, that was mostly the case, as an extra player meant extra costs for the organizers. Additional money needed to be put up for bringing to a game someone who would enter the court just in case, standing in for the injured starter. It was easy to distinguish between the starters and the reserves, as the former were clearly the supreme athletes. As noticed by Pat Riley, a Hall of Fame coach and himself an NBA reserve during his playing days, in 1984: "There was a time when you sent in a substitute and crossed your fingers, hoping he wouldn't hurt you too much. But the game has changed in the last couple of years. There's so much more talent now you can't afford a letdown when you go to your bench. It's important to have players who can go in and give you a lift."[1]

In the 1980s, 1990s and early 2000s starters played mostly huge minutes even during the regular season. Keeping the starters on the court simply guaranteed wins. Legendary players, like Larry Bird (38.4 career minutes per game) or Isiah Thomas (36.3 career minutes per game), whose careers could have been prolonged with load management, retired too early because of playing time. This is the luxury afforded to modern-day superstars thanks to deeper, better benches. The 2019 champions, the Toronto Raptors, are a prime example of what a solid bench can do for a superstar's career. Kawhi Leonard, traded from the Spurs, was coming off a quad injury that limited his performance to just nine games the season prior. To keep the player happy—Leonard was a free agent the next season—and healthy for the postseason, the Raptors limited his playing time, while putting bench players on the floor. In the regular season eight players—Pascal Siakam, Danny Green, Serge Ibaka, OG Anunoby, Fred VanVleet, Leonard, Norman Powell[2]—appeared in at least 60 games, playing at least 20 minutes per game. This allowed Leonard to play 39.1 minutes per contest in the 24 games the team needed to play in order to win the championship title. In the finals the Raptors used an eight-man rotation, with the eighth man, Norman Powell, playing 11 minutes per contest. The average number of minutes for the ninth and tenth player of that finals rotation—two for Patrick McCaw and 0.17 for Jeremy Lin—was the lowest by any NBA champion in the 2000s.[3]

With the best players becoming much more powerful, when it comes to them being able to join the teams of their liking and/or teaming up with whoever they want, like LeBron James and Chris Bosh joining Dwyane Wade in Miami or Anthony Davis and Paul George forcing their franchises to trade them to Los Angeles (to the Lakers and Clippers, respectively), it becomes understandable that teams focus more on bringing in 12 and not just five quality players. There is no better proof of that development than the August 23, 2020, game between the Raptors and the Nets. In Game Four of the first round the Raptors bench scored a league-record 100 points in the 150–122 win, clinching their team's progression to the next series. Coach Nick Nurse played all 12 of his players, 11 of them for at least ten minutes. Each bench player scored at least two points, while four scored in double figures—Norman Powell had 29, Serge Ibaka 27, Terrence Davis had 14 and Matt Thomas 12 points.

In professional sports, the bench carries mostly negative connotations. Being on the bench means not playing, hence an action contrary to that of a professional player, whose obligation is clearly to play. Players often feel that they are wasting their time and talents when not playing at least 30 minutes per game. With visible frustration they talk about being "glued" or "chained" to the bench. They are "banished" to the bench for not performing well enough. A benching may be considered a disciplinary action—when an athlete loses a starting spot, it may be either a sign of disrespect or a consequence of the disrespect shown to the rules of conduct set by authority figures (coaches or team executives). Things like showing up on time and not missing practice are important for chemistry building, because they help to convince role players that they are judged by the same criteria as the superstars.

However, benching does not always work. Marvin Barnes, one of the most talented and problematic professional basketball players of the 1970s, was reprimanded numerous times by his coaches by starting games on the bench. Nicknamed "Bad News," before one game for the ABA Spirits of St. Louis the power forward was talking to a lady throughout the warm-up, and his coach, sick of his antics, decided to move him to the bench. When Barnes eventually entered the court, he completely dominated the game, finishing with "40 points and 20-some rebounds."[4] The disciplinary action did not work, and Barnes continued to cause trouble, slowly descending into drug addiction. Following the NBA-ABA merger in 1976, he became a bench player and remains one of the best players to never fully realize their potential.

The bench still serves as a threat to the starters' well-being whenever they transgress or have a couple of bad games. By the turn of the century the player most disciplined by being forced to begin games on the bench, for either missing practice or being late to actual games, was Isiah Rider, then on the Portland Trail Blazers. One of the more curious reasons why he did not start a game was because he had to go to the bathroom and came back onto the court just in time for tipoff. Rider was benched in favor of journeyman Jim Jackson, then on his third team in two years. Jackson would eventually play for 12 teams in 14 years—an NBA record he shares with Tony Massenburg and Chucky Brown. Instead of "learning his lesson," Rider continued to cause even more trouble. When asked by a reported how he felt coming off the bench, Rider simply told him to "shut up." He was traded to the Atlanta Hawks in exchange for fellow shooting guard Steve Smith after three seasons in Oregon.[5]

While questionable as a disciplinary tool, it is even more doubtful to consider the bench as representative of the pecking order on a modern-day team, as it was viewed in the past. Pat Washington, the wife of Kermit Washington, the Los Angeles Lakers' 1973 first-round pick (fifth over-all), experienced the ostracism that comes with being *associated with* a reserve firsthand. When she asked the wife of another teammate if they could sit together during a game, the woman replied that Washington was a bench player, while the woman's husband was the starter and, as she justified it, they could not sit together, because, after all, "does the bank president socialize with the tellers?"[6] This clearly changed as players like Kevin McHale or Andre Iguodala were instrumental to the success of their teams and continued to come off the bench for, respectively, the Celtics and the Warriors. Their voices were heard even from the bench.

A sixth man is tasked with either igniting his team with new energy when it's trailing or upholding the tempo of the game when it's leading. These obligations are clearly difficult, as not all players are capable of a careful reading of the game. Possessing that ability may position a player to become a great coach in the future, as was the case with Don Nelson, Phil Jackson or Pat Riley, who were also parts of championship teams during their playing days. All three were included in the Top 10 Coaches in NBA History, assembled on the league's 50th anniversary in 1996. By being afforded less responsibility regarding the on-court events, they could observe the inner workings of some of the best teams in basketball history, while focusing more on doing what was necessary off the court to make their teams successful.

Nelson won five championships on the Boston Celtics (1966, 1968,

1969, 1974, 1976) and got his number retired by the team. In 1969 it was Nelson's shot that sealed the championship for the Celtics against the Lakers. With the game clock running down in Game Seven of the NBA Finals, Nelson caught the ball lost by his teammate John Havlicek as he was running outside the key and almost immediately shot it: "I shot it so poorly. It must have gone up 20 feet in the air and came down right through."[7] The ball bounced off the back rim and went in, making the score 105–102 for the Celtics, who won 108–106. Despite having the better team and home-court advantage, the Los Angeles Lakers lost to the Celtics in the finals for the sixth time in nine seasons. What made that shot even more painful for the team from Los Angeles was that it had let Nelson go in 1965, as he barely cracked the rotation, only for the Celtics to pick him up. Nelson's playing time increased from 6.1 to 23.5 minutes per game after the move, and he went on to average ten or more points in nine of the 11 seasons he spent in Boston.

A season later the Celtics did not make the finals, and the Lakers were playing against a different team, the New York Knicks, in the last series of the postseason. While the Knicks had a star-studded roster of Walt Frazier, Bill Bradley and Willis Reed, it was a bench player on that team, Phil Jackson, who would win the most championship rings of the group— 11 as a coach, six with the Chicago and five with the Los Angeles Lakers. As a player with exceptionally long arms, Jackson made for a great reserve defender, and that was his primary function on the Knicks teams that won the NBA Championship in 1970 and 1973.

Just like Jackson, Riley won four championships with the team he coached, the Lakers (1982, 1985, 1987, 1988), and later one with the Heat (2006). During his playing days, he was also a role player on the team from Los Angeles. When former Celtics great shooting guard Bill Sharman became the coach for the Lakers in 1971, he said to Riley, "The only way you're gonna make this team is to be the best-conditioned athlete on the team. Otherwise, you're going to be useless to me."[8] This is where the seeds for Riley's obsession with conditioning were planted, later to blossom during his coaching and executive career on the Lakers, the Knicks and, especially, the Heat, where he has built a whole culture around conditioning and fitness. It was his conditioning practices that earned him the nickname "Coach Hitler"[9] and made his relationship with the Lakers' players sour, leading to Riley resigning his position after a 63–19 season.

Steve Kerr was another great coach who was a sixth man throughout his career. Kerr played in 910 NBA games, starting just 30. He continued to be an important long-distance shooter on the Chicago Bulls and the San Antonio Spurs, winning three titles with the former and two with the latter. It was his mid-range jumper that sealed the 1997 NBA Championship for the Bulls against the Jazz with six seconds left in the game. In the last postseason of his career, at 37 years old, Steve Kerr entered Game Six of the 2003 Western Conference Finals with the score 63–50 for the Dallas Mavericks. Despite playing an average of just 2.6 minutes in the previous five games, Kerr ignited the Spurs comeback, going 4/4 from three and having three assists. The Spurs won that game and progressed to the finals against the Nets, which they won 4–2.

On the Bulls and the Spurs Kerr could study how great coaches, Phil Jackson and Gregg Popovich, handled superstar players and clashing egos. Before taking on a head coaching job with the Warriors, Kerr said, "You can't have All-Stars sitting on the bench. You must have solid veterans who come in and can play when necessary but will support the team when they are not playing."[10] And yet when on the job he decided to put a one-time All-Star and the 2014 All-NBA Defensive First Team member, Andre Iguodala, on the bench, just a few months after the player earned both distinctions. Before the start of the 2014–15 season, Kerr said to Iguodala, "You've earned the starting spot but I think it's best for the team if you come off the bench. If we don't bring you off the bench, we're just not going to get as much from our second unit."[11] Iguodala was adjusting throughout his first season, but in the end it paid off—the Warriors won three NBA Championships in five seasons, while Iguodala was the 2015 NBA Finals MVP.

While he is now the paragon of what a modern-day bench player is supposed to be, Iguodala found it hard to adjust to the rhythm of the game when not being present on the floor since the opening tip. Kerr kept telling him to "find the flow," which, as the player was to find out, meant not that he was asked to create offense, but to get his teammates involved by controlling the pace of the game. While in his autobiography Iguodala admits that his own rhythm did not always match that of his team, he still decided to sacrifice his personal statistics for the greater good.[12] Despite not being totally comfortable with his role, thanks to accepting it, as well as trusting his head coach and believing in his teammates, he won three NBA Championships with the Warriors. Iguodala also made the 2020 finals as a member of the Heat.

If he would have won the title against the Lakers, Iguodala would be just one title short of another great bench player, whose athleticism and defense allowed him to make an impact in the league, despite coming off the bench. Michael Cooper has spent his whole NBA career on the Lakers, for 12 seasons finishing flashy passes thrown by Magic Johnson and taking on the other team's swingmen on the other end of the floor. He was named 1987 NBA Defensive Player of the Year and made the NBA All-Defensive First Team five times and the All-Defensive Second Team three times. This was all while coming off the bench. Most importantly for Cooper, though, he won five NBA Championships: "The winning is why I play. So when I'm on the wing against a Jordan or a Bird, and they have the ball and nothing is between them and the basket but me, well, that's the moment I live for."[13] While he was primarily a defender, the most memorable moment of his career came on the offensive end. In Game Two of the 1987 NBA Finals against the Celtics, Cooper went six of seven from three, setting a record for three-pointers made in a finals game. The record was beaten in the 2010 finals by Celtic Ray Allen, who made eight three-pointers against … the Lakers.

The most important shot of Allen's career came three years later, in Game Six of the 2013 finals. With seven seconds left, Allen made a step-back three following a rebound and a pass from Heat teammate Chris Bosh. The shooting guard's shot tied the game, 95–95, and the Heat were able to beat the Spurs in overtime, tying the series 3–3. Allen was the sixth man on that team, for the first time in his career coming off the bench at age 37. He did not start a single game for the Heat that season. In comparison, up to that point he appeared in 1,148 games and was not a member of the starting lineup in just eight of them.

Next year the Heat again faced off against the Spurs, but this time the team from San Antonio made easy work of LeBron James, Dwyane Wade and company, winning the finals in five games. This was the team's fifth NBA Championship, the fourth won by the trio of Tim Duncan, Tony Parker and Manu Ginobili. While the first two were starters on those Spurs teams, Ginobili was the sixth man, starting 349 games of the 1,057 he played in the NBA, all of them under Coach Gregg Popovich. Selected with the 57th pick in the 1999 NBA Draft, the Argentinian entered the NBA three years later, at age 25. Ginobili is an example of a player who could do it all: dunk, shoot from long distance, pass, steal and block. Throughout the years he was greatly involved in his team's success. Some of his best playoff games include Game One of the 2005 finals, in which he had 26 points and nine rebounds, and Game Six of the 2007 Western Conference Finals, in which he had 33 points, 11 rebounds and six assists.

Those are just some examples of NBA sixth men—exceptional players to whom this book is devoted. In it I want to highlight the importance of the bench to the careers of players of various backgrounds, abilities and physical conditions. That is why I think it is important to start with a bit of history, with a chapter devoted to the "first sixth men," to the pioneers who made the role relevant in the NBA. The central figure in this chapter is not a player though, but Red Auerbach, the legendary coach and executive, who was the first to recognize how bringing one of the best players on the team off the bench was beneficial for team success.

Some players, who would later make the Hall of Fame, actually started their careers as sixth men, learning the game from the comfort of the bench. Although being high draft picks, Clyde Drexler, Scottie Pippen and Kobe Bryant were reserves for at least one season. These and other players are described in the second chapter. The third one is devoted to reserves who have made such an impression on other team executives or coaches that they were traded for or signed by them, and made a significant impact—either positive or negative—when inserted into the starting lineups of their new teams. On the example of three players associated with the Seattle SuperSonics and Oklahoma City Thunder—Detlef Schrempf, Jim McIlvaine and James Harden—this chapter highlights two things. The first concerns said players: how bringing in a starter may benefit the team, cause enormous chemistry issues or hurt the team giving away a bench player. The second is more about how such decisions regarding the roster may be one of the causes of a franchise moving to a different city.

In the fourth chapter, I describe players who willingly moved to the bench in order to win championship titles. With players who have never won a title looked down upon by some fans and journalists, Bob McAdoo and Mitch Richmond were able to add NBA Champion to their Hall of Fame resumes. The reason for picking those two players is that they have played for the same franchise and, despite being great players, played very different parts in the postseason success of the Lakers. The fifth chapter highlights great playoff performances by bench players, who uplifted their teams and made their postseason success possible. While not all of these players won championship titles, they have proven with their play that, despite not making the starting lineups on their teams, they belonged in the best basketball league in the world. Some of them, like Sam Cassell or Robert Horry, came up big in the playoffs multiple times, while others, like Nate Robinson, have enjoyed only one great postseason in their careers.

The sixth and seventh chapters are somewhat connected, as the former focuses on two players who, despite serious health issues, were able to remain in the NBA and win championship titles thanks to accepting reserve roles on their teams. Both centers, Bill Walton and Alonzo Mourning owe the second chapters of their careers to the bench, as they were no longer the focal points on their teams, yet important enough to help them win. In the seventh chapter I present the examples of the opposite, with players' egos getting the best of them and them not accepting bench roles. The most prominent player analyzed in this chapter is Michael Jordan, who refused to come off the bench as a member of the Washington Wizards.

The eighth and ninth chapters are connected as well, as they present two prevalent types of sixth men. The former presents high-volume scorers, fast, agile players, who need just two or three made shots to get going and inspire a run that may lead their teams to victory. I write in the

Red Auerbach was the first coach to recognize the importance of the sixth man (1995).

present tense, because, as of now, they are still active NBA players. The ninth chapter of the book focuses on big men who came off the bench and revolutionized how the game of basketball is played. By moving away from the basket, passing the ball like point guards or performing with unparalleled energy, they changed the expectations regarding big men in the modern NBA.

The last chapter presents players who for some reason did not "crack the rotation." They are, however, worthy of more than just a brief mention in this book. After that chapter the reader will find three tables, which show how players who have won the Sixth Man of the Year Award (Table 1) and those who have never won the award (Table 2) performed during their best seasons coming off the bench. The third table shows exceptional postseasons by players who were either bench players during the regular season or came off the bench during the playoffs.

This book I hope paints a comprehensive, complex picture of the way the bench was and is used in the NBA. While far from complete, it aims to shed light on basketball players who at some point of their careers were cast out of the starting lineups of NBA franchises. Not all of them embraced being reserves, but being (or refusing to be) sixth men is a vital, if sometimes omitted, part of their career narratives.

1

The First of the Sixth Men

Irv Torgoff
> *Forward. In the BAA: 1946–1949.*

Frank Ramsey
> *Guard/Forward. In the NBA: 1954–1964.*

John Havlicek
> *Guard/Forward. In the NBA: 1962–1978.*

While, as described in the introduction, the position of the sixth man on any given team is much more nuanced than it seems at first glance, it is appropriate to appreciate the three pioneers who have largely contributed to its meaning in today's basketball. A basketball team is like an organism, in which some parts may be faulty, while others may seem out of place or, quite plainly, be in need of readjustments. The coach is responsible for keeping the organism alive for as long as possible, but it is the front office's function to keep it well-balanced and properly nourished. The "parts" must accept their place in an organism and understand that only in that way can it function properly as a whole. Sam Anderson writes that

> basketball's defining challenge, once you get past the physical stuff, is social. More than any other American sport, it is a game of civics. Every player, on every play, has to find the proper balance between self-interest and self-sacrifice—a threshold that moves with just about every bounce of the ball. The game is fluid, with everyone shifting roles and responsibilities more or less constantly. The calculus of selfishness versus self-sacrifice can be crushingly complex. A properly balanced team can make that calculus feel manageable. An unbalanced team can make it hopeless.[1]

The need for balance applies not only to the five players who are on the court, but also to the seven who are sitting on the bench, watching the events on the court. Sixth men must know what will be expected of them once they enter the game. For them, the move to the bench is not a demotion or a disciplinary measure. Instead, by getting into a game that already

15

began they are able to influence it while performing to the best of their abilities.

Red Auerbach was the visionary coach who understood the significance of the bench player and turned it into one of the most prominent roles in modern basketball. His reasoning was as follows:

> When a game or a half starts, both teams get into a certain rhythm…. After a little while, a little bit of fatigue sets in and everyone begins to lose just a little. My thought was, "If I send one of my two or three best players into the game at that point and he's completely fresh, he's going to be able to take advantage of people. He'll probably make some plays right away because his legs are fresh, In turn, that gives my other guys a burst of energy and picks up the whole team."[2]

The head coaching job on the Washington Capitols was his first professional basketball gig. Before, he coached in high school and in the navy, but he made such a big impression on team owner Mike Uline that it was hard for him to imagine someone else taking over the team. Uline was among the 11 team owners who embarked on a dangerous and risky project—figuring that, after World War II was over, people were in need of entertainment (and would pay big money to be entertained), they decided to form a basketball league. They named it the Basketball Association of America.

The man at its helm was Maurice Podoloff, who also happened to be the president of the American Hockey League. Approaching the league as a business and not a tool of popularizing the sport of basketball, before the inaugural season, along with team owners, he laid out some ground rules: "A franchise would cost $1,000, with each franchise limited to a salary cap of $40,000, excluding the coach and trainer's salaries. The teams would be named for their respective cities, rather than for the businesses owning them, and the home teams would keep the gate receipts. College players could not be signed until their class had graduated."[3] The season started on November 1, 1946.

The teams were divided into two divisions: Eastern and Western. The Eastern Division consisted of the Boston Celtics, New York Knicks, Philadelphia Warriors, Providence Steamrollers, Toronto Huskies, and Washington Capitols, while the Western Division was formed by the Chicago Stags, Cleveland Rebels, Detroit Falcons, Pittsburgh Ironmen, and St. Louis Bombers. Each team would play 60 regular season games, which were longer than in other leagues—48 minutes to the usual 40. This development made it obligatory for teams to invest in better benches, filling them with quality players. After the end of the regular season, the second team from the Eastern Division faced off against the third team from the Western Division, while the third team from the Eastern Division played the second team from the Western Division in the quarterfinals, which were a three-game series. The best teams in both divisions played the series' winners. The winners of the semifinals faced off in a best-of-seven series in the finals.

Even some years after the league was created, players from visiting teams had to go to the radio and promote not only the game they were about to play in, but even the game of basketball itself, as its rules were still hard to grasp for some of the fans. A year later, in 1947, the league was cut down to eight teams, due to insufficient popularity of the sport. The conditions in which the games were played were far from perfect. Uline Arena, in which the Washington Capitols played, was infested with rats. This was long before the place became known as the location in which The Beatles played their first-ever concert on American soil. The arena, which Uline originally intended to be an ice-skating rink—himself being an owner of a couple of profitable ice plants during a time when refrigerators were not as prevalent and affordable—was finished in 1941.[4] It immediately became home to the Washington Lions hockey team, which folded after two years, but was resurrected by Uline in 1947, following the popularity enjoyed by the Capitols in their first-ever professional season.

Before it even began, Auerbach firmly believed that he was the right man for the Capitols. He boldly declared to Uline: "You need a coach. I can coach and I know enough guys to get a team put together quickly that will be good right away."[5] While the job as a high school coach and teacher was more respectable, Uline was willing to pay Auerbach twice as much for his services as he would make in school. The coach assembled the team roster by telephone, making around 300 calls. Unlike other teams, who have built their rosters on local talent, Auerbach recruited players from all over the country:

> Players from big cities, for example, were usually good ball handlers; so, that's where my guards came from. With few exceptions, forwards and guards who could run and drive came from the Midwest. You got your rebounders from wherever you could, but not from New York, which was mainly noteworthy for its guards. The majority of the one-handed shooters, of course, came from the West Coast.[6]

One of said players was an all-around talent from Brooklyn, capable of playing all five positions, the 6'2" Irv Torgoff. His name is not the first—or second, third, or sixth for that matter—that comes to mind when discussing the sixth man in professional basketball. In fact, as with most basketball pioneers, who were responsible for popularizing the beautiful game in its early days, when it was not yet organized, let alone televised, he remains just an interesting footnote when discussing the first coaching job taken on by a brash 29 year old hailing from the same borough as Torgoff, Red

Auerbach. While Frank Ramsey of the Boston Celtics is associated with pioneering the sixth man role in professional basketball, Torgoff was the original sixth man—a role he was assigned by Auerbach.

Torgoff was born the same year as his coach, 1917, but while Auerbach got into coaching immediately after graduating, Torgoff wanted to become a professional basketball player. First, in the 1939–40 season, he played for the Detroit Eagles of the National Basketball League. Then he was a member of the Philadelphia SPHAs (Southern Philadelphia Hebrew Association) of the American Basketball League, and the Long Island Grumman Hellcats on the independent circuit, touring the country or playing the teams visiting Long Island while on tour. The Hellcats, consisting of Long Island University graduates, were owned by Grumman Aircraft Co. and named after its World War II fighter plane. On the SPHAs he contributed to the team's 1943 championship, igniting his teammates with a 70-foot shot at the end of the second half of Game Seven of the finals.[7] He won three championships in six years in Philadelphia, before joining the Washington Capitols of the Basketball Association of America in 1946.

In the BAA's first season the Capitols were indeed the best team— until playoffs came, that is. Auerbach preferred to play fast-break basketball, with rebounders quickly throwing the ball downcourt to rushing guards and swingmen. He would later perfect that style with the aid of Bob Cousy and Bill Russell in Boston. The Capitols were truly dominant, fired up by the red-hot temper of their coach. Auerbach was always shouting and gesturing at the sidelines during games, and before them he would make sure that the players knew each one was important, as it seemed that he held grudges against every other head coach in the league. The team finished with a 49–11 record, the best in the league, losing just one home game throughout the season. After starting the season 2–3, the Capitols even went on a 17-game winning streak. By the end of the season they went on another streak, this time winning 15 games in a row, before it was snapped with just three games to go in the regular season. In the playoffs they were eliminated by the Chicago Stags, losing 2–4.

Torgoff played in all but two games of the regular season, averaging 8.4 points per game. He appeared in games at guard, forward and center, handling the playmaking duties and defending the basket. He also participated in an on-court altercation with an opposing coach that, if it had occurred today, would lead to both men being suspended and heavily fined. Paul Birch, the coach of Pittsburgh Ironmen, made his players live up to their team's name—they played tough, defensive-minded basketball, often using their elbows to stop opponents from getting to the basket. Their coach, however, sometimes resorted to verbal abuse. One time, in an event described by Pittsburgh's Moe Becker—who resented his own coach—to Charley Rosen:

> "Irv Torgoff was with the Caps, and he was having a field day. Nobody could guard him, including me. Birch was always riding opposing players, and he called Torgoff a 'kike.' I resented this, and I cursed at Birch from my seat on the bench." Birch kept after Torgoff, and their argument escalated to the point that they swapped a few punches in the waning moments of the game. The refs quickly banished both of them.[8]

During their next season the Capitols regressed to a 28–20 record. Torgoff appeared in 47 games and was averaging 7.2 points per contest. His team again lost the Western Division Tiebreaker to the Chicago Stags. In the following season, 1947–48, the Capitols made the finals, but lost to George Mikan's Lakers. Torgoff however was no longer on the team. In his last season in the BAA, he played in Baltimore and Philadelphia, having a much lesser role on both teams, finishing the season with an average of four points per game. In 1948 he joined the Trenton Tigers of the American Basketball League, making his return to the league in which he won three championships as a member of the SPHAs, but appeared in just four games. His team finished the season with a 4–16 record. At the age of 32 Torgoff was done with professional basketball, while Auerbach's career was just getting started. He ended his career with 25 percent field goals and 77 percent free-throws made, stats that seem appalling from today's perspective.

After an 115–53 record in three seasons, Auerbach resigned from the Capitols, due to Uline's unwillingness to accept his plan to rebuild the team. The BAA was merging with the National Basketball League (NBL),[9] and the team needed to get more competitive in order to win in this new environment. Auerbach took on an assistant's job at Duke University, but left after a couple of months to join the Tri-Cities Blackhawks after a 1–7 start to the 1949–50 season. The owner gave Auerbach a free hand in shaping the roster, and the coach made trades involving 28 players. Just like in his early Boston days, he was operating without a scout or a general manager, making all the personnel decisions and evaluating the talent on his own. Thanks to his moves the team went 28–29, 29–35 overall, and still made the playoffs. They lost to the Anderson Packers in the Western Division Semifinals. The 1949–50 season would be Auerbach's lone losing one in his 24-year coaching career, both in high school and in the pros.

In the next season, 1950–51, at the age of 32, Auerbach took over the Boston Celtics, a team that did not win more than 25 games during a single season, and made the playoffs only once in the BAA's/NBA's four-year history. Picking first in the 1950 draft, Auerbach famously passed on local hero Bob Cousy, as he considered the point guard too flashy, and wanted to build the team from scratch starting with a big man. Auerbach said later that he was not too impressed with Cousy's play.[10] Luckily for him, Cousy fell into his lap anyway, as he was selected with the third pick by Auerbach's former team, the Blackhawks, despite really wanting to play in Boston. The team traded him to the Chicago Stags, who folded—as did five other teams—before the start of the season. The Chicago players were assigned one by one to the teams that remained in the league, until there were three players left. Their names were put into a hat and Celtics owner Walter Brown drew Cousy's. Auerbach changed his mind about the player before the start of the season and named Cousy, a rookie, team captain.[11]

In 1951 the team acquired shooter Bill Sharman from the Fort Wayne Pistons, who picked the 1950 second-round pick in the dispersal draft after Sharman's original team, the Washington Capitols, folded. The Celtics sent Chuck Share, the man drafted in front of Cousy, to the Pistons. Share did not play a single game for the Celtics, deciding to play in the Waterloo Hawks—a team from the National Professional Basketball League, which was a short-lived organization formed by small-market teams that did not make the NBA—instead. The Celtics still had the rights to Share and, by trading them to Fort Wayne, they got an exceptional shooter and future Hall of Famer in Sharman. With that move, their backcourt was set for years to come, as Cousy and Sharman would win four NBA Championships together, until Sharman's retirement in 1961.

Auerbach used his connections from the navy to recruit players, who, due to their military backgrounds, were used to following orders. That is why they had no problems with doing what Auerbach wanted. Before every season the team would enter training camp, going through two practices a day for two weeks, and then play in fourteen games in fourteen days. He did not set any curfews, nor did he suspend his players for being late. Other coaches would send them to the bench in order to punish them for their insubordination, while for Auerbach the bench players were just as important as the starters.

In 1953, with the fifth overall pick, he drafted Frank Ramsey from the University of Kentucky, where he just finished a 32–2 season, capped off with an NCAA Championship. At that time, in the state of Kentucky, basketball was viewed as a college experience, not something associated with the pros. Not many people actually knew about the NBA's existence. That was why Ramsey did not want to join the league and returned to the university despite being drafted. Back at Kentucky he enjoyed an unbeaten season, which ended prematurely, because three players on that team graduated and would not participate in the final tournament.

While skeptical at first, Ramsey decided to give professional basketball a try. The 6'3" player, despite being such a high pick, was coming off the bench, as he was too small to play against forwards and centers, so it was natural for his coach, and for Ramsey himself, that he would provide rest for either Cousy or Sharman, who were simply better players. Ramsey's main characteristic was recognizing the flow of the game—by sitting on the bench in the first few minutes of the game he could see which players were having a bad day. Once he entered the court, he could have a significant impact on defense, immediately knowing what needs to be done to stop the opposing players. In his first NBA game Ramsey scored 15 points and had five fouls, playing with equal ferociousness on both ends of the floor. He finished the season averaging 11.2 points per game. After it was over, Ramsey went to the navy for a year.

In 1956 the Celtics drafted center Bill Russell. Ramsey rejoined the team in January of 1957 and after shaking off some initial rust—he scored just 12 points in the first three games—was able to contribute to the team's first NBA Championship. In the second game of the finals, against the St. Louis Hawks, he made eight of his 11 shots, finishing with 22 points, while the Celtics won that game 119–99. In the next finals, in 1958, the teams would meet again, and this time Ramsey pretty much took over the series on the offensive end for the Celtics, finishing with three double-doubles and an average of 19.7 points per game. He scored 29 points in Game Three and 30 in Game Five, both losses. His performance is largely forgotten because the Celtics lost the series to the Hawks 2–4, the last time an all-white team would win an NBA Championship.

In the next playoffs Ramsey was even better, finishing the postseason with an average of 23.2 points per game. In eight of the 11 games the Celtics played in, he had 20 or more points. In the finals the Celtics swept the Minneapolis Lakers. Ramsey scored, respectively, 29, 20, 17, and 24 points in the four games. Vern Mikkelsen of the Lakers said about that series: "When we played them in 1959, we were pretty even five-on-five, but then, just when we were getting dog-tired, I'd look up, and here would be Frank Ramsey coming off the bench, fresh as a daisy."[12] *Sports Illustrated* called him "the best substitute this game has ever seen."[13] Later in his career, Ramsey would indeed play as a forward, having the speed advantage over much taller players.

He also introduced the NBA to flopping, even penning with Frank Deford an illustrated article on the "art," bearing the title "Smart Moves by a Master of Deception."[14] It contained instructions and illustrations on how to trick referees into whistling cheap fouls on the opponents. He retired in 1964 with seven championship rings which he won in nine seasons as a pro, and career averages of 13.4 points, 5.5 rebounds and 1.8 assists, playing 24.6 minutes per contest. Before Ramsey called it quits, the Celtics already had a new versatile scorer and relentless defender to take his place as the sixth man on the team.

The 6'5" swingman John Havlicek, and Jerry Lucas, the 6'8" center, who was a great rebounder and shooter—the latter then a rarity for players of his height—were the leaders of the 1960 Ohio State team that won the sole NCAA Championship in its history. They also made the 1961 and 1962 finals, but lost in both games. The third best-known name on that team was Bobby Knight, a reserve who did not even make the team in his first year in college and averaged a mere 3.8 points per game. He would later go on to have an illustrious coaching career, for 19 years working at Indiana University, where he won three NCAA Championships and was named Big Ten Coach of the Year eight times. It was Knight who said to Havlicek, "You should go kiss Red Auerbach's ass when you meet him,"[15] after his teammate was drafted by the Celtics—a team, which was perfect for Havlicek's style of play. The seventh pick in the 1962 draft, Havlicek, was not too impressed with the Celtics facilities though, especially coming from Ohio State.

Havlicek was another versatile athlete who also excelled at other sports and was picked by Auerbach. Havlicek and K.C. Jones were both drafted by NFL teams, while Bill Sharman and Gene Conley played in the MLB.[16] Apart from having great hands, which also made it easy for him to play as wide receiver (and participate in the Cleveland Browns training camp), Havlicek also had great speed and conditioning. The Browns actually bought him a car, but they decided to cut him before the season started. Ever since the first Celtics scrimmage the player showed what would become his main characteristics: "a style peculiar to Havlicek and, since it requires the physiology of an Arabian saddle horse, impossible to imitate. Havlicek runs and runs (scoring, rebounding, defending tenaciously, making key passes, setting up plays), and when his opponent begins to go under, he runs some more."[17] He earned the nickname "Hondo" from the 1953 John Wayne movie of the same name, as he reminded his teammates of the main character with his strong, silent persona. Instead of talking, he kept on running, long after other players went to the bench with tired legs, while he would barely break a sweat.

Havlicek immediately made an impact on the Celtics, as he won three NBA Championships in his first three seasons in the league. With averages of 14.3 points, 2.2 assists and 6.7 rebounds, he was named to the 1962–63 All-Rookie First Team. He would finish his career with most career points and assists from that draft class, while his Ohio State teammate, Jerry Lucas, had the most rebounds. Lucas was selected first overall the same year as Havlicek, but sat out the whole 1962–63 season due to contractual issues with the Cincinnati Royals. It was also in that draft that another Hall of Famer and Celtics legend joined the NBA—in the third round, with the 17th pick overall, the Chicago Zephyrs selected Don Nelson. "Nellie" spent ten seasons on the Celtics, after three unsuccessful years in the league—one on the Zephyrs and two on the Lakers. Never playing more than 27.5 minutes per game in a season, the forward became another in the long line of Celtics' sixth men, whose contributions to five NBA Championships with the Celtics were appreciated with his number 19 shirt being retired by the team.

Coming back to Hondo, the most famous moment of his career lives on in Celtics folklore partially due to a memorable call by Johnny Most, the team's radio announcer. Never hiding his bias toward opposing teams, it was Most who turned one play made by Havlicek into the stuff of legends. In the 1965 playoffs, on their way to the third NBA Finals in a row, the Celtics encountered a significant roadblock—the Philadelphia Sixers, who have acquired Wilt Chamberlain in a mid-season trade from the San Francisco Warriors. The team relocated to San Francisco from … Philadelphia in 1962. Chamberlain, who was born in Philadelphia, did not enjoy playing on the West Coast and after two and a half seasons was able to return to his city of birth. Interestingly, in 1968 he would once again demand to be traded, this time from Philadelphia to a team on the West Coast, the LA Lakers.

The Eastern Conference Finals were evenly fought, and the teams took turns winning—Boston the odd, and the Sixers the even games. With the series tied 3–3 and the home team leading by one point, after a series of ten straight points scored by Wilt Chamberlain, there were only five seconds left on the game clock. Russell was inbounding the ball, and it hit the backboard, giving the Sixers the last chance to score. With the Celtics standing very close to the Sixers' players, Hal Greer found it really hard to find an open man. Havlicek was standing next to Chet Walker, and with the corner of his eye he saw the ball about to go over his hand. With his hand he tipped it toward his teammate, to which Most reacted by shouting, "Havlicek stole the ball!" The Celtics were able to retain possession and dribble out the clock, advancing to the finals. The call remains one of the most memorable and recognizable in league history.

Playoffs were actually a time when Havlicek performed better than during the regular season. He played in the postseason 13 times and averaged 22 points, 6.9 rebounds and 4.8 assists. In comparison, in the regular season, he was averaging 20.8 points, 6.3 rebounds and 3.5 assists. He retired with the most games ever played in the NBA with 1,441 overall and 1,270 in the regular season, while also being—at that time—the only player in league history to make at least 1,000 points in 14 consecutive seasons (one season more than Cousy or West). He was one of the first relatable superstars in the NBA, but one who did not really look the part, like the gigantic Russell, imposing Chamberlain, elegant West or flashy Cousy. While all of these players were hard workers, Havlicek seemed like he had

John Havlicek made All-Star and All-NBA teams while coming off the bench (1978).

built himself from the ground up, because his natural gifts were not as evident when he played. Plus, he ran like crazy throughout the duration of whole games, furthering the impression that he achieved success due to pure determination. Peter Carry of *Sports Illustrated* wrote about him: "He has unobtrusively grown from the fast, young defensive substitute into about the best player in the team's history—aside from Russell."[18]

Havlicek eventually became the starter and even had an impressive farewell tour during the last season of his career. On the 29th of January 1978 Havlicek announced that he was going to retire at the end of the season. Cousy's farewell tour was the reason for the way Havlicek ended his NBA career. He said, "I wanted something like that. Of course it is a gate hype. But the NBA has been great to me. It set me up for life. The fans are responsible, and the franchises, too. If I can help out and get some more people in the buildings, I'm happy to do it."[19] His teammate, fellow Hall of Famer Dave Cowens, considered the tour more of an apology made by the league and opposing fans, as Havlicek was underappreciated and undervalued throughout most of his career. Getting standing ovations in various NBA arenas, the 38 year old was finally getting his due.

In his second season in the NBA, 1963–64, Havlicek led his team in scoring and made the All-NBA Second Team while coming off the bench. No one had done that up to that point or since. This honor stands as proof that with Havlicek Auerbach perfected the formula for the sixth man—a player who would read the game off the bench and make an immediate impact once entering the court. Whether it was necessary of him to score, pass or defend, Havlicek was willing to do it all in order for his team to win.

With Ramsey and "Hondo" began a long, impressive tradition of Celtics bench players, like Satch Sanders, Don Nelson, M.L. Carr, Paul Silas, Kevin McHale, Bill Walton, Rodney Rogers, James Posey and Marcus Smart. The history of sixth men would not be complete without the mentioning of Red Auerbach's innovative strategy of moving some of his best players to the bench, but it was also said players who have made the Celtics a historically great team. Without them the team from Boston definitely would not have 17 championship banners hanging from the rafters.

2

From the Bench
to the Hall of Fame

Kobe Bryant
   Guard. In the NBA: 1996–2016. Seasons as a bench player: two. 13th pick, 1996 NBA Draft.
Steve Nash
   Guard. In the NBA: 1996–2014. Seasons as a bench player: three. 15th pick, 1996 NBA Draft.
Tracy McGrady
   Guard/Forward. In the NBA: 1997–2013. Seasons as a bench player: five. 9th pick, 1997 NBA Draft.
Kevin McHale
   Forward. In the NBA: 1980–1993. Seasons as a bench player: nine. 3rd pick, 1980 NBA Draft.
Clyde Drexler
   Guard. In the NBA: 1983–1998. Seasons as a bench player: two. 14th pick, 1983 NBA Draft.
Scottie Pippen
   Forward. In the NBA: 1987–2004. Seasons as a bench player: two. 5th pick, 1987 NBA Draft.

In this chapter I want to focus on players who began their NBA careers on the bench and after some time "graduated" to the starting line-ups on their teams, eventually ending up in the Basketball Hall of Fame. Selected with high picks in the draft, they needed some time to adjust to the physical—in comparison to college or high school basketball, they were used to—style of play and the draining 82-game season schedule. The transition to the life of a professional athlete is always difficult, and it is hard to expect teenagers or young adults to immediately make a significant impact on their teams, as only a selected few players, like Moses Malone, Michael Jordan or LeBron James, were able to do. Here I want to present how the season(s) spent coming off the bench allowed the players discussed to not burn out too quickly, but rather lit a competitive fire underneath them and eventually allowed them to shine in the best basketball league in the world.

It is understandable to begin with Kobe Bryant, since he is the most accomplished player from all of those mentioned above. The Lakers legend is fourth in NBA career points with 33,643, holds five NBA Championships and one MVP trophy. His jersey numbers—as he played with two: 8 and 24[1]—are both retired by the Los Angeles Lakers. Bryant aimed for greatness even before he entered the league, as already before the draft he and his father Joe, a former professional basketball player himself, made it clear that they wanted Kobe to play in Los Angeles, and once team general manager Jerry West let it be known that he wanted Bryant as well, the player refused to work out for any other team. In his book *Boys Among Men* Jonathan Abrams describes the whole process of Bryant falling into the Lakers' lap with the 13th pick. The highlights of said process included Joe Bryant calling Isiah Thomas, who was then executive vice president of the Toronto Raptors, to dissuade him from picking Bryant with the second pick; the Bucks owner vetoing Mike Dunleavy's trade "pyramid scheme" that could have brought the team Bryant and a couple of future draft picks; and the Nets' John Callipari deciding to pick Kerry Kittles over Bryant after being convinced by the former's agent to do so.[2] Bryant was selected by the Hornets but was immediately traded to the Lakers for center Vlade Divac. The team's starting center was replaced less than a month later with the biggest free-agent name of the summer—other than Michael Jordan, who was clearly going to remain in Chicago, despite seriously considering a $25 million contract offer from the New York Knicks—center Shaquille O'Neal.

The team from Los Angeles was however in its deepest crisis so far. The fans had experienced four championship dynasties but were at the time in one of what Andrew van Buuren characterizes as their black holes—"the years between dynasties, when the team wasn't blessed with great talent or coaching, and so [they] get lost in the shuffle of our memories." As an example of the lack of attention that these years get from van Buuren, consider the amount of time that these seasons received in the NBA's official documentary complementing the ten-disc DVD set *Los Angeles Lakers: The Complete History*. In it the 16 unsuccessful years are condensed to two and a half minutes.[3] Of course when it comes to a team as successful as the Lakers, said "black hole" denotes the lack of finals appearances, because in the years 1991–1996 the team failed to make the playoffs only once. Del Harris, the 1995 Coach of the Year, had a solid roster, as, apart from O'Neal and Bryant, the Lakers had point guard Nick Van Exel and shooting guard Eddie Jones. With the two being already established NBA players, it was evident that Bryant would have to take on the bench role, as the team would be looking for the best position for him, allowing the young player to share the court with the other Lakers.

The management, coaches and players were carefully grooming the 18 year old to be their star player, and they brought in veteran shooting guard Byron Scott to serve as his mentor. Scott was selected with the fourth pick in the 1983 NBA Draft and spent a significant part of his first year coming off the bench as well. He started 49 of the 74 games he played for the Lakers as a rookie, but in the 1984 playoffs, in which the team made it to the NBA Finals, he did not start even once. Instead, team coach Pat Riley decided to start Michael Cooper, who was a quintessential sixth man. Scott eventually became the starter and a vital part of the Showtime Lakers that would go on to win three NBA Championships. When Scott returned to the Lakers, after two seasons on the Pacers and one with the expansion Vancouver Grizzlies, he was 36 years old. The veteran described how he would always come early before practice to get his treatment, and Bryant was already in the empty arena, with no lights on, working on his game.[4]

Even though he was determined to immediately become an important player for the Lakers, Bryant would have to patiently wait for his chance. He did not even enter the court during the first NBA game he was declared eligible for, and played for 16 minutes combined in the next three. He scored a total of six points and had five turnovers. With time he was able to improve and even earned the nickname "Showboat" from Shaquille O'Neal due to his willingness to dunk the ball and please the crowd with impressive plays. Bryant hated the nickname and considered it disrespectful.[5] The fact of the matter was that the young player was eager to make a name for himself, either with his play or fictional relationship with pop star Brandy, who cheered him on during the 1997 Slam Dunk Contest, which Bryant won. After a very successful All-Star Weekend—he also scored 31 points during the rookie game—the pressure was on coach Harris to up Bryant's playing time, which he reluctantly did.[6] Bryant ended the season with six starts in 71 games, averaging 7.6 points in 15.5 minutes per game.

In the playoffs the Lakers progressed to the second round, where they faced off against the Utah Jazz, who were on their way to their second trip to the finals in two seasons. In what would turn out to be the last game of the series, with the Jazz leading 3–1 and the score being tied 87–87, the Lakers had the ball with 11 seconds left. O'Neal was no longer on the floor, as he fouled out in the fourth quarter. Harris decided that Bryant would take the last shot, which he airballed. The Jazz won the game in overtime, while Bryant had three more airballs. After the game Harris said, "I spent over half of the year being criticized for not playing Kobe, now I'm getting criticized for playing him."[7] After the game, instead of going home, Bryant went to the gym and worked on his shot. He continued to do so throughout the summer and came back a different, better player.

For the 1997–98 season Bryant continued to be a bench player, but his playing time went up to 26 minutes per game. His friend and rival for the position of starting shooting guard, Eddie Jones, was stumping Bryant's progress, as he was a very solid player, averaging 16.9 points and 2 steals per game, and it was evident that he should be traded if the team wanted to maximize Bryant's potential. The 19 year old earned praise from Jordan himself, and his reputation grew to the point that, a little over half a year after missing the most important shots of his career, he was voted by fans to be a starter in the 1998 All-Star Game. Jones, Van Exel and O'Neal were selected by the coaches to be the Western Conference reserves.

Much was made of the duel between Bryant and Jordan during the game. It was seen as changing of the guard of sorts, since it was almost certain that Jordan would end his basketball career after that season, while Bryant's was just taking off. The Laker was another in the long line of players who were dubbed "The Next Michael Jordan."[8] The most (in)famous of that informal group was Harold Miner, who earned the nickname already as a high school player because of his dunking ability. When at college in USC he not only wore number 23—presumably because 32, the one worn by Julius Erving, was taken—but was also sticking his tongue out just like Jordan. He also borrowed mannerisms from other players, like rubbing his fingers against the soles of his shoes like Larry Bird or Alex English's free throw routine, but once the comparison to Jordan was made, it was the only thing people saw. The player himself said long after his basketball career was over that the nickname "helped [him], but it hurt [him] too."[9] Miner won two slam-dunk contests, but was unable to adjust his style of play to the NBA. That, plus knee injuries, limited his professional career to four seasons and 47 starts in 200 games.

Bryant on the other hand possessed the work ethic that matched— or even was superior to—Jordan's and the same competitive spirit. Despite the praise and the progress, coach Del Harris continued to bring Bryant in slowly, allowing him to start just one of the 79 games he would go on to play in the 1997–98 season. His playing time went up, and Bryant was now averaging 15.4 points. He was beaten only by the Suns' Danny Manning for the Sixth Man of the Year Award. With Eddie Jones and Rick Fox as the starters, the team won 61 games that season and made the Western Conference Finals, where it once again lost to the Jazz. After going 6–6 at the beginning of the lockout-shortened 1999 season, Del Harris was replaced by former Laker Kurt Rambis, who allowed Bryant to do whatever he wanted on the court. Rambis was an inexperienced coach pressured by the front office to play the shooting guard more, and he did just that in order to keep his job.[10]

He lost it after the season was over. Harris already tried to start both Jones and Bryant, but the team struggled, and mid-season Jones was traded along with Elden Campbell to the Hornets for Glen Rice and veteran J.R. Reid. Freeing up Bryant, as well as bringing in Phil Jackson, allowed the Lakers to finally succeed in the postseason.

After a tumultuous eight years, which involved three NBA championships and a well-documented feud between Bryant and O'Neal, the latter was traded to the Miami Heat, while team coach Phil Jackson decided to retire. Jackson described the dysfunction within the team in the memoir *The Last Season*. He characterized Bryant as someone who "can be consumed with surprising anger" and "rebels against authority."[11] After just one season in which Bryant missed the playoffs for the first time in his career, he and Jackson had settled their differences, and the coach was back in Los Angeles. Instead of further attempts at changing Bryant's attitude, Jackson allowed the player to be himself and organized the team's offensive strategy so that it would cater to his best players' strengths.[12] They won two championships together, which left Bryant one short of Jordan's six. His last run at the title was supposed to come in the 2012–13 season, after the Lakers were eliminated in the Western Conference Semifinals for two seasons in a row.

During the summer of 2012, a year after Chris Paul was not allowed to move to the Lakers due to "basketball reasons"—a perplexing reason given by league commissioner David Stern concerning his vetoing of the trade of the then-Hornets point guard—the team brought in another future Hall of Fame playmaker, Steve Nash. The two-time league MVP in 2004 and 2005 was 37 years old, with a well-documented history of back problems, and holding the dishonorable distinction of being the only MVP in league history never to play in the NBA Finals. When he returned to the Suns in 2004 as a free agent—as the team from Arizona drafted Nash in 1996, but more on that in a moment—he co-authored, along with coach Mike D'Antoni, one of the biggest turnarounds in league history. The Suns improved from 29 wins in the 2003–04 season, to 62 a year later.

With Nash on the roster, the points per game average improved from 92.4 the season prior, to 110.4. D'Antoni and Nash led the Suns to two Western Conference Finals, but after a couple of disappointing playoff exits D'Antoni left in 2008 to join the Knicks. D'Antoni immediately recognized who he had in Nash, as the coach himself was a point guard during his playing days, however, unlike Nash, he "always rued a certain lack of mental toughness, and a dubious outside touch, that kept him from really making it."[13] On a more personal level, D'Antoni, just like Nash, also had an older brother who was the superior athlete, yet did not realize his potential. While the player and the coach enjoyed a rather successful run together in Phoenix, they met again in the most unlikely of places, considering the rivalry between the two teams—Los Angeles.

Along with Nash, the Lakers brought in Dwight Howard, a 6'11" center, three-time Defensive Player of the Year, whose Magic lost to Bryant's Lakers in the 2009 finals. The trade that brought in Howard included four teams, 12 players and five draft picks. Nash was brought in for two first-round and two second-round draft picks. Just like Howard, Nash also had some history with the Lakers, who had eliminated the Suns in the 2010 Western Conference Finals. Bryant felt personally responsible to put away the team from Phoenix, which in the first round of the 2006 playoffs not only progressed despite being down 1–3 to the Lakers—who at the time were only the eighth team in league history to give away such a huge lead—but won the crucial Game Seven by 31 points.[14]

With Bryant, Nash, Howard, and Pau Gasol on the roster, the Lakers were expected to make a deep playoff run, but general manager Mitch Kupchak fired second-year defensive-minded coach Mike Brown just five games into the new season. Following five more games that the team played under interim-coach Bernie Bickerstaff and Lakers fans chanting "We want Phil" in reference to Phil Jackson, who did not get his deal extended after the team was swept by the Dallas Mavericks in the 2011 Western Conference Semifinals, Kupchak decided to not bring back the beloved coach, but instead hired Mike D'Antoni.

D'Antoni was Bryant's favorite player growing up, so it made perfect sense that, to appease their star, the Lakers brought in the esteemed coach, whose fast-paced offense could be a perfect fit for the once–Showtime team, had the average age of the starting lineup (with Nash, Bryant, Metta World-Peace, Gasol and Howard) not been almost 33 years, with Howard being the only player under 30. Jackson himself said, "The players don't match well with the system. I like Mike as a coach, just not with this personnel."[15] The season did not bring the sixth championship to Bryant, nor the first one to Nash. Instead, the two struggled to play together, as both needed the ball to be efficient, while Dwight Howard was unable to accept a lesser role on offense and found himself struggling to learn the pick-and-roll with Nash, who himself took partial blame for the underperforming team: "I'm not as efficient as I've played in the past. This is not quite what I'm capable of."[16] The Lakers were the last team in the league to make the playoffs that season and were swept in the first round.

D'Antoni's failures at Denver, New York and Los Angeles should not overshadow the success he enjoyed in Phoenix and Houston. He is one of the most revolutionary coaches in recent basketball history, a true follower of Don Nelson's quick, position-less play, but not the first experimenter on the team from Arizona, which somewhat explains why the Suns decided to give him a chance in the first place. Danny Ainge, who has spent half of his career as a bench player, retired from the NBA after the 1994–95 season. Ainge began his only stint as an NBA head coach after eight games of the 1996–97 season. The Suns went winless in those first eight games, and the man in charge, Cotton Fitzsimmons, resigned. He was supposed to pass the reigns to Ainge after the season, but instead the unprepared rookie coach had to step in. Ainge lost his first five games, making the 1996–97 0–13 start the worst in franchise history. The fact that the team managed to make the playoffs with a 40–42 record and took the second-seeded Seattle SuperSonics to five games[17] was in equal parts due to Ainge's coaching and Bryan Colangelo's trade for Jason Kidd, at that time the most promising point guard in the league.

Kidd would go on to have a Hall of Fame career, finishing second all-time in assists with 12,091. The third player on the list, Steve Nash, was Kidd's substitute on the Suns. With Kevin Johnson, Rex Chapman, Wesley Person, Kidd and Nash, Ainge had five guards who could play in the starting lineup. And while he was willing to play three of them at the same time, Nash was usually stuck on the bench—he averaged 10.5 minutes, making 3.3 points and 2.1 assists per game. The 15th pick in the 1996 draft was no stranger to adversity, and he would show that he could handle it quite well, demonstrating significant improvements in his second season.

The fact that Nash even made the NBA, let alone the first round of the draft, seemed unlikely just a couple of years earlier. The Canadian point guard who learned how to play basketball in British Columbia was only able to get on the radar of Santa Clara University because he impressed one of the assistant coaches attending the game between Canada's U-19 team and Long Beach State University.[18] He struggled as a freshman, playing behind John Woolery, who would dominate Nash during team workouts. Woolery was averaging 8 points and 5.2 assists that season, and Nash in no way looked like a future MVP, nor as an elite point guard, that he would eventually become. His coach at Santa Clara, Dick Davey, said, "He was a tough-minded son of a gun. He wanted to be as good as he could possibly be. He was so deranged about the game—had a great feel and a love for the game."[19]

In the 1997–98 season Ainge started playing one of the first original versions of small ball basketball, with the 6'10" forwards Danny Manning and Clifford Robinson often at the center position, the explosive Antonio McDyess being the power forward, and with a combination of natural guards in Jason Kidd, Rex Chapman, Kevin Johnson, Steve Nash and George McCloud (who was a small forward, but joined the league as a point guard and on the 1989 draft night earned comparisons to Magic Johnson). In that lineup Nash was often the shooter coming off picks. During his second MVP season Nash said about his first time in Phoenix, "To this day, one of my biggest accomplishments was getting minutes my second year."[20] That was not an easy task, considering the competition.

The fact that he played 21.9 minutes per game Nash also owed to the team's starting point guard, who had a pass-first mentality and preferred to distribute the ball rather than go for a layup. A pass-first player himself, Nash had to adapt in order to make the Suns' rotation, so he worked on his shooting. His scoring ability proved to be a big part of his game later on, after he was traded to the Mavericks thanks mostly to Donnie Nelson, who was the assistant coach on the Suns during Nash's time there, but in 1998 joined the Mavericks as assistant general manager, behind his father and head coach, Don. Nash struggled during his third season in the league, his first as a starter in Dallas. He was even getting booed by his own crowd, but with time formed an effective partnership with coming-of-age superstar Dirk Nowitzki.

When the Mavericks owner Mark Cuban decided not to match the Suns' contract offer for Nash in the summer of 2004, he believed that the player, who was 30 years old at the time, would soon start suffering from back problems that would not allow him to remain a productive member of an NBA team. Following the decision, Don Nelson said, "I never dreamed we'd lose Nash, or any other player of his magnitude."[21] Nelson would resign the following season, citing Nash's departure as one of the reasons for his loss of interest in coaching. The turmoil, which actually brought the Mavericks their first finals appearance, occurred as Nash was in the midst of the best year of his career, even better than his previous MVP campaign, averaging 18.8 points, 10.5 assists and 4.2 rebounds, while the team's second-best player and his main target, Amar'e Stoudemire, was injured throughout the season. With Stoudemire out, Nash needed to handle more of the shooting responsibilities, just like he did in his second season on the bench in Phoenix. Shaun Livingston, an important reserve during the Golden State Warriors championship seasons, said of Nash, "He was the first dude I remember seeing pull up from three on the break. Crazy."[22] It was thanks to Livingston and other members of the Warriors that Nash finally got his championship rings, serving as player development consultant for the team from the Bay Area.

Another Hall of Famer who retired without a ring and who had close ties with Bryant was Tracy McGrady. The two, along with Antoine Walker, were the faces of the Adidas marketing campaign that was supposed to rival Nike's dominance as the number-one basketball shoe brand in the world. McGrady and Bryant immediately struck up a friendship after the teenager from Auburndale, Florida, came to visit the Laker in his Los Angeles home. He spent almost two weeks there, while the two players engaged in one-on-one games on a daily basis.[23] McGrady was an unknown player just a couple of years earlier, until he made an impression at the Adidas-owned ABCD Camp when he was just 17. Two years later he was one of the most highly recruited players in the draft. He signed a shoe deal with Adidas before he was actually selected—the deal was signed between workouts for the Lakers and the Pacers.[24] McGrady was projected to be the fourth high school player drafted in the top 20 during the span of three years, along with Kevin Garnett, Kobe Bryant, and Jermaine O'Neal. For nine years O'Neal held the record of being the youngest player ever to participate in an NBA game (18 years, 53 days), as he was 19 days younger than Bryant, who made his NBA debut a month before the Blazers center. The record was eventually beaten by Lakers prospect (and Bryant's teammate) Andrew Bynum, who was 18 years and 6 days old when he made his first appearance on NBA hardwood.

McGrady entered the floor of an NBA game for the first time when he was 18 years, 160 days old, as a member of the Toronto Raptors. He came onto the court during the first game of the season, against the Miami Heat, who were among the best teams in the league, as they made the 1997 Eastern Conference Finals just a couple of months earlier, where they were overpowered by the Chicago Bulls. The Raptors were just learning the ropes, as they finished their second season in the league with 30 wins, nine more than in the one before, and were expected to show even more progress in the 1997–98 season. The rookie got to play only six minutes in his first game and ended it with zero shots taken, zero points, one rebound and one turnover. Selected with the ninth pick in the 1997 draft, McGrady was expected to be a work in progress. After all, he was a kid from small-town Florida who was forced to move to not only a bigger city, but also a different country. His first professional coach, Darrell Walker, was not fond of his star rookie and predicted that with his poor work ethic McGrady would be out of the league within three seasons.[25]

The coaching change in the middle of the season brought in Butch Carter, who started giving McGrady more playing time, but he was also reluctant to make McGrady a full-time starter. Things got complicated for the player the next season, when in the 1998 NBA Draft the team acquired his third-cousin, Vince Carter, in a draft-day trade with the Warriors. McGrady found himself once again on the bench, behind Carter, who played the same position as the younger, yet more experienced, family member. Still, if things would have turned out differently, McGrady might have been preparing for another season in a different city, over 500 miles away. A city with a well-established basketball culture, that was the capital of professional basketball in the '90s.

Jerry Krause, the general manager of the Chicago Bulls, really liked

McGrady when he was in high school and even attended some of his games. By trading Pippen, who was very vocal about his hate for the GM and the fact that he was the 142nd highest-paid player in the league, yet one of the top 15–20 players overall, Krause intended to solve three problems at the same time: get rid of a negative influence in the locker room, bring in an exciting new player who could learn from Michael Jordan, and prove that *he* was the mastermind behind turning that Bulls team into a dynasty.[26] Earlier, Krause intended to sell Pippen and Luc Longley to the Celtics for the third and the sixth picks in the 1998 Draft. The Celtics' team president and coach at the time was Rick Pitino. Pitino was vocal before the draft that he really wanted McGrady, but he chose point guard Chauncey Billups and shooting guard Ron Mercer with the picks he once offered the Bulls. Interestingly, Pitino's Celtics won against the eventual champions, the Bulls, in his first game as team coach. The game remains the brightest moment of his chaotic tenure with the Celtics.

The Pippen-for-McGrady deal obviously did not go through, as team owner Jerry Reinsdorf decided to run the trade by Jordan, who openly refused the move, recognizing how vital Pippen was for the Bulls' franchise at the time. Krause however did not give up on McGrady, and in the summer of 2000, when he was available as a free agent and showed no signs of staying in Toronto—apart from the little playing time he saw during his three years there, the kid from Florida could not stand the cold—Krause attempted to sign him, along with Tim Duncan and Grant Hill, who all were free agents at the time.[27] The Bulls had the necessary cap space, yet because of the public status of the feuds Krause had with coach Phil Jackson and his best players, Jordan and Pippen, none of the three went to Chicago. Hill and McGrady joined the Magic, and Duncan considered it a possibility as well, but he decided to remain in San Antonio.

Years later McGrady admitted he regretted leaving Toronto and going to Orlando, as Carter and he could have had more team success.[28] That remains one blemish on McGrady's otherwise stellar NBA career—he never played in more than seven games during the playoffs, as his teams were knocked out in the First Round in the eight-out-of-nine times they even made the postseason. His only chance to appear in the finals occurred after he was signed by the Spurs in April 2013, in a move that was supposed to deepen the roster. McGrady had not played in the NBA at all that season; instead, he was a member of Qingdao of the Chinese Basketball League, averaging 25 points, 7.2 rebound, 5.1 assists and 1.55 steals in 29 games. With the Spurs he would appear in just six games during that postseason, missing all of his field-goal and free-throw attempts in the total of 31 minutes he was on the court. That was the closest McGrady got to winning an NBA Championship title, as the Spurs fell to the Heat 3–4.

Just a year after he left the Raptors to sign with the Magic, the team from Toronto was one Vince Carter miss away from making the Eastern Conference Finals, after a hard-fought series with the Philadelphia 76ers, who were led by Allen Iverson. The Raptors made their playoff debut a season before, in McGrady's third year on the team. They were swept in a three-game first round series by the more experienced New York Knicks. At the beginning of the season McGrady began playing more as a shooting guard, and he even started all three games of the series. Despite having veterans Antonio Davis and Charles Oakley on the roster, the Raptors stood no chance with the team that had made the NBA Finals the season prior.

The 1999–2000 season would turn out to be a breakthrough for McGrady, who notched 15.4 points, 6.3 rebounds and 1.9 blocks. The last stat corresponded with the player spending more time as a shooting guard, as the 6'8" McGrady was taller than most of his opponents playing the same position. He was third in voting for the NBA Sixth Man of the Year (*ex aequo* with Cedric Ceballos) and sixth in voting for the Most Improved Player awards. A year later he made such progress that he finally earned the Most Improved Player award, after averaging 26.8 points, 7.5 rebounds and 4.6 assists on a Magic team that was seriously harmed by the injury of the other big-name free agent, the 28-year-old Grant Hill. Hill was supposed to be the team leader, yet his season ended after just four games with an ankle injury. He was signed to a seven-year deal worth $93 million. Throughout the course of the deal Hill would appear in just 200 games, as he was constantly unable to return to full health. With the next best player on the team being rookie Mike Miller, McGrady had to mature quickly and become the main scorer for the Magic, while the size and length of Hill's contract seriously limited the team's chances of signing other significant free agents.

McGrady would go on to lead the league in scoring for two seasons in a row, averaging 32.1 points per game during 2002–03 and 28.0 during 2003–04. He was then traded to the Houston Rockets, after asking for the move following the Magic finishing last in the league in 2004. McGrady and the Chinese giant Yao Ming could have formed a championship-caliber duo, yet they never stayed healthy long enough to make a deep run into the NBA postseason. Nicknamed "The Big Sleep" due to his facial expression, which made him look uninterested and tired, McGrady was anything but. He ended his career with averages of 19.6 points, 5.6 rebounds and 4.4 assists, making 43.5 percent of his shots. While the end of his career was rather unimpressive, as he would bounce around from team to team, not able to make an impact on the Knicks, the Pistons, the Hawks or the Spurs, in his prime he was one of the best scorers in league history.

For proof one must look no further than the 13 points he scored in 35 seconds at the end of the game between his Rockets and the Spurs, on the 9th of December 2004. With 49 seconds left and the Spurs leading by ten, a lot of home fans were already heading toward the exits. The Rockets were able to stop the team from San Antonio on four consecutive plays, while McGrady made four three-pointers in a row and one free throw. The last of said three-pointers was a runner, that McGrady was able to make after stealing the ball and rushing toward the opposing basket with two seconds left in the game. The Spurs would go on to win the 2004 NBA Championship, which makes McGrady's performance all-the-more impressive, despite occurring in a regular season game.

The performance stands out in NBA history, but it probably would not have been possible without the program put in place by team president Isiah Thomas, who brought along the teenager slowly and took care of his needs before resigning after he was not able to purchase a bigger part of the Raptors in the middle of McGrady's rookie season. Thomas was one of the executives responsible for the influx of high school players into the NBA, as he not only brought in McGrady in 1997, but also wanted Bryant in 1996, as well as Kevin Garnett in 1995. The success enjoyed by said players prompted NBA teams to draft 18-year-old athletes, who were mostly raw, inexperienced and underdeveloped, which led to mixed results when it came to their basketball careers. Some, like LeBron James or Dwight Howard, succeeded, while numerous others failed and were out of the league in a couple of years. In 2006 commissioner David Stern introduced a rule that a player was eligible for draft after being at least one year removed from high school. This was a highly controversial decision and is commented on till this day, as young players are forced to either go to college for one season or play overseas, instead of fulfilling their NBA dream.

Garnett was the one who ignited the outpouring of young players to the league, and it was one talk that Thomas had with his close friend that helped to turn him into the fifth pick in the NBA Draft. The tough kid from Chicago caught the eye of another Chicago native, Thomas, who wanted to take him with the seventh pick in the 1995 draft, the first in Toronto Raptors' history. However, he got a phone call from Kevin McHale, the Celtics legend and the man with whom he had been close since high school. Taking into account the intense rivalry between McHale's Celtics and Thomas's Pistons, the men were forced to keep their friendship a secret as their teams were battling in the Eastern Conference Finals.[29] McHale was now the general manager of the Minnesota Timberwolves, the team from his home state, who held the fifth pick in that draft. Instead of treating him as a rival, Thomas said honestly, "If you don't take him, I'm definitely taking him."[30] McHale decided to gamble on Garnett, and he developed into one of the best power forwards in league history. Garnett could not have imagined a better mentor, as McHale himself was one of the greats—in 1999 he became a member of the Hall of Fame. Larry Bird wrote about him, "I have always said that Kevin could have been an MVP any year he put his mind to it. He has every tool,"[31] which is enormous praise coming from a three-time MVP himself.

McHale won three NBA Championships as a member of the Celtics. He made six NBA All-Defensive Teams, was once selected to the All-NBA First Team, and was a seven-time All-Star. He retired with career averages of 17.9 points, 7.3 rebounds and 1.7 blocks per game. His best individual performance came on the 3rd of March 1985, when he scored 56 points against the Pistons, at that time the most in Celtics history. That record stood for nine days, as team leader Larry Bird beat it against Atlanta, with the Hawks bench memorably reacting with laughter to some of his improbable made shots. During that season McHale was a sixth man, but once he entered the starting lineup in February, following Cedric Maxwell's injury, for the next four seasons he would become the starter, while Maxwell was traded after the season to the Clippers for backup center Bill Walton. The Hall of Famer started 400 of the 971 games he played in the NBA, but he averaged 31 minutes per game throughout his career, which shows how important of a player he was for the Celtics. Along with Bird and Robert Parish, they formed one of the best frontcourts in league history, known as the Big Three. McHale was another in the long line of Celtics sixth men, starting with Frank Ramsey and John Havlicek.

Prior to the 1980 draft Celtics president Red Auerbach won the coin flip for the number-one pick. He however decided to trade down in the draft and acquired the third pick from the Warriors plus their center Robert Parish, as he heard that the Warriors' owner, Al Attles, wanted to select center Joe Barry Carroll, whose acquisition would make Parish expendable.[32] The Celtics also traded the 13th pick in that draft. Attles was desperate to take Carroll, so he accepted the trade offer from Auerbach.[33] Parish actually wanted to leave Golden State anyway if the team would not meet his contract demands. Joe Barry Carroll was nicknamed "Joe Barely Cares" for the lack of emotion he had shown on the court, but the name itself seemed to overshadow his basketball skills.[34] The trade that brought him to Golden State is considered to be Auerbach's masterstroke, even though Carroll retired with averages of 17.7 points, 7.7 rebounds and 1.6 blocks, which were strikingly similar to those of McHale.

In his rookie year, McHale won an NBA Championship, as his Celtics beat the Houston Rockets. He played 20 minutes per game and averaged 10 points and 4.4 rebounds. In his twelfth NBA game McHale set a franchise record with six blocks in one game, which, just as with his scoring record, was broken rather quickly, this time by Robert Parish. In the Eastern Conference Finals the Celtics were losing to the Sixers 1–3 but were able to fight back winning the next three elimination games by a total of five points. McHale played a crucial role in the win, blocking Andrew Toney's shot that could have sealed the win for the Sixers. With that win the Celtics ended their 11-game losing streak in Philadelphia and progressed to the finals, which they won for the first time in five years—at that time an eternity for the "spoiled" Celtics fans. Up until 1986 it was the biggest championship "drought" in team history. After 1986 the Celtics won the title only once, in 2008.

In his second season McHale played better and earned 33 starts, but during the next two seasons he was again the team's designated sixth man. Peter May writes that team coach Bill Fitch "instantly recognized McHale's value as a game-changing weapon off the bench. McHale could play two positions, but he also had the capability to tilt the playing field simply by his presence on the floor." Fitch himself said that "all things considered, Kevin should go down in history as the absolutely ideal sixth man."[35] Playing McHale off the bench was a sign of the influence Red Auerbach still had on the coaches that came after him, as McHale was a better player than Maxwell, yet entering the game when the other starters were tired, he was supposed to give them new energy with his play.

The player, whom Alex Ward accurately described as "6 feet 10 inches tall, most of it elbows and knees,"[36] during the next two seasons was voted Sixth Man of the Year. Playing for Bill Fitch and later K.C. Jones, McHale was better fitted for the bench role, providing relief for either Bird or Maxwell, jumping in as the team needed either points, blocks, rebounds or all three. Pistons' head coach Chuck Daly said that "The first thing on any Celtic scouting report is to watch out for McHale, not Larry Bird."[37] What is interesting is that Bird was critical of his teammate's work ethic, as he thought that McHale should have achieved more during his career.[38] McHale ended his third NBA season with averages of 14.1 points, 6.7 rebounds and 2.3 blocks. A season later he averaged 18.4 points, 7.4 rebounds and 1.5 blocks. He crushed the competition in both votings, as in his first time being named the NBA's Sixth Man of the Year, McHale got 59 votes out of 76 available. In 1985 he got 57 votes out of 78 available.

In second place, *ex aequo* with Dan Issel of the Nuggets, with five votes in 1985, came another future Hall of Famer, the 22-year-old shooting guard Clyde Drexler. It is a common mistake to believe that the Blazers passed on Michael Jordan because of already having a similar player in Drexler in the 1984 NBA Draft. The team from Portland, holding the second pick, decided to select center Sam Bowie instead of Jordan, who went with the third pick to the Bulls. The common belief then was that teams were built from the center, and Bowie was the second-best center available in the draft, ranked only below Hakeem Olajuwon, a Nigerian-born former soccer goalkeeper, who did not play basketball until he turned 15. With great hands, quick feet and remarkable coordination, he was a surefire first pick. The Blazers had to pick between Bowie and Jordan, although, at that time, it did not seem such a hard choice. Even the general manager of the Bulls, Rod Thorn, felt the need to justify his decision to pick Jordan: "There just wasn't a center available.... What can you do? ... We've taken a step in the right direction. Jordan isn't going to turn this franchise around. I wouldn't ask him to. I wouldn't put that kind of pressure on him."[39] The truth was that only a few knew how good Jordan actually was, and no one expected he would become this good.

Bowie on the flipside was a much-hyped prospect, a high school phenom, who averaged around 28 points and 18 rebounds at Lebanon High School in Pennsylvania. He was steadily progressing as a college player at Kentucky, but by the end of his sophomore year he landed awkwardly on his left foot after a dunk. After the game the doctors found a stress fracture in his left tibia. He continued to practice throughout the summer, not knowing that the fracture had not fully healed. Bowie was forced to sit out not one, but two seasons, since the bone could not heal naturally, and it had to be surgically repaired. He was granted an extra year of play by the NCAA and made the first team All-American, hiding the pain he was still feeling. He also hid it when being checked by the Blazers team doctor.[40] A healthy Bowie was a truly dominant player, dunking the ball on the one end of the floor and blocking shots at the other seemingly at will. The 7'1" center simply appealed to the Blazers more than Michael Jordan, and Clyde Drexler was not the only reason behind their decision.

Drexler was never rated as highly as Jordan—to be honest, nobody was and probably nobody ever will be—and even when it came to selecting the Dream Team, despite finishing second in the 1992 MVP voting, following the best season of his career, he did not make the first ten of the players selected to go to the Barcelona Olympics. The last two roster spots were a subject of discussion, as they were considered to be either given to two outstanding college players, because it was just too hard to pick between Christian Laettner and Shaquille O'Neal, or maybe one of them would be given to Isiah Thomas, famously left out of the roster on Jordan's request. The late selection furthered the relatively passive, but visible, animosity between Jordan and Drexler, especially after the two faced off in the NBA Finals and Jordan set an NBA-record six three-pointers in a half of a game, dominating the Blazers' shooting guard.

In Jack McCallum's podcast devoted to the Dream Team, in which the esteemed basketball writer comments on the interviews he had recorded for his 2012 book, *Dream Team: How Magic, Larry, Charles, and the Greatest Team of All Time Conquered the World and Changed the Game of Basketball*

Forever, there is a very telling snippet from the talk McCallum had with Drexler. Thirteen years after retiring from professional basketball, Drexler says that he was "bigger, faster, stronger [and] did everything [Jordan] could do, except shoot more."[41] McCallum quickly dismisses that notion by a quote from Jordan himself, who describes Drexler as "a poor man's Michael Jordan." The comparisons between the two seemed absurd when they were still active players, and they are more absurd even now. There was also was no merit to them during the 1984 draft, after Drexler was coming off a rather unremarkable rookie season.

Back in college in his home state of Houston, he was described as "all subtlety and swirl and perhaps the finest athlete in the college game."[42] After three years on the Cougars, Drexler was selected with the 14th pick in the 1983 NBA Draft by the Portland Trail Blazers. The Rockets held the first pick, and they picked the best player available, center Ralph Sampson. In his first season in the NBA, Drexler was on the bench, playing 17.2 minutes per game behind either starting shooting guard Jim Paxson or small forward Calvin Natt. He averaged 7.7 points and 1.9 rebounds, but made himself stand out with his dunking ability, which earned him a spot in the 1984 Slam Dunk Contest. The competition was reintroduced in a new form after seven years, when it featured 22 participants, one from each NBA team.

Drexler was not even the sixth man on his team. That role belonged to power forward Kenny Carr, who, despite starting 57 of the 82 games he played in that season, got one vote for the 1984 Sixth Man of the Year Award, finishing far behind the recipient, Kevin McHale. The sixth pick in the 1977 draft, Carr would be by today's standards considered a bust, as he failed to become a starter on the Lakers, yet was able to contribute for the Blazers for four seasons, after joining the team as a 27 year old. After the 1984–85 season it was Drexler who ended up after McHale, improving his stats to 17.2 points, 6 rebounds, 5.5 assists and 2.2 steals per game, while starting 43 of the 80 games he appeared in.

In his fourth season in Portland Drexler became the best player on the team, but he refused to take on the leadership role, as he did not react too kindly to criticism. He found himself arguing with veteran coach Jack Ramsay and his successor, Mike Schuler, over matters such as "Drexler's lackadaisical practice habits, his sometimes questionable shot selection, his lack of discipline in Portland's half-court offense and his failure to assert himself as a team leader."[43] Don Nelson, then coach of the Golden State Warriors, in 1990 called Drexler the most overrated player in the league, because, "He chips away at what an organization's trying to do. He's the worst of all kinds because he comes off as polite. He's religious, devoted to family. Yet in the context of a team, he's destructive."[44] Still, it was Drexler who led a stacked Blazers team twice to the NBA Finals, where it lost to the Pistons (1990) and the Bulls (1992). During the 1994–95 season Drexler, after playing 11 and a half seasons for the Blazers and averaging 20.4 points, 6.1 rebounds, 5.6 assists and two steals per game, asked for a trade. The team was rebuilding, and he did not want to develop new players.[45] While there was initially a possibility that he could go to the Sonics, Drexler joined the Rockets, where he intended to help his home state team to repeat as NBA Champions. After three and a half seasons Drexler ended his NBA career. His number was retired by the Blazers and the Rockets.

During his last two seasons in the NBA, Drexler was playing along-side Olajuwon and Charles Barkley, who joined the Rockets following a promising, yet ultimately disappointing four seasons in Phoenix. When Drexler retired, the team brought in another veteran in hopes of one last championship run. Scottie Pippen, 33 years old at the time, was still the youngest of the three future Hall of Famers. Having spent his whole pro-fessional basketball career in Chicago, the 6'8" small forward became one of the best defenders in basketball history—which in no small part was due to his everyday practices with Michael Jordan—and won six NBA Champi-onships. Underpaid for years, he finally signed a big contract—$67 million over five years—with the Bulls and was immediately traded to the Rock-ets. In order for his team to afford Pippen, Barkley took a large pay cut and signed a one-year contract for $1 million, showing how committed he was to winning his first NBA Championship. Injuries, Barkley's questionable work ethic and Pippen's struggles to learn the Rockets' system led to disap-pointment, and a season later Pippen was traded to the Trail Blazers. The move was executed by Blazers general manager Bob Whitsitt, who origi-nally drafted Pippen in 1987, yet traded him for the eighth pick in that draft, center Olden Polynice, and two second-round picks back when he was the general manager of the Seattle SuperSonics. Referring to that twist of fate, Pippen joked: "I guess I owe Bob twice."[46]

Pippen got really close to finally making a trip to the finals without Jordan in 2000, but his team buried a chance to win a decisive Game Seven against the Lakers in the Western Conference Finals despite leading 71–55 by the end of the third quarter, until Brian Shaw made a three-pointer with four seconds left. The shot gave the Lakers hope, and they went on an incredible run, which would result in them winning the game 89–84. The game influenced the fate of both franchises, and while Pippen remained a starter for the Blazers for four more seasons, first as a small forward and then as a point guard, the team collapsed, while the Lakers went on to win three NBA Championships. Even though the Blazers were getting worse with each season, Pippen remained a good teammate, something he was known for throughout his career—Steve Kerr, who played with him on the Bulls and the Blazers described him as "easy to talk to, and unselfish and giving."[47]

He did not however seem like that to the public following his contract dispute with the Bulls' management. In 1991 Pippen signed a seven-year, $18 million contract with the team.[48] With time though, as the salaries skyrocketed—in the summer of 1996 a yet unproved forward Juwan Howard became the NBA's first $100 million dollar man, signing a deal worth $105 million over seven years—he found himself 122nd when it came to salaries in the NBA. Back when he signed the contract he was happy that he had financial safety and could remain a provider for his extensive family—he had 11 older siblings, two of whom were handicapped, and so was his father. In case of an injury, the deal served as "insurance policy" for the player.[49] With the rules changed and the rights to renegotiate the contract prohibited, he was stuck with his long-term deal. Just a couple of years earlier the deal seemed a small miracle for a raw, athletic and skinny prospect out of Central Arkansas.

Jerry Krause, the general manager of the Bulls, said that looking at Pippen, he recognized his potential as someone who could one day be a great defender mostly due to his physical gifts: "a guy with long arms and quick feet and big hands … who was not a good shooter."[50] While the shooting could be worked on—Jordan himself was not a great shooter when he entered the NBA—the athletic gifts could not be duplicated. The Bulls' strength coach Al Vermeil appreciated Pippen's fluidity, meaning he did not waste as much energy when running on the floor as other players. He was extremely durable, while also being a great jumper.[51] Jordan was presumably happy with the pick—at least that is what Jerry Krause claimed in his interview with Adrian Wojnarowski for the latter's podcast—because Pippen was simply tough.[52] Toughness was a quality Jordan enjoyed the most, as he was constantly testing his teammates during workouts, talking trash and belittling them in order to harden them for the playoffs, when they needed to step up.

Jordan, recognizing Pippen's talent, took it upon himself to toughen his new teammate, becoming a teacher for the player from a relatively small college, and decided to invest in him.[53] Capable of playing and guarding all five positions, as he was a point guard in high school, and his athleticism allowed him to stop taller opponents, Pippen became the perfect complementary player to Jordan, who could showcase his offensive talents while Pippen handled the toughest defensive assignments. Before he became that type of player though, the small forward was a reserve for the Bulls, not even starting one game during his rookie year, while playing 20.9 minutes behind Brad Sellers, the 7'0" forward, who was constantly mocked, ridiculed and abused by Jordan because the management chose him over guard Johnny Dawkins, whom Jordan considered the obvious pick in the 1986 draft.[54]

Sellers lost his place in the starting lineup already in the 1987 playoffs, as he started just four games to Pippen's six. It was however only after Sellers was traded away that Pippen became a full-time starter. In his seventeenth season in the league, 2003–04, he returned to Chicago, but played in just 23 games, starting six of them. By then the Bulls were a totally different team, as they went through three head coaches and finished the season with 23 wins.

Right: **Clyde Drexler started his Hall of Fame career on the bench (1992).**

3

From the Bench to a Starting Role (on a Different Team)

Detlef Schrempf
> *Forward. In the NBA: 1985–2001. Bench: Pacers. Starter: SuperSonics.*

Jim McIlvaine
> *Center. In the NBA: 1994–2001. Bench: Bullets. Starter: SuperSonics.*

James Harden
> *Guard. In the NBA: 2009– . Bench: Thunder. Starter: Rockets.*

The NBA offers only 150 starting spots for the best players in the world and, considering such factors as personal preferences, luck and salary cap, it is evident that a bench player on one team could be not so much a starter, but one of the two or three best players on another one. Sometimes it does not take a breakout season for such an athlete to get the opportunity to showcase his abilities. For example, Jermaine O'Neal, drafted by the Portland Trail Blazers with the 17th pick in the 1996 draft, had spent four seasons on the bench until he got his chance to start for the Indiana Pacers. After just one season as a starter, O'Neal made the All-Star Team and won the 2001–02 Most Improved Player award. Because of poor grades O'Neal could not attend college, but after being drafted, that did not matter much. Nicknamed "The Kid," the player was brought along slowly by the Blazers' organization, which was well aware of his potential. O'Neal himself was confident in his abilities, as he declared, "A couple of years from now, I'm going to be an NBA All-Star," before playing even a single game in the NBA.[1] That would not be possible in Portland, as the team was bringing in new, produce-now players on his position almost every year and, in consequence, stunting his growth. He needed to be traded in order to maximize his potential.

There have been numerous talented players who simply did not get the opportunity or support necessary to develop their game. While there

45

are some players labeled as busts, who came into the league carrying great expectations and failed to make it in the NBA, it is safe to assume that there are no accidental players in the league. Even though it is convenient for some fans and journalists to label players as "bums" or "failures" in order to get clicks, followers and likes, every athlete who has put on an NBA team's uniform during a regular season game is capable of playing basketball and has an understanding of the game on a level well beyond that of an average person. The reason for the failure—understood here as an inability, and not a depiction of a given person—is a culmination of factors, but one of the most important is the circumstances. Given the chance, those with the right work ethic indeed become at least serviceable players for a couple of seasons.

Before I get to the three players analyzed in this chapter, I want to point out something that the NBA-oriented reader undoubtedly already noticed—all three players whose career narratives will be presented here have played for the Seattle SuperSonics/Oklahoma City Thunder. By narrowing my focus to one franchise, I want to highlight two things. First, I want to show how one team is capable of: noticing the talent which the other team overlooked; overrating and overpaying for mediocre talent, to the point of destroying a good team; and not appreciating enough the talent that it has and breaking up a potential dynasty. Second, while it can be argued that three such players may be found in the history of each of the other 29 NBA teams, Seattle/Oklahoma is special because of the relocation that took place in 2008, effectively ending high-profile professional men's basketball—luckily the city still has the WNBA's Storm—in Seattle. While it is unreasonable to blame the demise of Seattle basketball solely on general manager Wally Walker's infatuation with Jim McIlvaine, the free agent signing may be considered the first step in the demise of the Sonics, just as they were turning around years of playoff futility, coming off a hard-fought 1996 NBA Finals series against the 72–10 Chicago Bulls. One former bench player did not kill a franchise, although his signing did play its part in the process.

Established in 1966, the SuperSonics (in 1969 the team changed its original spelling by adding the second capital "S") were part of the city's rebranding "from a loggy old frontier town into a shiny technotopia of glass and light," which explains the futuristic name of the team.[2] Seattle paid $1.75 million to the NBA for the privilege of housing one of the five expansion teams, rounding up the number of NBA teams to 14. Thirteen years after the team was established (and 11 after completing their first NBA season) Seattle celebrated its first championship. The city would have to wait until 2014, when the Seahawks won the XLVIII Super Bowl, for its team to emerge triumphant in a professional sports league. Following the 1978 championship, the Sonics appeared in the finals a year later, but lost to the Bullets, who have won their sole championship in that series. The year of 1996 was the last time that the NBA Finals were played in Seattle (the Thunder made the 2012 finals, but lost 1–4 to the Heat).

In 1983 the team that paid the NBA less than $2 million to be part of basketball royalty was sold to Barry Ackerley for $21 million. In the '80s the team made the Conference Finals twice, but also failed to reach the playoffs three times. In the '90s the Sonics became one of the teams to watch, impressing fans and experts alike with their high-flying, fast-paced offense and hard defense. Led by the point guard–power forward duo of Gary Payton and Shawn Kemp, and coached by George Karl, the Sonics were in the top three of the Western Conference when it came to their regular season record five times, but made the finals only once. In 2001 Howard Schultz bought the Sonics for $200 million. The founder of Starbucks was sold the team only after promising that they would stay in Seattle, and when he sold the Sonics to an ownership group led by Oklahoma businessmen Clay Bennett and Aubrey McClendon for $350 million in 2006, he made them promise the exact same thing. However, the businessmen had other plans and in 2008 moved the team to Oklahoma City.

When hurricane Katrina hit New Orleans in 2005, the New Orleans Hornets arena was only slightly damaged, but the area around it was completely flooded. League commissioner David Stern came up with the idea of temporarily moving the team to Oklahoma City, while New Orleans was healing from the wounds suffered from the natural disaster.[3] The people in Oklahoma quickly embraced the Hornets, despite the team rebuilding, with a roster consisting of NBA journeymen like Speedy Claxton, Marc Jackson and Marcus Fizer and promising, but still rather raw, players like Chris Paul, David West and J.R. Smith. "Embraced" may actually be too small of a word to describe the enthusiasm with which Oklahomans welcomed their first professional sports franchise, even though it was just a rental: "OKC's arena was almost always sold out, and it became instantly notorious as one of the loudest places in the league." Furthermore, "attendance in Oklahoma City was far higher than it had ever been in New Orleans,"[4] which meant that the city made sense as a possible NBA location in the future, despite the small market.

Meanwhile in Seattle, the league and the owner were struggling to get funding for a new sports arena. After Schultz bought the Sonics, they have made the playoffs only twice, and while Seattle was considered a basketball-crazed city by outsiders and Sonics players themselves, the basketball fandom there was fading. Ray Allen, who played for the Sonics during that time and was traded a season before the team moved to Oklahoma, wrote in his autobiography: "I'd always believed the Sonics would never leave Seattle, given such enthusiastic support from the fans at KeyArena. Turns out, those fans represented a relatively small sample size."[5] Detlef Schrempf, one of the key members of the 1995–96 Sonics, who still has close ties with the city of Seattle, said about the Thunder: "There's nothing left from the Sonics, really. There's no tradition. It's a totally new organization, a different city."[6] Schrempf felt that the leadership and the politicians did not do enough to keep professional men's basketball in Seattle. It was revealed in leaked e-mails not long after the two Oklahoma businessmen bought the team that the acquisition was made with the clear intention of relocation.[7]

Schrempf played for six seasons for the Sonics, the longest he has been on one team during his NBA career, which also included three and a half seasons in Dallas, four and a half in Indiana, and two rather frustrating years in Portland. The frustration was caused by the issues with team chemistry on the Blazers. In his first season there, 1999–2000, Portland had the deepest roster in the NBA, as the bench players on that team (Jermaine O'Neal, Brian Grant, Schrempf, Bonzi Wells, Greg Anthony) would have easily been starters on other teams in the league. The expectations were high, and the team acquired big names in the summer: "Scottie [Pippen], Steve [Smith], Detlef—what can you say…. If we can't get it done now, I don't know when we ever will" said Brian Grant, the reserve power forward.[8] The team had the highest salary in the league ($73.9 million), more than double of the $34 million salary cap. The starters (Arvydas Sabonis, Rasheed Wallace, Scottie Pippen, Steve Smith, Damon Stoudamire) themselves were earning more than full rosters of 25 teams in the league.[9] The Blazers came very close to the Finals, as they were able to come back from a 1–3 deficit against the Lakers in the Western Conference Finals to force a Game Seven, in which they took a 71–55 lead late in the third quarter, yet lost 84–89, outscored 13–31 in the fourth quarter.

During that season Schrempf started just six of the 77 games he played in, his lowest number of starts since the 1992–93 season, the last on the Pacers. During the 2000–01 season the Blazers came back even stronger, with veteran additions of Dale Davis and Shawn Kemp, both former All-Stars. Schrempf started the season as inactive, since he was seriously considering retirement, but the Blazers saved an open roster spot for him, and he rejoined the team in January. Not long after the All-Star break the Blazers were 40–18, but finished the season 50–32, seventh in the Western Conference. The frustrations within the team grew, and they culminated on Easter Day, during the game with the Lakers, when Rasheed Wallace threw a towel in Sabonis' face to retaliate for the team center accidentally hitting Wallace in the face during a flop. Instead of admitting that the team's best player was in the wrong, the coaches left Wallace in the game without a comment. After that Schrempf got up, cussed out the members of the staff and sat by himself at the end of the bench. When head coach Mike Dunleavy wanted to talk to Schrempf about his behavior, the player responded, "You can kiss my ass."[10] This was not the first time the German offended the coaching staff—as a member of the Sonics he refused to credit the coaches with the improvements that allowed him to enjoy his only All-NBA selection in 1994–95.[11] Despite his behavior, he continued to play on the Blazers, who were swept by the Lakers in the First Round of the playoffs.

That was the end of a rather unlikely basketball career that spanned f 22 seasons, four in college, at Washington University, and 18 in the NBA. Born in West Germany, Schrempf's primary love was soccer, but he quit after arguing with his coach and injuring his foot. At 13 he fell in love with basketball, despite such obstacles as being unable to find a basketball court or enough players to play pickup games, due to the sport's lack of popularity in his homeland.[12] Thanks to the connections he had made while playing basketball, he was able to spend one year in Centralia High, Washington, where he made such an impression on college coaches that he stayed in the U.S. and was recruited by Washington University. As a freshman he saw little playing time (11.2 minutes per game), but during his second year the number of minutes per game he would spend on the court tripled. Capable of playing all five positions, the 6'10" Schrempf earned comparisons to Magic Johnson for his ball handling ability. The player welcomed them, saying, "If I could choose, I'd like to play more like Magic. I get satisfaction passing the ball."[13]

Before Dirk Nowitzki, Schrempf was the original Wunderkind, and he was the first German who joined the team that drafted the future Hall of Fame power forward, the Dallas Mavericks, with the eighth pick in the 1985 draft. In the same draft, with the 17th pick, the team from Dallas grabbed another player from West Germany, the 7'1" center Uwe Blab. Nowitzki was picked ninth in 1998 by the Milwaukee Bucks, but was traded for the sixth pick, Robert Traylor, to the Mavericks. While Nowitzki started 24 games in his rookie year, Schrempf was named the starter for a total of 22 games during the three and a half seasons he has spent on the Mavericks. Blab started just one game during his four seasons in Dallas.

The expectations were relatively high regarding Schrempf. Sam Goldaper of the *New York Times* predicted that he should make an immediate impact on the team, as "his open-court game fits in with Dallas's galaxy of shooters: Mark Aguirre, Rolando Blackman, Derek Harper and Brad Davis, all plus-.500 shooters from the field."[14] Instead he found himself coming off the bench behind either Aguirre or Sam Perkins, the starting forwards on the Dick Motta-coached Mavs.

In his third season on the Mavericks, Schrempf was discussed as a possible trade target for the Knicks in exchange for center Bill Cartwright, whom the team from New York was actively shopping due to his injury history and the fact that they already had a great center in Patrick Ewing. Ewing had to play as power forward if he was to share the court with Cartwright. The move did not happen, and Schrempf spent another year on the Mavericks, playing fewer minutes per game than the season before due to the rise of another sixth man, Roy Tarpley, the second-year power forward selected with the seventh pick in the 1986 NBA Draft.

After playing 18.7 minutes and averaging 7.5 points and 7.1 rebounds per game during his rookie year, Tarpley was given a more important role on the Mavericks next season. Playing 28.5 minutes per game, he was making 13.5 points and grabbing 11.8 rebounds, showing substantial improvements and earning the title of the 1988 NBA Sixth Man of the Year, decisively winning (67–13) the vote with Utah's Thurl Bailey, a power forward who, playing behind Karl Malone, was averaging 19.6 points and 6.5 rebounds. The Mavericks made the Western Conference Finals that season, but lost to the eventual champions, the Los Angeles Lakers. Already at the time Tarpley was having problems with substance abuse—he died at 50 due to liver failure—having entered rehab before the start of his breakout NBA season. In 1988–89 he played in just 19 games due to knee injuries and was still having issues with drugs and alcohol. After that season the Mavericks extended his contract—the five-year, $9 million deal that he signed in 1989 was the highest in franchise history. As Jack McCallum put it:

> The Mavs did not just stick with Tarpley, a potential superstar, through several alcohol- and drug-related incidents; they built the franchise around him. But he failed two drugs tests and refused to take a third, thus striking out under the NBA's drug policy. He was banned from the league just before the start of the 1991–92 season.[15]

When McCallum's article was published, the Mavericks were on the brink of becoming the worst team in league history. They won 11 games (13.4 percent), failing to "beat" the 1972–73 Sixers, who have won just nine games, for that dubious title. Tarpley made a return to the NBA in the 1994–95 season, following a successful stint in Greece, but was permanently banned from the league for the same reasons as earlier.

During the same 1992–93 season, when the Mavericks were the league's bottom feeders, Schrempf was enjoying his first NBA season as a starter for the Indiana Pacers. Team GM Donnie Walsh acquired the 26 year old for the 31-year-old center Herb Williams in the middle of the 1988–89 season, and the German was given a bigger role on his new team. The trade was made because of Tarpley, as the Mavericks needed a big man to fill in for the potential superstar while Tarpley was in rehab. Schrempf was still coming off the bench, but coach Dick Versace moved him from small forward to power forward, and the switch better suited his game. He started his first full season with the Pacers 15 pounds heavier, yet was able to retain his speed, passing ability and shooting touch.[16] He finished the 1989–90 season with averages of 16.2 points, 7.9 rebounds and 3.2 assists, all career-highs, while starting just 18 games. He lost the voting for the Sixth Man of the Year Award to Ricky Pierce by a decisive margin of 69 votes (77–8). Pierce was averaging just 2.8 rebounds and 2.3 assists, but also making 23 points per game on the Milwaukee Bucks. Since the sixth man is mostly associated with offensive abilities, which make his presence on the court with the starters superfluous, a scorer like Pierce was the obvious choice over an all-around player such as Schrempf, at least from a basketball purist's perspective.

A year later though, Schrempf won the award while posting very similar numbers as the year before—16.1 points, 8 rebounds, 3.7 assists per game. The Pacer beat the Suns shooting guard, Dan Majerle—13.6 points, 5.4 rebounds, 2.8 assists per game—by just one vote, 38–37. Pierce got just six votes, despite averaging 20.5 points, 2.4 rebounds and 2.2 assists, which was not really that big of a decline in each of the three major statistical categories to validate such a small number of points from the 96 media representatives. It is possible that voter fatigue played its part in the process, especially since Pierce not only made the All-Star Team that year, but also already won the award in the past, in 1987. The Pacers finished the season 41–41 under coach Bob Hill and were eliminated in the first round of the playoffs. In the 1991–92 season the team showed no improvement, winning one game less and again getting eliminated in the first round. Still, Schrempf was once more the recipient of the Sixth Man of the Year Award, now noting 17.3 points, 9.6 rebounds and 3.9 assists. His best game of that season came on February 11, 1992, against one of the worst teams in the league, the Orlando Magic. Schrempf scored 26 points and grabbed 23 rebounds. He scored 20 or more points in 26 games and had the third-highest point average on the team, behind esteemed shooters Reggie Miller and Chuck Person.

This time Majerle was third in the voting, while the runner-up was Šarūnas Marčiulionis of the Golden State Warriors, enjoying a breakout season under Don Nelson. It was Nelson's son, Donnie, who befriended Marčiulionis while touring the world with a basketball team representing Athletes in Action, a Christian sports organization. The swingman was selected by the Warriors with the 127th pick in the 1987 draft and joined the team two years later, becoming the first Soviet player to play in the NBA. The 6'5" Marčiulionis led all NBA guards in field-goal percentage in the 1991–92 season and was awarded with a five-year, $10.4 million contract extension by the Warriors after his third season in the league. However, he was soon plagued by injuries and would play just 30 games next season, and miss the whole of the 1993–94 campaign with a knee injury, just like his teammate, starting point guard Tim Hardaway. Despite the injuries, the Warriors managed to win 50 games that season. Marčiulionis would spend three more seasons in the league, each on a different team—the Sonics, the Kings and the Nuggets—but lost his explosiveness while struggling to stay healthy for the duration of a whole 82-game season.

During the 1994–95 Sonics season, Marčiulionis was coming off the bench behind Schrempf, who was playing his second season in Seattle. Moved back to the small forward position, the German took some time to adapt to playing in the frontcourt next to Shawn Kemp, following a great year on the Pacers, which he finished with averages of 19.1 points, 9.5 rebounds and six assists. The then 30-year-old Schrempf was the only player in the NBA who made the top 25 in the aforementioned three statistical categories. A few months after the trade, Phil Taylor of *Sports Illustrated* wrote that "it was the acquisition of the versatile, 6'10" Schrempf that many observers believe may put championship rings on the Sonics' fingers."[17] The Pacers traded him to the Sonics for Derrick McKey, who has spent six seasons in Seattle and was acquired because new coach Larry Brown wanted him for his defensive abilities. In the 1994–95 season Schrempf made the All-NBA Third Team, and a season later his team has made the NBA Finals, where the Sonics lost to one of the best teams in NBA history, the 72–10 Chicago Bulls.

In the summer following the 1996 finals the team made one key acquisition, which would shape its future for years to come. Shawn Kemp was the best Sonics player during their finals run, yet he was making just slightly above $3 million dollars, due to the contract renewal he had signed in 1994. The contract was non-negotiable until October 1997, following the collective bargaining agreement, which prohibited the player from renegotiating his contract for three years after signing an extension. This caused a lot of grief and frustration for Kemp, who eventually demanded a trade following a turbulent 1996–97 season. Interestingly, he signed the deal following an unsuccessful trade attempt which would see him change teams with another famously underpaid superstar. Kemp was so beloved in Seattle that when the team considered trading him (along with Ricky Pierce and a first-round draft pick) for Scottie Pippen in the summer of 1994, the fans were outraged. Owner Ackerley responded by vetoing the trade, even though Karl and Bulls GM Jerry Krouse had already come to terms. The Sonics did not have a GM at the time, as Bob Whittsitt, that season's Executive of the Year, was fired after the playoff loss.

In 1997 Kemp was traded to the Cleveland Cavaliers, where he immediately signed a seven-year contract for $107 million, becoming just the fifth player in NBA history—after Juwan Howard, Alonzo Mourning, Shaquille O'Neal and Kevin Garnett—to sign a contract for $100 million or more. He got what he asked for—albeit on a different team—when he complained to the press before the start of the 1996–97 season: "When you play for seven years and you've proved yourself to be an All-Star, then you see guys who haven't proved themselves sign for millions of dollars, you have a right to be upset."[18] The interview was the consequence of Kemp sitting out three weeks of training camp and missing five exhibition games. After the Sonics lost to the Rockets in the second round of the playoffs, Kemp said that he never wanted to play for the team again.[19] After the trade Kemp spent three seasons in Cleveland, during which he took the team to the playoffs only once.

Although he stated otherwise on numerous occasions, it was evident that the reason for Kemp's frustration with the Sonics was the signing of the reserve center from the Washington Bullets, Jim McIlvaine, by general manager Wally Walker in 1996 free agency. Originally the Sonics wanted to sign Brian Williams, who played just seven games for the Bulls during the 1996–97 regular season, but played in 19 games in the playoffs as a substitute for Luc Longley. During the Bulls' 1997 title run, Williams averaged 6.1 points and 3.7 rebounds in 17.7 minutes per game. In Game Three of the finals, which the Bulls lost, he had 16 points and 6 rebounds. Instead of joining the Sonics, Williams decided to sign a seven-year, $45 million deal with the Detroit Pistons. In 1998 he legally changed his name to Bison Dele to honor his Cherokee ancestry. On July 8, 2002, Dele mysteriously disappeared while on a boat near the coast of Tahiti, never to be seen again.

When Shaquille O'Neal moved to the Los Angeles Lakers in the summer of 1996, teams in the Western Conference were forced to upgrade their center positions. By then teams were not necessarily built from the center, but it was still the norm, and mediocre tall big men were in high demand. The Sonics' coach, George Karl, characterized the situation as follows: "We hired the 7'1" McIlvaine to be our Shaq-stopper,[20] but the guy he stopped instead was his new teammate. Shawn Kemp resented Mac's seven-year $33.6 million deal, and I didn't blame him…. Shawn would be making about a million less than the unproven new guy."[21] The 32nd overall pick in the 1994 NBA Draft, McIlvaine had a rather pedestrian rookie year, playing fewer than 10 minutes a game (9.7 to be exact), grabbing 1.9 rebounds, scoring 1.7 points and blocking 1.1 shots per game.

He was the team's third center, behind the 7'7" Romanian Gheorghe Muresan and veteran Kevin Duckworth. Duckworth, the 1988 NBA Most

Improved Player of the Year and two-time All-Star, was the starting center on the Portland Trail Blazers teams that made the NBA Finals in 1990 and 1992. With his game continuing to regress—the process already began in Portland—due to weight issues and injuries, Duckworth spent only two seasons in Washington, before being traded to Milwaukee. After the 1995 trade, McIlvaine became the reserve center, and his playing minutes increased to 14.9 per contest. He did not show much improvement on the offensive end, finishing the season with 2.3 points per game, but it was his defensive skills that made him such an interesting player for the Sonics. His 2.1 blocks per game were good for ninth place in the league, the same as Shaquille O'Neal and better than Vlade Divac, Shawn Kemp or one of the best defensive centers in the NBA, Ervin Johnson. Johnson was great for the Sonics during the 1995–96 regular season, but was moved to the bench during the playoffs, and the team decided not to prolong his contract following his poor performances in the postseason.

The management was impressed by a different player, whose team did not even make the playoffs, while he himself started just six games in the 1995–96 season. During those six games, the last six of the season, against three of the worst—Raptors (twice), Timberwolves and Celtics— and two of the best—Magic and Bulls—teams in the league, he was averaging 4.7 points, 6.2 rebounds and 5.2 blocks per game. In the last game of the season, against the eventual champions, McIlvaine had six points, nine blocks and 11 rebounds. The Bullets lost by ten points, with the Bulls resting their starters (only Scottie Pippen played 30 minutes) before the playoffs.

The contract was largely discussed even before McIlvaine played a single game for the Sonics, as he was considered overpaid, making more than Kemp, Pippen, Karl Malone or Mitch Richmond. Phil Taylor of *Sports Illustrated* tried to be optimistic about the deal:

> if McIlvaine provides the interior defense the SuperSonics need to transform them from last season's NBA finalists into this season's champions, he will seem like a bargain. His 2.08 blocked shots per game ranked 10th in the league even though he averaged only 14.9 minutes, and his projected 6.67 blocks per 48 minutes was the best such mark in the league.[22]

However, he concluded that: "If Sonics had been careful, they wouldn't have gambled on signing McIlvaine in the first place. Now they hope that, come June, they will be rewarded for their risk."[23] A good shot-blocker and not much more, McIlvaine, somewhat predictably, failed to develop into a good offensive player, but, more importantly, he caused the aforementioned rift between Shawn Kemp and the Sonics. Kemp's frustration was visible on and off the court, as he led the league in fouls (320 in 81 games) and was late for team flights and practices. McIlvaine had 247 fouls in 82 games, but he played just 18 minutes per game, which means that per 48 minutes he averaged 9.37—second in the league behind Felton Spencer of the Golden State Warriors.

Kemp was also benched for four games late in the season and was rumored to have a drinking problem.[24] He was traded to the Cleveland Cavaliers, who acquired him and Milwaukee Bucks veteran point guard Sherman Douglas. The team from Wisconsin got the Cavs' Terrell Brandon and Tyrone Hill. The Sonics got Vin Baker, who, as it turned out, also had a drinking problem. The move started the decline of the franchise, despite a promising beginning—Baker made the All-NBA Second Team, and the Sonics won 61 games in his first season in Seattle, but were eliminated in five games by the Lakers in the Western Conference Semifinals. McIlvaine, the center who was supposed to make the difference on the defensive end in such a series, was playing just 10.4 minutes per game, despite being named the starter in four of them. He made a total of just five blocks and grabbed nine rebounds.

After the season the Sonics traded McIlvaine to the Nets and signed veteran Olden Polynice, the player who the team traded away Scottie Pippen for on the 1991 draft night. The center said about his predecessor: "No offense, but last year when that guy was on the court, Seattle was playing four-on-five. Anything I can add will be an improvement."[25] Despite being stronger at center, the team failed to make the playoffs for the first time in eight seasons. Baker regressed from 19.2 points and eight rebounds to 13.8 points and 6.2 rebounds per game. The team also got rid of head coach George Karl, whose contract was not extended. With Paul Westphal on the bench, the Sonics were able to win just 25 games in the lockout-shortened 50-game season. Up until the aforementioned 2008 move to Oklahoma City, the team went to the playoffs only three times and only once made it past the first round. In 2007, with the second pick in the draft the Sonics selected Kevin Durant, the eventual Rookie of the Year, who scored 42 points in the last game played by the Sonics, the 126–121 win over the Golden State Warriors.

The team won 20 games during its last season in Seattle, and this time, with another lottery pick, it selected Russell Westbrook. The point guard–small forward duo of Westbrook and Durant was supposed to form the core of the new franchise, a fresh start for a new team. In that draft the soon-to-be Thunder also selected Serge Ibaka, who joined the team a season later, 2009–10, and would eventually become its starting power forward. In the summer of 2009, after another bad season, the Sonics/Thunder were in the lottery again, this time picking third. With the first pick in franchise history they selected James Harden from Arizona State. In three years, with a second, fourth and third pick in three consecutive drafts, the team from Oklahoma acquired three future MVPs. While Harden had earned that title in Houston, in the summer before his departure the Oklahoma City Thunder became the first team to have three players chosen to represent the United States in the Olympics.

Durant and Westbrook were immediately named the starters, while Harden was coming off the bench. He was fine with being a complementary player. "Harden, unusually for a young player, told the team that [becoming an elite backup] was exactly what he wanted. He was more than willing to come off the bench."[26] As a freshman at Arizona State, Harden turned around a program that lost its record 15 straight games the year earlier. As an 18 year old, he was averaging 17.8 points and 3.2 assists per game. He entered the draft a year later, following an improved season on the Sun Devils (20.1 points, 4.2 assists per game). Pete Thamel of the *New York Times* wrote about his game at the time:

> He is a maestro of subtlety. He has an effective jab step, uses his shoulders to clear space and has a lethal pull-up jumper. His most impressive statistic may be that he attempted 253 free throws this season, an average of 7.7 per game. One of his defining traits is his ability to lean into defenders to draw fouls.[27]

However, there were also some concerns regarding his game, which came from the way he finished his career at Arizona State. In his final college game, in the second-round loss to Syracuse in the NCAA Tournament, Harden went just 2/10 from the floor, including 0/5 from three. Jonathan Givony described the game as "yet another NCAA tournament performance ... that will raise eyebrows even amongst [Harden's] biggest supporters."[28] He was referring to the first-round game against Temple, which Arizona State won 66–57, despite Harden's poor shooting performance (1/8 from the floor, four turnovers, seven rebounds, three assists, three steals).

As a rookie Harden did not start a single game, and ended the season with averages of 9.9 points, 3.2 rebounds and 1.8 assists per game. He scored 20 or more points in four games. Harden was a surplus player on a roster with two ball-dominant players, whose presence limited his on-court time on the Thunder. "The problem was that Harden was clearly too good to be a backup. He was a precious node of order among the chaos of an NBA game. You could give him the ball and get out of the way and trust him, almost every time, to do something dangerous with it."[29] Along with Westbrook, Durant and Ibaka, the 2010 Thunder won 52 games and became the youngest team in playoff history. In fact, a year later they became the second-youngest team to make the NBA postseason.

In his second season Harden showed vast improvement, but it was during his third season in the NBA that he turned from a good reserve player to one of the best shooting guards in the league. Steve Kerr, then a TNT analyst, suggested that Harden would in fact become the league's best shooting guard after Kobe Bryant and Dwyane Wade retired. Serving as an addition to the team's nucleus of Durant and Westbrook, "Harden has embraced and maximized the sixth man role for the Thunder, averaging a robust 16.8 points while taking just 10 shots a game this season. He is ruthlessly efficient (49.1 percent shooting), a deft playmaker (3.7 assists a game) and a perfectly low-maintenance counterpoint to his flashier teammates."[30]

The 2012 Sixth Man of the Year was averaging 17.6 points, 5.2 rebounds and 3.3 assists—which was an improvement in the two first categories in regards to his regular season stats of 16.8 points, 4.1 rebounds and 3.7 assists—in the first three rounds of the playoffs, and the Thunder had made their first of what was supposed to be multiple finals' appearances. In the NBA Finals though he struggled, noting two 2/10 shooting nights and finishing the five-game series with 37.5 field-goal percentage plus an average of 12.4 points per game. The inexperienced Thunder were beaten by the established stars of the Miami Heat, but they were poised for a quick return to the finals. Their triumph seemed just a matter of time. Harden himself said after that season that "a dynasty is being built here."[31]

Three days before the new one began, Harden was traded to the Houston Rockets (along with Cole Aldrich, Daequan Cook and Lazar Hayward) in exchange for Kevin Martin, Jeremy Lamb, two first-round and a second-round pick. Looking for an opportunity to extend Harden's contract and avoid the player becoming a restricted free agent during the next summer, the team offered him $52 million for four years. Having already committed multi-year contracts to its four starters, Durant, Westbrook, Ibaka and center Kendrick Perkins, the team wanted to avoid paying the luxury tax, which meant that it had to stay under the salary cap. Harden asked for the league maximum $60 million for four years, and the team's final offer was $55.5 million. Sam Anderson points out that

> the $4.5 million gap was symbolic: a test of Harden's civic commitment to the Thunder. If he wasn't willing to give up that fraction of a maximum salary, he probably wouldn't be willing, later, to sacrifice more important things: playing time, shots, individual glory. Such trade-offs were at the heart of Sam Presti's vision of long-term success.[32]

Harden was already sacrificing his game and playing time to accommodate his teammates, so there was no need to ask him to sacrifice even more.

In Houston he joined a Rockets team that was desperate for success. The 1994 and 1995 NBA Champions had made the Western Conference Finals in 1997 and until Harden's arrival had been to the second round of the playoffs only once, missing the postseason eight times. The

Detlef Schrempf won back-to-back Sixth Man of the Year Awards in 1991 and 1992 (1990).

analytics-obsessed Rockets' GM Daryl Morey for years wanted to bring Harden to Houston.

> An hour before his first Rockets game, Harden signed a five-year, $80 million deal—OKC had been offering $54 million for four years—and then he dropped 37 points in a win over the Pistons. Two nights later he scored 45 in Atlanta. "Back then," Morey says, "his ability to drive and be efficient was something like the best in NBA history. At least that's the data we had. It's always good to start with someone who's the best ever at something."[33]

In the eight years that followed, the Rockets did not miss the playoffs, and it was now Harden who was the centerpiece of a franchise, complemented by such superstars as Dwight Howard, Chris Paul, and Russell Westbrook, who became his teammate in the summer of 2019.

With Westbrook's departure the once-promising Thunder were now a part of NBA history, relegated to the role of one of the ultimate what-if teams. Durant, Westbrook and Harden all became league MVPs, and for years have been among the top-10 players in the league. In 2016 the Thunder again made the Western Conference Finals and had a 3–1 lead over the Golden State Warriors. Durant joined the Bay Area team the following season and won two NBA Championships. Following his departure Westbrook made league history averaging triple-doubles for three seasons in a row. Before him only one player finished an NBA season with at least ten points, ten rebounds and ten assists per game—Oscar Robertson in the 1961–62 season, while playing for the Cincinnati Royals. After three first-round playoff exits, before the start of the 2019–20 season Westbrook was traded to the Rockets.

With that move a team that came to life partially due to an acquisition of a disappointing bench player was dismantled because of its failure to recognize the potential of its own bench player. Giving too much money to an unproven reserve was the beginning of the demise of the Sonics, while not being willing to pay a future superstar what he turned out to be worth put an end to a potential championship nucleus of the Thunder. This somewhat tragic story would not have been possible without the acquisition of another great bench player, Detlef Schrempf, who proved to be a great complementary option for the superstar duo of Payton and Kemp. Two ball-dominant players, Payton and Schrempf, were able to coexist and win basketball games just like Westbrook and Harden were doing in Houston. Both duos failed to win NBA Championships.

4

Champions Off the Bench

Bob McAdoo
Center. In the NBA: 1972–1986. NBA Champion: 1982, 1985.
Mitch Richmond
Guard. In the NBA: 1988–2002. NBA Champion: 2002.

Nothing solidifies a basketball player's legacy more than a championship. While superstars are presented as individuals in a team sport, unique in their basketball abilities, they are also evaluated on the basis of team success. Just one championship is enough to elevate the status of a given player and ingrain him into the tissue of the local society. When LeBron James won the first championship in Cleveland Cavaliers history, in the post-game interview he shouted, "Cleveland, this is for you!" as if he really thought that he won the title for his city, and the 52-year (and 147-season-long) championship drought would solve the problems of its inhabitants. If anything, the title helped in reaffirming the narrative of the prodigal son, who returned to his home state and led his team to the promised land. It did nothing to change the day-to-day lives of Ohioans.

Winning a title is more important for the career narrative of a player than really useful in evaluating his individual career. While the championships won at the end of their careers do not make these players great, the championships shed a different light on their earlier achievements, making them appear no longer in vain, as is the case with exceptional players who have never won a title. Their stories are supposed to be filled with agony, pain and frustration, simply because they failed to win a couple more games of basketball. That is why great power forwards like Charles Barkley or Karl Malone are often not regarded as highly as Tim Duncan or Kevin Garnett, both NBA Champions. And it was not like Barkley or Malone were not giving their all in order to win. Barkley demanded a trade from the Phoenix Suns after his team was eliminated twice by the Houston Rockets in the 1994 and 1995 playoffs, on their way to back-to-back NBA Championships, and then lost 1–3 to the San Antonio Spurs in the

60

first round of the 1996 playoffs. Barkley joined the Rockets before the start of the 1996–97 season, in which the team of veterans—Olajuwon, Drexler, Mario Elie, Kevin Willis, Eddie Johnson, and he—made the Western Conference Finals, but was eliminated by the Utah Jazz. For the next two seasons the Rockets were unable to get out of the first round of the playoffs, losing once again to the Jazz and then to the Lakers.

Malone was the best player on the Jazz teams that eliminated the Rockets, and would later on, following numerous failed attempts at winning the title, join the Lakers. The power forward spent 18 seasons on the Jazz and played in two finals in a row, in 1997 and 1998, during which his team fell to the Michael Jordan–led Chicago Bulls, both times, losing the series 2–4. When his Hall of Fame teammate, point guard John Stockton, ended his career in 2003, Malone signed with the Los Angeles Lakers as a 40 year old. He had the worst regular season stats of his professional career and appeared in just 42 games, but his team indeed made it to the 2004 NBA Finals, where it was upset by the Detroit Pistons. Malone had a very bad series, attempting just six shots per game and making good on a total of eight said attempts. He averaged just five points per contest, despite playing 31.2 minutes per game. He did not play in the last game of the series because of the left knee injury that kept nagging him all season.

A superstar joining an already-established, winning team is always problematic, as it often involves the new arrival taking a backseat to players who have already made the team successful. There is also the issue of whether it is because of the superstar's arrival that the team is able to remain dominant, or is he just profiting from his teammate's play? Seen that way, a superstar's move to a superior team may in fact negatively impact his legacy. Such may be the case with Kevin Durant, who joined the Golden State Warriors after they eliminated his team, the Oklahoma City Thunder, in the 2016 Western Conference Finals, despite the Thunder being up 3–1. The 2014 MVP and four-time NBA scoring champion became a member of a team that just went 73–9 and lost in the NBA Finals to the Cleveland Cavaliers. As Ethan Strauss put it,

> The Warriors still boasted of world-beating record in the games Durant missed. Many pondered whether the Warriors would be fine if KD's slot were manned by a merely competent small forward, instead of one of the very best ones ever…. If he choked, the world would have come down on him…. When he came through, on the biggest stage, it was taken for granted.[1]

Throughout history there were obviously also cases of great players joining great teams after being way past their primes, only to retire with a championship ring. Two prominent cases were that of Gary Payton and Michael Finley, who have won NBA Championships, respectively, in 2006 and 2007. Payton was 35 years old and past his prime—which included being the only point guard in NBA history to win the Defensive Player of the Year award, as well as nine All-NBA selections—when he joined Malone on the Lakers. After the season the Lakers traded him to the Celtics, where he embraced the mentor role to younger players, despite early objections. He enjoyed being on that team so much that, after a mid-season trade with the Hawks for Antoine Walker, he returned to Boston after a buyout, stating that he felt obligated to come back.[2] He played the same role next season, as he joined the Miami Heat to be the backup to Jason Williams, who was famous for his flashy plays as much as for his bad on-court decisions. More importantly, Payton rejoined O'Neal, who was traded by the Lakers after they lost the 2004 finals to the Pistons. This time Payton won the title. He retired a season later, after the aging, injury-ridden Heat were unable to make it out of the first round of the 2006 playoffs.

His teammate on that team could have been Michael Finley, a shooting guard/small forward, who was the sole star on the Dallas Mavericks before teammates Steve Nash and Dirk Nowitzki matured as basketball players. Finley spent eight and a half seasons on the Mavs, averaging 19.8 points per game, after being a part of the Jason Kidd trade with the Phoenix Suns on the 26th of December 1996. Finley was in his second year in the league then. In 2001 he signed a seven-year contract with the Mavericks, but was amnestied by the team before the 2005–06 season. Facing the decision with whom to sign, Finley joined the Spurs instead of the Heat, stating, "To be a part of a championship team, I'm excited. This is the closest I've ever been to a championship. I'm looking forward to the challenge of helping this team repeat."[3] Ironically, it was the Dallas Mavericks who made the 2006 finals. However, in 2007 the Spurs won the title, sweeping the Cleveland Cavaliers. While being a reserve for his first two seasons in San Antonio and despite coming off the bench in just 20 games of the 626 he played for the Mavericks, all in his first season in Dallas, in the 2007 playoffs Finley started all 20 games the Spurs played in on their way to their fourth championship in franchise history.

In this chapter I will focus on two players who joined the Los Angeles Lakers, a team which already held multiple NBA Championships and is regarded as historically great. Both of these players are Hall of Famers, and they both accepted the bench role behind superior players after moving to California. However, while the first one, Bob McAdoo, contributed to the 1982 and 1985 titles as a serviceable backup to Kareem Abdul-Jabbar, the second one, Mitch Richmond, appeared in just two playoff games for the 2001–02 Lakers, playing a total of four minutes and scoring three points, while a substitute for Kobe Bryant. McAdoo was a player ahead of his time, a 6'9" center who was also a shooter, while Richmond was a conventional shooting guard. Both played on bad teams in their prime, and won championships as bench players.

The main difference, apart from playing different positions, was their contributions to the championship titles the Lakers won. While Richmond's career was practically over when he became a member of the Lakers at age 36, McAdoo was 30, and because of his reputation, he was ostracized by many teams in the league. The second pick in the 1972 draft, McAdoo earned Rookie of the Year honors and a season later, after a move from power forward to center, was the league's leading scorer, averaging 30.6 points per game. He would retain that title for three seasons in a row, with averages of 34.5 and 31.1 points per game in the following two seasons. For that three-season period he also averaged 13.8 rebounds and 2.5 blocks per game. During his third year in the league McAdoo was named the league MVP. However, in the middle of the 1976–77 season, his fifth on the Braves, the team that drafted him traded him to the New York Knicks.

The reason? The Buffalo Braves simply did not win. It did not matter that McAdoo averaged 37.4 points in the 1975 playoffs, including a 50-point game, when his team lost the seven-game series against the Bullets and was blown away by an average of 13 points in the four losses. Even his teammates criticized McAdoo. Jim McMillian said, "When Mac gets 45 or more points, we usually get beat. It happens seven out of ten times."[4] McMillian, the 1972 NBA Champion with the Lakers, knew what was necessary for a team to win, as it was his insertion into the starting lineup as small forward in the place of Elgin Baylor that ignited the still-standing NBA record of 33 regular season wins in a row.

The Braves were a new team in the NBA, entering the league in 1970, along with the Portland Trail Blazers and the Cleveland Cavaliers. In their first three seasons in the league they have not won more than 22 games, including McAdoo's rookie year. In his three-year reign as the scoring champion the team entered the playoffs, but did not make it beyond the second round. McAdoo was blamed for his team's shortcomings because of a couple of misperceptions. For one, he was considered too skinny, weighing just 210 pounds, because of which he was thought to be a defensive liability, easily overpowered by stronger opponents. Yet, as pointed out by Sean Fury, "while McAddo didn't have the reputation as a player who intimidated others in the paint on defense, he finished in the top six in blocks three straight years with the Buffalo Braves. He crashed the boards, finishing third in rebounding one season, fourth in another."[5] He led the league in rebounds in the 1974–75 season.

Furthermore, he simply did not play like other centers on offense. McAdoo was a shooter, who did want to accommodate anybody and change his style. Once, his Braves' coach, Jack Ramsay, urged him to stop shooting so much during a game, and McAdoo refused to shoot at all. The coach then called his star player and said, "Mac, whatever I told you earlier, forget it."[6] McAdoo loved to shoot from mid-range and had unmatched confidence in his shot, no matter if he was open or closely guarded by much more physical, taller centers. Despite being so dominant, effective, and unique, McAdoo was not known outside of basketball circles. While some journalists recognized him as "the finest shooter and the most astounding outside scoring machine ever to play basketball," and praised him as "sincere, thrifty, brave and honest,"[7] he was constantly asked to play like a regular big man—close to the basket.

McAdoo was traded by the Braves to the Knicks after demanding a new contract, worth $500,000 a year. At 25 years old, he was tasked with being the next great big man of the New York franchise, four years removed from its second championship. He seemed just the opposite of the hard-nosed, powerful big man who was the integral part of the two-time NBA Champions, Willis Reed, yet faced the same expectations. Reed famously played through a thigh injury in Game Seven of the 1970 NBA Finals against the Lakers, inspiring his teammates to win their first championship.

McAdoo signed a five-year contract, but was traded to the Celtics during his third season on the team for three first-round picks and Tom Barker, a 6'11" center, who was a traditional big man. Surrounded by other superstars, such as Walt Frazier, Earl Monroe and Spencer Haywood, McAdoo was able to take the Knicks to the playoffs only once. Not willing to continue, and fighting overpaying for a player who did not deliver on his promise, they traded McAdoo to Boston, a place which was, as the player himself put it after spending just half a season there: "a graveyard where black players went to die."[8] Bill Russell brought to light the racism he encountered in Boston, and it seemed that since his time things have not changed much, despite the team breaking various color barriers, like drafting the first black player, having the first black head coach and putting an all-black five on the court during a professional basketball game.

McAdoo then joined the Pistons, where he would once again familiarize himself with losing—the Pistons won just 16 games in his first season there. McAdoo missed the last 15 games of that season, due to problems with his left foot, as well as a pulled groin muscle. In 1980–81 he appeared in just six games, with the team intentionally benching him, in hopes of developing younger players, while continuing to lose games to have a better chance at drafting a highly coveted prospect, the 7'4" Ralph Sampson out of Virginia. Instead of sitting out the season, as the Pistons intended for him, he joined the young New Jersey Nets team, but due to injuries and issues with coach Larry Brown, he played in just ten games. Once the season was over, McAdoo was out of his large contract and, at 30 years old, was also out of the league.

It was only because of an injury to power forward/center Mitch Kupchak that the Lakers decided to sign McAdoo on Christmas Eve of 1981, despite his reputation as a malingerer and malcontent. First-year head coach Pat Riley had no doubts that he "was the ideal guy. Everywhere else Mac had played, he was expected to carry the load every night. This team is too strong for any one player to be a disruption."[9] With Magic Johnson and Kareem Abdul-Jabbar getting all the media attention, McAdoo could focus on what he did best—playing basketball.

As a member of the Lakers, McAdoo obviously needed some time to get into game shape and scored just a total of eight points in his first four games. This included a 15-minute performance against his former team, the Pistons, in which he had four points and six rebounds. He ended the season with averages of 9.6 points and 3.9 rebounds, not starting a single game of the 41 he appeared in. While during the season his production was spotted, as he would score four points one game and 30 the next one, he found his rhythm during the playoffs and was instrumental in the Lakers championship run. Playing for 27.7 minutes per game, he averaged 16.7 points and 6.8 rebounds, including five performances in which he scored 21 or more points. In the six-game finals series against the Sixers he was making 16.3 points, while grabbing five rebounds and blocking 2.3 shots per contest. McAdoo made the key defensive play of the series, blocking Julius Erving and putting a stop to a Sixers third-quarter run in Game Six. He made such an impression on the opposing team that the Sixers wanted to sign him to play behind Moses Malone, but McAdoo stayed on the Lakers.

There he made three further consecutive NBA Finals. The Lakers lost to the Sixers in 1983 and the Celtics in 1984. The last series was especially hard fought, as it involved a lot of pushing and verbal arguments, with the Celtics winning Game Seven in Boston. Next season the teams once again met in the finals, and once again the teams fought hard, not always within the rules. McAdoo got into a fist fight with Kevin McHale. After Game Three, Boston coach K.C. Jones said, "McAdoo is playing out of desperation to get a contract. When he gets his contract, he'll go back to being the same old McAdoo, bouncing from team to team."[10] After the Lakers won Game Six in Boston Garden, the players and the fans showed the team the ultimate respect, saluting them for their triumph. Considering the fact that McAdoo spent four seasons in L.A. and was one of the players responsible for getting the team to four NBA Finals in a row, it was evident that what Jones did was just talk, supposed to discourage one of the Lakers' best players. After the 1985 finals McAdoo was signed by the Sixers, because the Lakers decided not to match their offer.

The Lakers won two more titles, in 1987 and 1988, then lost in the finals in 1989 and 1991. Following a relatively brief period of irrelevance, in the summer of 1996 they have made two roster moves that were instrumental in them turning their fortunes around. With the signing of Orlando Magic center Shaquille O'Neal and the draft-day trade that brought in rookie Kobe Bryant for center Vlade Divac, the Lakers laid the foundations for a championship dynasty that would succeed—but not surpass—Michael Jordan's Chicago Bulls.

There were a couple of links between the '90s Bulls and the 2000s Lakers—both teams were coached by Phil Jackson (and assistant Tex Winters), and both had Ron Harper, Horace Grant and John Salley on their rosters. While the Bulls had Jordan, the Lakers had Bryant, who modeled his game on the Bulls superstar, and had similar work ethic and attitude. Another, not so obvious, link is Mitch Richmond, the Hall of Fame shooting guard, whom Jordan described as the toughest opponent he ever had to guard.[11] While on the Lakers he played his part in pushing Kobe Bryant in practice for one season, 2001–02. It would turn out to be the last of Richmond's illustrious professional career, which began in 1988, after he was selected fifth overall by the Golden State Warriors.

Learning about the selection, his mom's friend told Richmond, "Don't worry about it. One day you'll make it to the NBA." The player had to explain to her that the Golden State Warriors were an actual NBA franchise.[12] With Don Nelson's arrival in the previous season as general manager, and his decision to return to coaching before the start of the 1988–89 season, the Warriors were about to become one of the most exciting teams in the league. Richmond was an important part of that team, along with small forward Chris Mullin and point guard Tim Hardaway, drafted a year later, forming Run TMC—a trio of athletic, quick shooters, whose offensive plays were equal parts improvisation, pace and beauty. The shooting guard earned the nickname "the Rock" for his natural strength, thanks to which he overpowered opponents. Nelson liked Richmond so much that he immediately put him into the starting lineup, making him the second rookie starter in Nelson's then 11-year coaching career.

Richmond and Mullin were able to play positions one through four, and with Hardaway and versatile Lithuanian rookie Šarūnas Marčiulionis, the Warriors introduced small ball basketball to the NBA. All four players were capable of driving to the lane and scoring from the outside, while also being great dribblers and passers. Marčiulionis was the reserve, put in when Nelson wanted his players to run the opposition into the ground. The Lithuanian's best season actually came after Richmond was traded to the Sacramento Kings for the 6'9" rookie Billy Owens. In 1991–92 the Lithuanian swingman averaged 18.9 points, 3.4 assists and 2.9 rebounds, and was second in the Sixth Man of the Year voting, losing to Detlef Schrempf of the Indiana Pacers, who won the award for the second time in a row. Both players were known for their versatility, contradicting the notion that the best sixth man should be primarily a scorer.

While Run TMC played beautiful basketball, Nelson still felt under pressure to "get big," so that his team would win. Instead of completely embracing small ball—something that would happen twenty years later, thanks to the 2004 rule change and subsequent success enjoyed by the Phoenix Suns, the Miami Heat and … the Golden State Warriors—he finally succumbed to the pressure, and, in order to get over the hump, traded Richmond to the Sacramento Kings. Nelson said the move was "the toughest I have ever made. Mitch has been much more than just a great basketball player for the Warriors. He's been a member of our family. Fortunately, as we say goodbye to Mitch, we know he will remain a good friend for life and become an NBA All-Star for years to come."[12] Richmond lived up to his nickname and became the rock for the Sacramento Kings team, that made the playoffs only once during his tenure there. On the Kings, from 1993 to 1998, Richmond made six All-Star Teams, and was named All-Star Game MVP in 1995.

While appreciated for his game around the league, among casual fans he was not well known due to the fact he was playing for a small market team, plus did not enjoy any team success. He was also not a flashy player, as with age he moved away from the basket and started to rely more and more on jump shots. Before the start of the 1997–98 season Richmond finally made a statement about the direction the team was heading by missing out on the team's preseason games. By mid-season he was almost traded to Atlanta, Miami or Los Angeles, but the exchange for shooting guard Steve Smith fell through, and the Heat were unable to get the Celtics interested in a three-team swap, while the Lakers refused to exchange much younger Eddie Jones for Richmond.[13] He would eventually join the team from Los Angeles, but three years later, which he spent on the Washington Wizards, where he was traded along with fellow veteran Otis Thorpe in exchange for Chris Webber. Webber was 25 at the time, while Richmond was 32 and Thorpe was 35 years old. His time on the Wizards was not pleasant, as he struggled with injuries, and was inconsistent, benched and booed by the fans in Washington.

While earning around $10 million a season and being the team top scorer during his first two seasons as a Wizard, he again failed to make the playoffs. Once Richmond became a free agent in the summer of 2001, he had earned five All-NBA selections, appeared in six All-Star Games and scored 20,237 career points, yet only tasted postseason basketball three times in his 13-season professional career. In hopes of playing on a winning roster, Richmond joined the 2000 and 2001 NBA Champions, the Los Angeles Lakers, signing a one-season contract worth $1 million. For the first time in his career Richmond was not a starter. In fact, his minutes per game were reduced by two-thirds to what they were in the 2000–01 season

Bob McAdoo was a former MVP who sacrificed a starting role in order to win NBA Championships (1985).

on the Wizards (32.9 to 11.1). Still, he was highly respected by his Lakers teammates, and despite playing just one game in the playoffs, entered the court with one minute left in Game Four of the finals and got to take (and make) the last shot of his career, as well as dribble out the clock, completing the sweep of the New Jersey Nets.

The other of Richmond's playoff games during that offseason came against the Kings in a highly controversial Western Conference Finals. The series was marred with bad officiating, especially occurring in Game Six. The two teams were so evenly matched that Richmond was extremely stressed during each game: "I would sit on that bench and after the game, my whole uniform would be soaked without playing. I was like, oh my god, I cannot believe I have an opportunity to get a ring and the Kings are going to win it?"[14] In the end they did not, and Richmond retired as an NBA Champion.

Richmond was undoubtedly a ringchaser, yet since he could not carry his teams to the finals—nor to the playoffs—he willingly took on a far lesser role on a better team, in order to win a championship title. While many players refuse to do so because of their egos, Richmond simply accepted the passage of time, and retired with an NBA Championship. McAdoo on the other hand refused to call it quits and, because of sheer luck, joined the Lakers and appeared in four NBA Finals in a row. They both serve as examples of the importance of championships for players' career narratives and prove that some superstars can only win once moving to the bench.

5

Playoff Heroes
Off the Bench

Sam Cassell
    Guard. In the NBA: 1993–2009. Memorable postseasons: 1994, 1995.
Robert Horry
    Forward. In the NBA: 1992–2008. Memorable postseasons: 2002,
        2005, 2007.
Boris Diaw
    Forward. In the NBA: 2003–2017. Memorable postseasons: 2006,
        2014.
Nate Robinson
    Guard. In the NBA: 2005–2016. Memorable postseason: 2013.

This chapter is devoted to players who either came off the bench during the playoffs or were career bench players and were able to help their teams win, or who entered the starting lineup during the season/postseason in question. The playoffs are a true testing ground for players, as this is where every game matters, and the triumph of a given team depends on physical as much as mental toughness of its coaches and roster. Unlike in NCAA, NFL or soccer cups, one loss does not immediately eliminate a team from contention, yet that does not mean that a team can take a night off. There is of course a lot of planning and strategy involved. Phil Jackson, who has won 11 championship rings as a coach (and two as a player), says that a team needs to "develop a oneness of thought and action, to find the space where together [it] can become more receptive to the spiritual growth that is required this time of year."[1] That oneness refers to certain sacrifices that players have to make for the greater good—winning—and it is up to the coaches to make sure everybody is on the same page. Superstars need to accept that in certain situations they will have to allow their teammates to make important plays, while bench players need to accept a decreased role. When the season is on the line, most coaches prefer to trust well-established players and veterans rather than rotation players, which is understandable. However, sometimes coaches are forced to abandon their original plans, seeing how greatly certain players are handling the pressure despite their young age.

Such was the case with Sam Cassell, a 6'3" point guard, whom the Houston Rockets selected with the 24th pick in the 1993 draft. Center Hakeem Olajuwon led the team coached by Rudy Tomjanovich, but it heavily relied on the play of guards. The rookie found himself competing for playing time with Kenny Smith, Vernon Maxwell, Mario Elie and Scott Brooks, but he made his presence known once he joined the team, although it was not only with his play, but also with his energy and talkative personality. Cassell's mother at some point reminisced that even when practicing by himself he used to talk to imaginary opponents. To that Cassell replied, "Nothing wrong with talking to yourself. As long as you don't start answering yourself, you're all right."[2] His teammates and his coach enjoyed his ferocity, as already during exhibition games Cassell would not back down against more experienced athletes like Scott Skiles, with whom the rookie got into a scuffle before the start of the season.

In his first NBA game Cassell got substantial minutes, went 1/7 from the floor, including 1/3 for three, had six rebounds, five assists but also four turnovers against the Jordan-less Chicago Bulls. However, just a day later against the Utah Jazz and John Stockton, one of the best point guards in league history, who was also a pesky defender, Cassell scored 15 points and lost the ball just twice. As the season progressed he gained his coach's and teammates' trust, and even started six of the 66 games he played in. Cassell's last game of the regular season was his best, as he had 23 points (the first time he scored 20 or more in a game) and eight assists, but the Rockets failed to win against the Nuggets.

In the first round of the playoffs, the Rockets played against the Blazers, whose starting point guard was Rod Strickland, the player Cassell was supposed to replace at DePaul University. Following a successful recruitment, the star of Dunbar High in Baltimore attempted the Scholastic Aptitude Test (SAT) but failed to score the 700 minimum required by the NCAA. Cassell spent a year in prep school and, after once again failing to meet the necessary minimum, transferred to San Jacinto. After another year he finally made it to Florida State, where he would eventually get his jersey number retired after averaging 18.3 points, 4.4 assists and 2.3 steals a game during his two years there.

Cassell failed to impress against Strickland and the Blazers but was an important part of the team in the Western Conference Semifinals against the Suns, who were trying to make the finals for the second year in a row. In Game Six, which proved to be the last of the series, Cassell made eight of his 12 shots and all four of his free throws and had four rebounds, seven assists and two steals. His and Kenny Smith's defensive play was also crucial in slowing down the Suns' second-best player Kevin Johnson, who missed 13 of his 22 shots, while still having 11 assists and ending up with 25 points, just three more than the reserve point guard on the Rockets. The difference was that Johnson was already an established NBA player, whose jersey the Suns would eventually retire, while Cassell was not even a lottery-pick rookie. In the Western Conference Finals the Rockets would lose just one game to the Utah Jazz, as they made their way to the NBA Finals against the New York Knicks.

The star centers on both teams already had some history, as they had met in the 1984 NCAA Finals, with Patrick Ewing's Hoyas emerging victorious against Olajuwon's Cougars. It was their first meeting in the playoffs as pros, since Ewing's Knicks up to that point had not made the finals, and the Rockets appeared there once, in 1986, during Olajuwon's second year in the league. After the Rockets' Game One win, the *New York Times'* William C. Rhoden observed that, instead of the two stars, it would be the guards on both teams who would decide the series' outcome. The Rockets' strategy was to drive toward the basket and kick the ball back to outside shooters. A key part of their style of play was Cassell, whom Rhoden characterized as "the Rockets' most creative player. He penetrates, dishes off and is generally a better defender than Smith."[3] Tomjanovich noticed that as well during the season, and started playing Cassell in the final quarters of games, a time when the five best players are usually left on the floor.

Starting point guard Kenny Smith was having a pretty bad series, as he was limited by the Knicks' point guard Derek Harper to 5.6 points (38.9 percent from the field) and 3.1 assists, while turning the ball over twice per game. Cassell was turning the ball over even more often (2.6 times to 2.9 assists per game), but was averaging 10 points (on 42.2 percent accuracy), 1.3 steals and 3.1 rebounds. He was especially great in Game Three, and while the 15 points he had in the game may not look that impressive (although it was about one-sixth of his team's points), Cassell made all three of his three-pointers and scored the last seven points for the Rockets, including two free throws with 2.4 seconds left in the game. After the game Cassell made no doubts about who was the real hero in the final minutes of play: "[Olajuwon] created it all. I was wide open, he made the pass, and I made the shot."[4] In the next game however he went 3/11 from the floor, and following another superb performance by the Knicks defense, after five games the New Yorkers were up 3–2. However, in Game Six, played in Madison Square Garden, Olajuwon dominated Ewing on both ends of the floor (30 points to Ewing's 17, 6/20 from the floor). Game Seven brought the worst shooting performance in NBA Finals history, as the Knicks' John

Starks, the man who made Game Six so close by scoring 27 points and could have been the hero if Olajuwon had not blocked his last-second shot with his fingertips, made just two of 18 shots from the floor, 11 percent of his shots. Ewing once again had 17 points, while Olajuwon finished the game with 25 points, ten rebounds and seven assists. The Rockets won their first NBA Championship.

A year later they once again made it to the finals, despite looking tired and vulnerable. In mid-season the team brought in Clyde Drexler for a relatively cheap price of Otis Thorpe, Marcelo Nicola, and a first-round draft pick. Drexler came to Houston with small forward Tracy Murray, who would play a minor role on the Rockets, and would lose his spot on the roster in the expansion draft, join the Raptors for a season, until finally finding his place in the league as a sixth man on the Wizards. He did not even enter the court during the 1995 playoffs for the Rockets, as the team was in a tough spot, after going 47–35 in the regular season and finishing sixth in the Western Conference. Without home-court advantage, every game that the Rockets played was very important.

In the first round the Rockets won against the third-seed Jazz 3–2, despite trailing 1–2. The Suns, whom the team from Houston faced off in the Western Conference Semifinals, were leading the series 3–1, yet the Rockets won three elimination games in a row, making it to the Western Conference Finals. The final game of the series ended with a crucial three-pointer by Mario Elie, which was followed by a "kiss of death" that the player blew towards the opposing bench. There the team faced the San Antonio Spurs, whose superstar was the center David Robinson, who was named 1995 league MVP. The season earlier Robinson had better stats and was the league's leading scorer, but Olajuwon was voted the best player in the league, as his team had a better record. This time the Spurs won more games, a then franchise record 62.

Robinson's 1993–94 scoring title did not come without controversy, as it was one of the closest races for the crown of the best scorer in league history. The contestants were Robinson and second-year center Shaquille O'Neal of the Orlando Magic. In the last game of the season O'Neal got 32 points against the Nets, while Robinson took it upon himself to destroy the Clippers, finishing the game with 71 points and solidifying his lead over the young and brash player. He won the scoring crown by 36 points (2,383 in 80 games to O'Neal's 2,377 in 81). In that game Robinson spent 44 minutes on the floor, and it was no secret that his primary objective was the scoring title.[5] The Spurs' coach even instructed his players to intentionally foul the Clippers so that the team could get back the ball quickly and give Robinson more time to score.

A year later, before Game Two of the Western Conference Finals and his team down 0–1 following a close loss to the Rockets, Robinson was awarded the MVP trophy. Standing next to Olajuwon, Kenny Smith, Clyde Drexler and Mario Elie were inspiring their teammate, insinuating that Robinson was holding Olajuwon's trophy, since he averaged more points (27.8 to Robinson's 27.6) and blocks (3.4 to his 3.2), but the Spurs were the best team in the league. Olajuwon pretended before the game that he was not bothered by Robinson's crowning ceremony happening in front of him, but his teammates knew that it did strike a nerve. He got 41 points and 16 rebounds, and the Rockets dominated the Spurs. At the end of the game he said to Smith, "Kenny, I'm going to his house to get my award," to which the teammate reacted with laughter, as everybody knew that Olajuwon was angry, despite being able to objectively admit that Robinson deserved the award.[6] The Rockets eliminated the Spurs in six games, and Cassell also played his part in the series, scoring 30 points, including going 12/12 from the charity stripe, and dishing out 12 assists in Game Five.

In the 1995 finals, the Rockets faced the Orlando Magic and their center-playmaker duo of O'Neal and Penny Hardaway. Cassell knew the opposing point guard very well, as during the summer after the Rockets won their first title, Hardaway and he played full-court one-on-one games in a Houston high school. In Game One the younger, more athletic Magic looked like they were going to outrun the Rockets, at one point getting up to a 20-point lead. In the second half, however, the team managed to come back and tie the game thanks to an incredible performance by Kenny Smith, who set an NBA record with seven three-pointers, made on 63.6 percent accuracy. The last of his long-distance shots went in just one second before the buzzer. Nick Anderson of the Magic missed four crucial free-throws. The Rockets won in overtime.

After the game Cassell said to Smith, "You can relax [in Game 2], because I'm giving you the night off." In the second game Cassell played almost the whole second half, finishing with 31 points, and he was unstoppable on offense no matter if he was driving toward the basket and getting fouled (11/12 free throws) or shooting from three (4/6). Obviously he was not as dominant or as consistent as Olajuwon, who scored at least 31 points in each of the four games of the sweep. The Rockets have repeated as NBA Champions, at that time only the sixth team in NBA history to win back-to-back titles. In an article comparing the Rockets to other teams who achieved that feat, Phil Taylor of *Sports Illustrated* lists Sam Cassell as the only "reliable reserve" on the team, which, according to Joe Dumars of the Pistons, who repeated as a member of the "Bad Boys" Detroit Pistons, actually makes their two championship runs even more impressive.[7]

That Houston Rockets team would not have won without forward Robert Horry, drafted just a year before Cassell with the 11th pick. The 6'9",

240-pound Horry without any complaints moved to the power forward position once Thorpe was traded for Drexler, despite playing thus far as a small forward. Horry was not even supposed to win one title on the Rockets, as the team traded him along with fellow 6'10" forward Matt Bullard on February 4, 1994, to the Detroit Pistons for Sean Elliott, the Spurs' lifer, unhappy during his only season outside of San Antonio. After two days the deal was canceled, as Elliott failed his physical, and both players returned to Houston. Elliott and Horry played crucial roles in Game One of the aforementioned 1995 series between the Spurs—Elliott returned to San Antonio after one year in Detroit—and the Rockets. It was Horry who scored the winning basket, an 18-footer with 6.5 seconds left, while Elliot missed a four-foot jumper in the last play of the game. The Rockets won 94–93.

The non-trade actually gave birth to Horry's "Big Shot Rob" moniker, by which he became known later on. He owed it to his playoff heroics, as he would often struggle to motivate himself to perform on his highest level during regular season games.[8] During his first six seasons in the NBA Horry was a starter, either for the Rockets, the Suns, or the Lakers, but then he was moved to the bench in favor of a struggling Dennis Rodman (who was released after 23 games), reserve center Travis Knight or veteran J.R. Reid, who joined the team mid-season, following a trade with the Hornets. After that season Phil Jackson took over the team, and another veteran, A.C. Green, who won two championships in the 1980s with Magic Johnson and Kareem Abdul-Jabbar, was named the starting power forward. Horry did not have a good relationship with Jackson. Even though he played for Jackson for four seasons, they reportedly had just one off-court conversation, about Horry throwing a towel at Phoenix coach Danny Ainge—an action that got him traded from the Suns.[9] Still, it seems no talks were necessary for that team to function properly, as from 2000 to 2002 the Lakers were able to win three championships in a row.

Horry's biggest career moment came during the Lakers' third championship run, in Game Four of the 2002 Western Conference Finals. With the Kings leading 2–1, Game Four would prove to be pivotal—had the Kings won, they definitely would get one more win against the Lakers when given three occasions to do so. In Game Four, with seven seconds left, the Kings were leading 99–97, squandering almost all of the 24-point lead they held at one point in the game. Similarly to Game Three of the 2002 Western Conference First Round series against the Blazers, Kobe Bryant had the ball and was driving into the lane to tie the score. Against the Blazers he kicked it out to Horry, who won the game for the Lakers with a three-point shot. This time the Kings defense was all over Bryant, but he still somehow managed to release a shot. He missed, and during the fight for the rebound, the ball was swiped by Kings center Vlade Divac, toward the top of the key, where it bounced further away from the basket and reached the three-point line. Robert Horry caught it and with 0.8 seconds left released the ball. He scored, and the Lakers won 100–99, tied the series, and eventually headed to the NBA Finals for the third time in a row.

The Lakers won the NBA Championship that year, but a year later they fell to the Spurs in the Western Conference Semifinals. In the off-season they signed Karl Malone, who left the Utah Jazz after 18 seasons. Horry himself claimed that Jackson wanted to bring in Malone ever since he took over the team.[10] In order to create the cap space necessary to sign Malone, Horry was released. He signed with the team that eliminated the Lakers and would win an NBA Championship sooner than any of his former teammates as a member of the Spurs. In the 2005 NBA Finals Horry would once again appear as Big Shot Rob, scoring 18 of his 21 points in the fourth quarter and overtime of Game Five against the Pistons. In that game Horry made four out of five three-pointers, despite a shoulder injury. Tim Duncan, Spurs legend, who was the starting power forward on that team, described his teammate's crunch-time heroics as "probably the greatest performance I've ever been a part of."[11] The Spurs took the 3–2 lead in the series and would eventually win the championship, Horry's sixth. The seventh came in 2007. This one was marred by some controversy though, as during Game Four of the Western Conference Finals, Horry checked Steve Nash, the point guard of the Phoenix Suns, into the scorers' table. Outraged Suns players Amar'e Stoudemire and Boris Diaw left the bench, both earning one-game suspensions. Horry was suspended for two games. The foul changed the momentum of the series which was tied 2–2, and effectively limited the Suns' chances at reaching the NBA Finals. The move can be seen as the consequence of Horry's willingness to do anything his team needed of him in order to win. Whether it was shooting a three-pointer or fouling the best player of the opposing team, Horry was dependable, no matter the circumstances.

It was Diaw, then suspended for Game Five of the series, who would later reemerge as a playoff hero for the Spurs. Just like Horry, he also had problems with motivating himself for regular season games. Diaw was drafted with the 21st pick of the 2003 NBA Draft, one of the best of all time, by the Atlanta Hawks. Extraordinarily gifted physically, Diaw would often arrive to workouts in flip-flops with a cup of cappuccino in hand. He was very peculiar about the quality of his coffee, and later on, as a member of the Spurs, installed an espresso machine in his locker because he did not like the coffee that was available in the arena. The inborn athleticism was one of the causes of his carefree attitude, and it sometimes seemed that he took his physical gifts for granted, as he struggled with weight issues throughout his career. Diaw's mother, Elizabeth Riffiod, played center for the French national team, while his father, Issia Diaw, was a high jumper for Senegal. Diaw was not the only NBA player whose mother played professional basketball—Yao Ming's mom played for her national team in China, just as Javale McGee's mother, Pamela, did for the United States, while Ray Allen's, Dwight Howard's and Gary Harris' mothers played pro ball as well.[12]

The 6'8" Diaw played point guard for the Atlanta Hawks, mostly coming off the bench, although he managed to start 62 games during his two seasons there. In his rookie season, under Terry Stotts, Diaw was able to communicate with his coach, who spoke French and had a more open approach to basketball. In his second season, 2004–05, playing for the inflexible Mike Woodson, the Hawks won just 13 games, with Diaw averaging 4.8 points, 2.6 rebounds, and 2.3 assists. The team from Atlanta was in need of a rebuild, and the management struck a deal with Joe Johnson of the Suns, who wanted to play as a point guard, which was impossible in Phoenix, as the offense was constructed around the reigning league MVP, Steve Nash. Johnson's deal was for five-years and $70 million, with $20 million paid out upfront. The Suns refused to match it, deciding that the restricted free agent was not worth that much as a fourth option behind Nash, Amar'e Stoudemire and Shawn Marion. The Hawks got him in a sign-and-trade in exchange for two lottery-protected first-round draft picks, a trade exception and Diaw.

Diaw found himself struggling to adjust to a rather restricted style of play, requiring players to stick to conventional positions, simply because he was too versatile to play a limited role on a team. Out of necessity, as Stoudemire went out with an injury and would play just three games throughout the 2005–06 season, Diaw was named the starting power forward/center. Luckily for him, the Suns' coaches were not basketball purists and did not care all that much about players holding on to roles associated with regular basketball positions. Instead, the team's style was supposed to accommodate the players. Just a couple of months earlier Diaw was defending the likes of Stephon Marbury, Steve Francis and Eric Snow on the perimeter, while on the Suns he found himself battling for rebounds with Tim Duncan, Carlos Boozer and Ben Wallace. He averaged just 2.9 free throw attempts per game, while his team was last in free throw attempts with 18 per contest, but that was due to the fact that the Suns played rather quickly and preferred to shoot from long-distance rather than from the interior.[13]

The other thing was that Diaw was a distributor rather than a dunking machine like Stoudemire, as he finished the season second on the team in assists, 6.2 per game, behind Nash. Diaw also started 70 of the 81 games he played in, averaged 13.3 points, 6.9 rebounds and one block per game, and was named the league's Most Improved Player. His best performances though came in that year's playoffs, in which he played for the first time in his career. The Suns were hoping for a championship run, as they had reached the 2005 Western Conference Finals, yet without Stoudemire repeating that achievement seemed harder than the season before. Still, Diaw stood in quite nicely for the superstar, despite playing a different, more team-oriented type of basketball. In the first round series against the Lakers, which went to seven games, Diaw scored 19 or more points four times, while in Game Seven he had 21 points, nine assists and six rebounds. Another important factor in the game was the Brazilian shooting guard Leandro Barbosa, who scored 26 points off the bench. Nash said afterwards: "L.B. and Boris lost their virginity today."[14]

The 23-year-old Diaw was up and down in the series against the Clippers, as he was literally overpowered by forward Elton Brand and center Chris Kaman, but the Suns managed to progress to the 2006 Western Conference Finals. There they would face off against Nash's former team, the Dallas Mavericks. In the first game of the series Diaw scored what would remain his career high, 34 points, on the way to Game One victory against the Mavericks. He ended one of the best performances of his career with a game-winning seven-footer, in a play that was originally drawn up for Nash. The point guard said after the game, "Boris is amazing, I'm very, very proud of him. He's just getting better and better. He's doing that on a big stage now. It's exciting to see a young player really want the ball. He's fearless when it counts."[15] The Suns were eliminated in six games, while Diaw finished that postseason with averages of 18.7 points, 6.7 rebounds and 5.2 assists.

The hopes were high for the next season with Stoudemire finally healthy, and Diaw, Nash, Marion, and Barbosa back, but the team was not able to enjoy the same success as before. Diaw regressed, and the fearlessness on which Nash, his teammates, coaches and management counted was not on display as often as during his breakthrough season. In February 2008 general manager Steve Kerr rebuilt the roster and influenced the Suns' style of play by bringing in Shaquille O'Neal in exchange for Shawn Marion. The tempo of play became slower to accommodate O'Neal, and some of the players used to the "seven seconds or less" mantra struggled. When D'Antoni left, replaced by former point guard Terry Porter, the problems intensified, and in order to "shake things up a little bit," as Kerr put it, in December 2008 Diaw and Bell were traded to the Charlotte Bobcats for Jason Richardson, Jared Dudley, and a second-round pick.[16] The trade was supposed to invigorate the Suns' offense, but after going 28–23 and placing ninth in the Western Conference, Porter was fired four months into his first head coaching job. He was replaced by Alvin Gentry, who turned out to be the perfect choice for the Suns, as he immediately reintroduced D'Antoni's offensive schemes and uptempo play. Gentry knew them very well, serving as the Suns' assistant coach since 2004.

In the 59 games Diaw played for the Bobcats (all starts) that season, he formed an efficient partnership with Emeka Okafor, because the second pick in the 2004 draft, the first player ever selected by the Bobcats when they were an expansion team, was handling the interior play along with small forward Gerald Wallace, which allowed Diaw to move away from the basket. Diaw found himself attempting 2.8 three-pointers per game, which he drained with 41.7 percent accuracy. While under Larry Brown, Diaw remained an important member of the rotation and started 258 games in a row for the Bobcats (a franchise record), once again a coaching change brought problems for Diaw, who was benched by a more traditional coach, Paul Silas. Silas, a three-time All-Star and NBA Champion as a player, complained about the things that made the power forward so exceptional—his outside game, passing and team-first mentality: "Some of the things that would go on, like not shooting the ball, passing all of the time, that doesn't help us. I needed hoops, and he could put the ball in the hoop. When that wouldn't happen, it was very disturbing."[17]

The Bobcats were in the middle of what would be the worst regular season in NBA history, winning just seven of the 66 games during the lockout-shortened 2011–12 season. Diaw asked the team to be released with hopes of joining a playoff team, and finally his contract was bought out. He signed with one of the best teams in the league, the San Antonio Spurs. While during the rest of the season he was mostly coming off the bench, in the playoffs Diaw started all 14 games for the Spurs, playing next to Tim Duncan. The Spurs were eliminated by the young and athletic Oklahoma City Thunder in the Western Conference Finals in 2012, but for the next two years it was the team from San Antonio that represented the west in the finals, where they would square off against the Miami Heat. "The Heatles" were able to change the momentum of the 2013 finals after Ray Allen hit the miraculous game-tying shot by the end of regulation in Game Six.

A year later though the Spurs completely dominated the Heat, in no small part thanks to Diaw, who proved hard to contain on both ends of the floor. While he did not score all that much, his spacing, rebounding (8.6 rebounds per game in the series) and passing (5.8 assists) were crucial for the Spurs' decisive win over LeBron James and company. His best game of that championship run came against the Oklahoma City Thunder in Game Six of the Western Conference Finals, during which he scored 26 points on Steve Adams (center), Serge Ibaka (power forward), Reggie Jackson and Derek Fisher (point guards). Diaw's versatility was the reason why he was so hard to defend, as power forwards and centers did not possess enough speed, small forwards and shooting guards strength, nor point guards the height necessary to contain him. He stands as proof that a player who can do a bit of everything should be allowed to play the way he wants—only then is his team able to get the most out of him and succeed.

Not all players are however appreciated for their sacrifices and their playoff heroics, and despite achieving significant success, they are forced to prove year after year that they belong in the league. Such was the case with Nate Robinson, the 5'9" point guard who up until his sophomore season at the University of Washington was considered to be a football player, rather than a basketball player. Ever since he became recognizable, height was always a part of the story when it came to Robinson. The small, muscular and energetic point guard had to work out for 23 NBA teams before the draft, even though he averaged 16.4 points, 3.9 rebounds, 4.3 assists and 1.7 steals during his last year in college. Everywhere he went, he would always encounter the same question: will a player of his height be able to make an impact in the league? One thing nobody questioned was Robinson's athleticism, as already in college he performed a couple of in-game dunks.

There was one more factor involved into what could be characterized as "the Nate Robinson experience"—yes, there were flashy plays and impressive scoring outbursts, but at the same time there was the risk that at any moment Robinson would make a questionable play. Throughout his career his assist-to-turnover ratio was two to one, which is an indicator of bad decision-making for a point guard. Selected with the 21st pick in the 2005 NBA Draft by the Phoenix Suns and immediately traded to the Knicks, Robinson got a reassuring phone call from general manager Isiah Thomas, who said, "If you were six feet tall I think you would have been the No.1 pick in the draft."[18] Taking into consideration that Thomas was talking about a draft that brought into the NBA point guards like Chris Paul, Deron Williams or Raymond Felton, and that he signed Jerome James to a five-year, $29 million contract and Eddy Curry to a six-year, $60 million contract, maybe he was not the best judge of player potential.

Thomas's bad off-court decision making was opposed to his brilliant on-court play for the Pistons, where he has been the floor general for 13 years. When it came to Robinson, his off-court decisions were rather innocent and playful (like jumping on a naked teammate in the shower because he owed him money), but on the court the "questionable" factor became known in his first play of the preseason. Fresh off the bench, when running toward the opposing basket, Robinson was so confident in his abilities and so full of energy that he decided to make an instant impression on his coaches with a monster dunk. He missed and threw the ball, and it bounced off the rim and hit him on his head.[19] Later on, also as a Knick, with 0.4 left in the first quarter of a game against the Nets, Robinson attempted to shoot a three-pointer at his own basket. The ball went in, and had it left his hand earlier, the shot would have counted against his team.

Robinson was one of the rare players who could combine spectacular and spectacularly bad plays in the course of minutes. He could rebound like a power forward, dunk over centers, who would often just get out of the way in order to avoid being posturized, and, most of all, he could shoot. The problem was that he loved to shoot even on nights when the ball was not going in. During those nights he would shoot even more, in order to get himself out of the slump. During the best season of his career, 2008–09, Robinson averaged 17.2 points, 3.9 rebounds and 4.1 assists while playing a career-high 29.9 minutes per game. Still, he had nights when he would go 2/11, 7/21, 4/18 or 6/23 from the floor. During that season he made 43.7 percent of his shots, which would remain his career high. His personal-best stats did not amount to much, as the Knicks had to endure another losing season. In the next one, 2009–10, after a 1–9 start, D'Antoni benched Robinson and Curry, and the team responded by winning nine of its next 15 games. In a similar way he did with hometown hero Stephon Marbury a season earlier, D'Antoni decided to not play Robinson, citing "his immaturity and poor defense" as the reasons for his decision. The coach ignored the fans' chants to put Robinson into games, and eventually the player's agent demanded a trade.[20] He did not made the playoffs during the four and a half years spent in New York, but he remained a fan favorite because of his dunking ability—he won the Slam Dunk Contests in 2006, 2009 and 2010.

Inevitably, Robinson was traded. He headed to the Celtics and made his debut a week later, against his former team, but played badly, making just two of his seven shots. In Boston he saw limited minutes behind versatile point guard Rajon Rondo. As a member of the Celtics, Robinson also made his playoff debut, playing a whopping six seconds in Game One of the First Round of the Eastern Conference playoffs against the Miami Heat. However, Robinson saw his minutes grow as the playoffs progressed, and in the NBA Finals against the Lakers, he played over 13 minutes three times. The Celtics lost to the Lakers in seven games, and in the middle of next season Robinson was traded to the Thunder, where he played just seven games in total (four in the regular season and three in the playoffs). After five games of the 2011–12 season the Golden State Warriors signed Robinson, who was without a team and working out on his own in his hometown, Seattle.

Once again, despite convincing stats (11.2 points and 4.5 assists per game), due to his bad decision making, the Warriors decided not to renew Robinson's contract. He was signed by the Chicago Bulls, with the intention that he would be the backup point guard behind Kirk Hinrich, who originally was supposed to be the backup for former MVP Derrick Rose, recovering from an ACL injury. In February 2013 Hinrich injured his elbow, and Robinson was named the starter. The player who rarely felt the trust of his head coaches finally got the support of Tom Thibodeau. Known for overplaying his starters and keeping them on the court for too long, even when games were already decided, he was the perfect coach for the highly energetic Robinson, who wanted to finally play as many minutes as possible.

With Robinson starting 23 of the 82 games in the 2012–13 season for the Bulls—the only time in his career he appeared in all regular season games—the Bulls won 45 games and were facing off against the Brooklyn Nets in the playoffs. The main stars on the Nets were point guard Deron Williams and swingman Joe Johnson. In the summer they would be joined by Robinson's former teammates Kevin Garnett and Paul Pierce (who were already past their prime) to form one of the most interesting and ultimately disappointing teams in NBA history. General manager Billy King sacrificed the team's future by trading away multiple first round picks for the stars. Already a season earlier the team gave up most of its cap space by taking on Johnson's ridiculous contract. While Johnson was a very good player, in 2010 the Atlanta Hawks signed him to a six-year deal worth $119 million, following the season in which Johnson made Third Team All-NBA for the first (and only) time in his career. In the summer of 2010, with a number of free agent big names available—James, Wade, Bosh, Stoudemire, Nowitzki, Allen, Pierce, etc.—it was Johnson who signed the largest contract. He would never average more than 18.8 points per game, but through the 2012–2015 seasons remained one of the four highest-paid players in the league.

The motivation for these trades was the way the injured Bulls beat the Nets in the 2013 playoffs. Hinrich was the starter during the first four games of the series, but in Game Four, with the Bulls leading 2–1, he suffered another injury and was out of the playoffs. This left Robinson the only point guard on the team, and he responded with the best game of his career. In Game Four he scored 34 points, making 60 percent of his shots, and, most importantly, leading his team to hard-fought victory. The team from Chicago needed three overtimes to beat the Nets, the final score being 142–134. Robinson scored 23 points in the fourth quarter, just one point short of Michael Jordan's Bulls record.

The Bulls lost the next two games despite Robinson scoring 38 points and dishing out 12 assists in the two games combined. Luol Deng, the team's starting small forward, was added to the list of injured players after Game Five against the Nets. In no small part was the amount of injuries that struck the Bulls caused by their coach's habit of relying too much on his starters—for example Deng played 44.8 minutes per game in the series. The

Bulls managed to beat the Nets, but in the next series they would face the reigning champions, the Miami Heat, led by James, Wade and Bosh.

In Game One of the series, taking place in South Beach, Robinson once again exploded. In his autobiography he described his stat line as "27 points, 9 assists, 10 stitches,"[21] because he was rammed by James while fighting for a loose ball. Robinson's mouth had to be stitched up, but he got back into the game. Before it began, LeBron was awarded the MVP award, and Robinson said that the ceremony lit the competitive fire underneath him and his teammates. The fire burned for only one game, as the Heat won the next four, making easy work of the injured and tired Bulls. The team from Chicago already had Hinrich under contract, and with Rose supposed to be back for the season, the Bulls did not re-sign Robinson. He was picked up by the Nuggets, but, due to injuries and lack of trust from coaches, played 88 games on three teams in three years.

6

Hall of Fame Careers
Saved by the Bench

Bill Walton
Center. In the NBA: 1975–1987. Three seasons missed because of a foot injuries.
Alonzo Mourning
Center. In the NBA: 1993–2008. Appeared in 137 out of 410 games because of a kidney disease.

Few players have been lucky enough to end their basketball careers on their own terms. This is obviously not synonymous with players retiring on top of their game, as winners. Rather, with the risk of career-ending injuries occurring during any game or practice, the feat is all the more impressive. It is one thing to recognize that one's skills are diminishing, and one should accept a lesser role in order to still be able to play the game that one loves. It is another to know when to say goodbye to the only occupation one has known for almost all of one's life and have no second thoughts or regrets. That type of ending is especially painful when it happens suddenly, due to an injury. It is obvious that such players make (sometimes several) attempts at a comeback, and even though they are not able to play at the same level, they can state that they have beaten the odds and continued playing basketball for a couple of seasons.

One of such players was Grant Hill, the small forward out of Duke, who arrived in the NBA with the third pick in the 1994 draft and quickly became heralded as the next Michael Jordan, even though his game was more reminiscent of Magic Johnson. The Laker was the player Hill actually looked up to growing up. When describing his NBA career up to his ankle injury, Hill said, "My last year in Detroit I really started to figure it out, in the sense that the game had slowed down, I added some tools to my game and I figured I had a four to five year window where I could play at a really elite level."[1] Following the injury and a sign-and-trade which allowed Hill to join the Orlando Magic, teaming him up with an up-and-coming

Bill Walton came back from numerous injuries to win an NBA Championship with the Celtics in 1986 (1987).

shooting guard Tracy McGrady (whose career, interestingly, was also filled with injuries), Hill played in 200 games out of 574 possible in the seven seasons he spent in Florida. He was not the same player as before, but continued to play in the NBA on a rather regular basis and retired as a 40 year old.

Retiring on one's own terms means also retiring when one wants to and not when it's suitable for one's future legacy. Whether it was because of money, pride or the search for that elusive championship ring, some athletes played way too long, marring the perceptions of their otherwise successful NBA careers. Images of Patrick Ewing playing for the Sonics and the Magic or Hakeem Olajuwon for the Raptors come to mind once the discussion turns to players who have played for too long just because they could not see themselves retiring yet. The same goes for Shaquille O'Neal's rather unsuccessful seasons on the Cavaliers or the Celtics. Karl Malone spent one season on the Lakers, arguably the worst of his stellar NBA career, because he wanted to win an NBA championship. Still, they ended their careers exactly when they wanted, although probably not in situations that they thought were adequate for players of their stature.

The same goes for Magic Johnson and Michael Jordan, who both gave up their ownership of, respectively, the Los Angeles Lakers and the Washington Wizards, in order to come back to playing organized basketball. Jordan's tenure with the Wizards is covered later in this book. Johnson returned to the NBA four years after being forced to retire because of testing positive for HIV in 1991. He continued to play in exhibition games and spent a year playing competitive basketball in Sweden and Denmark. On the 22nd of March 1994 he was named the head coach of the Lakers, who were 28–38 at the time and risked missing the playoffs for the first time since 1976. He went 5–1 during his first six games, but finished the season with the same number of wins and 11 losses. The Lakers finished ninth in the conference, nine wins short of a playoff spot. A year later the team returned to the postseason under coach Del Harris, who was named Coach of the Year. In July 1995 Johnson said about his playing career, "I'm never coming back. That's it."[2] At the beginning of next year he started to work out with the team.

In his first game back, on the 30th of January 1996, Johnson came off the bench for the Lakers and had 19 points, ten assists and eight rebounds in 27 minutes of play, serving an important role in a ten-point win over the Golden State Warriors. Five games later, against the Hawks, Johnson had the only triple-double of the season, the last of his career. He appeared in 32 games and started nine, serving mostly as the sixth man for the Lakers, who were, at least in comparison to the time up until his first retirement, rather ignored—in comparison to the coverage they have received during their Showtime days that is—by the media and the fans. After Johnson's announcement regarding his return, the number of fans wanting to attend the games he was supposed to play in, in Los Angeles as well as those where the Lakers were the visiting team, immediately grew, while TNT added their games to its broadcast schedule. The team was 31–19 before Johnson's arrival, and finished the season with 53 wins, good for the fourth spot in the league. The 6'9" point guard, who was actually playing the small forward or power forward positions when sharing the court with the starter, the 6'1" Nick Van Exel, was even fifth in the voting for the Sixth Man of the Year Award with nine votes. He retired for good after the Lakers were eliminated in the First Round by the Rockets, but not before some controversy. While he would eventually call it quits, immediately after the series Johnson enumerated the things that the

> Lakers should do to make him more comfortable next season (for which he is not yet signed), including allowing him to play point guard 40%–50% of the time. If L.A. is unwilling or unable to accommodate that desire, Magic announced, "then I'll say O.K., thanks, it's been nice. There's five, six or 10 other teams I know already that want me."[3]

Johnson inspired a whole generation of players to play just like him. He had the size of a small forward or power forward, yet was able to make spectacular plays and keep up with smaller players who were playing at his position. Although he is worthy of a detailed analysis, his career was not saved by the bench, because he was 36 at the time and appeared in just 32 games, and there was not really anything to save. Magic Johnson was simply so respected that his former team allowed him to return after four seasons away from the NBA. He did not contribute to his legend in any way by returning to the league. Instead, here I want to focus on two players whose careers were prolonged because of their conscious decision to sacrifice a starting role in order to remain in the NBA for a couple of years longer.

I was also considering a third name for this chapter, Derrick Rose, who was the youngest league MVP at just 22, yet because his career is still active, and he is not a member of the Hall of Fame yet, I have decided to narrow my focus down to two centers who had been the focal points of their teams prior to their misfortunes—one was injured, the other seriously ill—and were able to swallow their pride in order to win an NBA Championships as sixth men. Rose is yet to win a title, yet there is little doubt that prior to his injury he seemed to be on the way to becoming one of the best point guards of the 21st century—which is no small feat considering the amount of talent that has flooded the NBA in the last 20 years. The first pick in the 2008 draft, Rose joined the Bulls, which could have created the narrative of the triumphant native son that would rival that of LeBron James—Rose was born in Chicago, like former great point guards Isiah Thomas and Tim Hardaway.

And while things seemed to be heading that way up to a point—in 2009 Rose was named Rookie of the Year, and two years later he was league MVP and his team was eliminated in the Eastern Conference Finals by the Miami Heat, then led by James, Dwyane Wade and Chris Bosh—in the 2011–12 postseason Rose tore his ACL. He had just renegotiated his contract with Adidas, which would make him $185 million during the next 14 years. Rose was truly a superstar in the making.

What must be noted here was that the Bulls could have landed two of the players that eliminated them from playoff contention two times during the next three seasons. In the summer of 2010 the Bulls were eager to get Wade and Bosh—a move which, if executed correctly, would create a starting lineup of Rose, Wade, Luol Deng, Bosh and Joakim Noah. After hearing about the possibility of bringing in the trio of James, Wade and Bosh by the Heat, Wade asked if the team from Chicago could create cap space for a third superstar. The Bulls failed or were reluctant to do so, and in consequence the three players moved to South Beach.[4] Wade eventually signed with his hometown team in 2016, with Rose already gone.

In the next season, 2011–12, Rose was limited to just 39 games in the lockout-shortened, 66-game season. During the season he suffered "turf toe, back spasms, pulled groin and foot injuries. He hasn't played more than two games in a row since suffering a foot injury on March 12, [2012]."[5] Upon his return, in the first game of the playoffs, Rose tore his ACL. The Bulls were leading 99–87 with less than two minutes left in the game, and the Bulls starters for some reason were still on the floor. After getting the ball Rose jumped up awkwardly, then landed holding his left knee. Rose missed the whole of next season and played ten games two seasons later. He was still playing through pain and below expectations, yet making around $19 million per season. In the last year of his contract he was traded to the New York Knicks. It would be the last season he would play as a starter. In the 2017–18 season he appeared in just 25 games for the Cavaliers and the Timberwolves. He was picked up by his former Bulls' coach Tom Thibodeau after being waived by the Utah Jazz, following a trade with the Cavs.

For the Timberwolves Rose was mostly coming off the bench, but on the 31st of October 2018, as a starter in a game against the team that waived him the previous season, he had a career night (up to this point). He had 50 points, four rebounds, six assists and two steals. After the Jazz missed three three-pointers in a row that would tie the game, the Timberwolves called a timeout, and an emotional Rose was surrounded by his teammates, who celebrated his achievement with him. He appeared in 51 games that season, starting 13, averaging 18 points, 4.3 assists and 2.7 rebounds per game.

Despite creating one of the feel-good stories of the season, he was just sixth in Sixth Man of the Year voting, as the Timberwolves did not even make the playoffs. In the summer of 2019 he became a member of the Detroit Pistons and had a similar season statistically. It remains to be seen if he will join the ranks of players whose NBA careers were saved by taking on a lesser role after suffering a serious injury.

The most famous player who salvaged his career by moving to the bench was Bill Walton, the 6'11" center[6] who dealt with foot injuries throughout almost all of his professional career. He played basketball with a broken foot, because the team doctor in Portland did not believe that he felt so much pain. He sat out three whole seasons and missed numerous games in many more, all because of the way he was built. When healthy, Walton was so dominant that, when the Blazers won the championship, they were referred to as "Bill and Company" by the *Oregionian*.[7] He changed the game of basketball, because, up until Walton or Bob McAdoo became famous college, and then professional, players, big men were regarded as stiffs, who were capable of making effective but not spectacular plays. Thanks to Walton's quickness, lightness and passing ability, as well as McAdoo's touch from mid-range, that perception changed. McAdoo was already analyzed in a previous chapter, so here I want to focus on Walton.

Even though he enjoyed great success as a pro, as well as in college, he never realized his full potential. Walton himself said, "Never measure yourself by what you have done, but rather by what you *could* or *should* have been able to do."[8] The fascinating thing about that quote is that he said it in reference to his college career, which he has spent at UCLA, becoming the starting center following Lew Alcindor's (Kareem Abdul-Jabbar's) departure for the NBA. Walton won two NCAA Championships and was named NCAA Final Four Most Outstanding Player as well, but considers his college career a disappointment. "His team won 88 games in a row … including two national championships, and Walton won the college player of the year award all three years he was eligible for it. In the 1973 N.C.A.A. final, Walton made 21 of his 22 official shots on his way to 44 points. Even then, his knees were almost too bad to play on; every game required an elaborate regimen of icing and heating, and often he was in too much pain to practice."[9] Despite the risk, the Trail Blazers could not pass up the possibility of drafting a big man with enormous potential, just as they did with Sam Bowie in 1984 and Greg Oden in 2007. In comparison to those two players though, Walton had a stellar and long NBA career, even though from the potential 1,066 games that he should have played in the span of the 13 seasons he spent in the league, he appeared in 468.

What made Walton so special? Off the court he was a redhead hippie with a beard, wearing a flannel shirt and jeans to almost every occasion. He was outspoken about his leftist political views and his vegetarianism. On the court, as the general manager of Portland Trail Blazers at the time, Stu Inman, put it, he was:

> A great shot blocker, a great concept of the game, great intelligence and he brought a special tempo to the game, there was a rhythm to his game and it was always the right rhythm. Most of all, his effect on his teammates. As long as he was there they all knew they would be in every game and they controlled their own egos. With him they always knew they could do it as a team.[10]

The opinion was given after Walton left Portland to join the San Diego Clippers as a free agent. League commissioner Larry O'Brien forced the Clippers to give away three players (Kermit Washington, Kevin Kunnert and Randy Smith) and a first-round draft pick as compensation for the small-market Blazers.

In his first two seasons Walton was averaging 13 rebounds, 4.5 assists, two blocks and 14.8 points per game, but he played in only 86 games. The fans were frustrated with his health, but so was Walton. As put by David Halberstam, "The one thing basketball had always been to him in the past, spiritual liberation, had been missing, and his paycheck, no matter how big, therefore, provided him with little sense of accomplishment."[11] He was playing in the best basketball league in the world—he appreciated the level of the competition in the NBA so much that he rejected a proposition from the ABA that would have made him twice as much money—but he wanted to perform in a specific way, by playing unselfish, beautiful basketball. He was the prototypical big man passer, under both baskets, either initiating the fast break after a good defensive stop or kicking the ball out to an open teammate for a shot. In his third NBA season Walton became obsessed with winning not only every NBA game, but also every pick-up game and every practice.

During the first two seasons in the league Walton played under Lenny Wilkens, who was also a player during Walton's rookie year. While he would eventually enter the Hall of Fame both as a player and a coach, he parted ways with the Blazers after two losing seasons and a 75–89 record. The team hired Jack Ramsay, who was fired a month earlier by the Buffalo Braves after turning the team from a 21–61 team to a playoff mainstay. Furthermore, Ramsay had the experience necessary to make things work with Walton, as he built the Braves team around Bob McAdoo, who was an out-of-the-box player as well. Ramsay served as the link between two exceptional big men, who played the game differently, yet were way ahead of their time. The sweet-shooting McAdoo paved the way for big men scorers like Dirk Nowitzki or Kevin Durant, while Walton inspired big men passers like Arvydas Sabonis, Chris Webber or Nicola Jokic.

During Ramsay's first season things started falling into place. The Blazers, who had not made the playoffs in their six-year NBA history, were playing electrifying, team-oriented basketball and, more importantly, finally winning games. This put a start to Blazermania which has swept the city of Portland and turned the team into the city's darling, which it remains until this day.[12] The fans felt they were experiencing something special, and they followed the team wherever it went. Bill Walton said about the time, "The newspaper used to publish our flight schedule, crowds would meet us in the middle of the night, hundreds of people."[13] Highly criticized earlier, Walton now became the central figure on the team that was bound for the playoffs for the first time in its history. In the Western Conference Finals they swept the favored Los Angeles Lakers, who were led by the player Walton followed at UCLA, Kareem Abdul-Jabbar. The Lakers center himself had a great series, averaging 30.3 points, 16 rebounds, 3.8 assists and 3.8 blocks in the four games, while Walton averaged 19.3 points, 14.8 rebounds, 5.8 assists and 2.3 blocks. Abdul-Jabbar was clearly the better individual player, but Walton was surrounded by players who better suited his playing style. In the Finals the Blazers were once again the underdogs, this time against the Philadelphia 76ers, who had acquired Julius Erving from NBA newcomers, the New Jersey Nets, one of four ABA teams that joined the league in the 1976 merger. After losing the first two games, the Blazers won the next four, including a decisive 130–89 triumph in Game Four. Walton was named the Finals MVP.

A year later he was named league MVP as well, despite appearing in just 58 games, which was exactly the number of games the Blazers won that season, improving the previous record by nine wins. On February 28, 1978, Walton took himself out of the game with the Sixers after playing just 13 minutes, complaining about the pain he felt in his legs and feet. That would be the last regular season game he would play for the Blazers, who until that moment were 50–10. He would make his return in the Western Conference Semifinals against the Sonics, coached by Lenny Wilkens. He left the second game of the series after playing for 15 minutes. After the game his left foot was diagnosed with a fractured bone. After the season, in July, Walton demanded to be traded to one of the four teams of his choosing (Clippers, Knicks, Sixers or Warriors), while also accusing the Blazers of mishandling his injury and misusing painkillers.

After a year away from basketball, Walton finally appeared on the court for the Clippers, who had been in their second NBA season, following the relocation from Buffalo, where they played as the Braves. The new name of the franchise came from the ships that sailed through the San Diego Bay. Just 26, Walton already had a long and well-documented injury history, and was risking his health every time he stepped onto the court. Walton was from La Mesa, San Diego County, so he was especially focused on the team doing well after his arrival. Now he was a self-proclaimed changed man. Instead of wearing casual clothes, he bought expensive suits, rode in limos and kept his opinions mostly to himself. He said about his changed attitude, "That year and a half that I couldn't play basketball I did a lot of thinking. I realized that life is much more enjoyable if people like you, and that you don't have to compromise your values to have that."[14] He might have been happier off the court in San Diego, but on it the injuries continued to bug him. He appeared in 102 games in five seasons he spent in his hometown, including two full seasons during which he did not enter the game even once (1980–81 and 1981–82).

In the middle of Walton's hiatus, in September 1981, real estate tycoon Donald Sterling announced his ownership of the San Diego Clippers with an open letter to the fans, in which he promised that he was intending to keep professional basketball in the city. San Diego had already lost its original NBA team, as the 1961-founded San Diego Rockets relocated to Houston ten years later. A season later San Diego launched its ABA team, the San Diego Conquistadors, who folded after three seasons, the same year they changed their name to the San Diego Sails, in 1975. A year after the letter Sterling made his first attempt to move the team to Los Angeles, but the move was blocked and investigated by the NBA. The Clippers eventually left San Diego in 1984. Walton until this day feels guilty about the relocation, showing strong belief that with his play he would have kept the team in the city: "It's my greatest failure as a professional in my entire life. I could not get the job done in my hometown. It is a stain and stigma on my soul that is indelible. I'll never be able to wash that off, and I carry it with me forever."[15]

Walton played one more season in Los Angeles with the Clippers, but only as a reserve. He started 37 of the 67 games he played in, averaging 10.1 points, nine rebounds and 2.1 blocks in 24.6 minutes of action per game. After another disappointing season—Walton had not appeared in the playoffs since the two games he played in 1978—the center demanded to be traded, and took it upon himself to find the team for himself, making a personal call to the Boston Celtics. The winningest team in NBA history had just lost to the Lakers, and Kareem Abdul-Jabbar was named the 1985 Finals MVP. With his shot-blocking ability, even for a limited period, Walton would substitute for either Parish or McHale, and the team would still be able to contain the best center in the league. Larry Bird, the back-to-back league MVP, was more impressed with what Walton could do offensively: "If we keep him healthy we can win a championship a lot easier than we could without him. He's the best passer I've ever seen in my life."[16]

Already in the first exhibition game he played as a member of the

Celtics in Boston Garden, often referred to simply as "The Garden" by basketball aficionados, he was overwhelmed by the atmosphere. Walton was hearing the fans chant, but he could not make out what they were chanting because of the noise, so he asked Larry Bird, "Are they chanting Jerry?" Bird replied, "No, they are chanting my name and you better get used to that," then he turned and made a three-point shot.[17] Walton may have been Bird's high school idol, but the pecking order was very clear in Boston. David Halberstam gives an equally interesting example of Bird's exceptional position on the team, but also the unparalleled confidence in his ability. Before one game during that season, in which Parish was out, Bird approached Walton and said, "I know what you're thinking. You're thinking you're going to get Robert's shots tonight, and you're going to get twenty points. Well, forget it. Those extra shots are mine."[18]

That Boston Celtics team is regarded as one of the best in league history. With the 67–15 record, they were fourth in regular season win percentage, after the 69–13 Lakers (1971–72), the 68–13 Sixers (1966–67) and the 68–14 Celtics (1972–73) at the time. In pursuit of reclaiming their championship title, the 1986 Celtics had to beat the team that dethroned them the year before, the Lakers. In their first regular season game against each other since that finals' series, Walton delivered an incredible performance—in just 16 minutes of play he had 11 points, eight rebounds and seven blocks. Walton and Parish held Abdul-Jabbar to 17 points, 6/20 from the floor. That Lakers team also featured Maurice Lucas, Walton's friend and former teammate on the Blazers. The two were so close that Walton named his son, Luke, after the power forward.

The Celtics had great confidence in their abilities, and they simply had fun playing basketball. With two of the greatest big men passers ever, Walton and the 6'9" Larry Bird, the Celtics embodied the principles of team-first basketball. Playing the fewest number of minutes per game up until that point of his career (19.3), Walton was averaging 7.6 points and 6.8 rebounds, also the lowest numbers of his career so far. However, he appeared in 80 games, which would become his personal best. The Celtics made it their point to rest him enough and provide him with proper medical care. For his contributions on and off the court Walton was voted 1986 NBA Sixth Man of the Year, getting 32 of the 78 votes available. While the players behind him, like Ricky Pierce or Eddie Johnson, had been statistically superior to Walton, the feel-good narrative of his season was just too promising to pass up. The Celtics won the championship that year, while Bird was voted league MVP for the third consecutive time. In the Finals the opposing center was once again successfully stopped by the duo of Parrish and Walton, only this time it was Ralph Sampson of the Houston Rockets, who played in the frontcourt next to Hakeem Olajuwon—the duo was known as the "Twin Towers," two centers playing alongside one another. Sampson noted 14.8 points and 9.3 rebounds per game, which were below his regular season averages of 18.9 points and 11.1 rebounds.

The next season though Walton appeared in just 10 games, as he re-injured his foot on a stationary bike and was again dealing with foot injuries. He played just 11.2 minutes per game, averaging 2.3 points, 3.1 rebounds and one block. He also appeared in the 12 games of the playoffs, making a vital contribution in the second game of the first round of the playoffs, grabbing nine rebounds and filling in for Parish, who was in danger of fouling out. In the 1987 NBA Finals Walton appeared in five of the six games in which the Celtics faced the Lakers, but he played just a total of 24 minutes, ten of which came in the final game of the series, a must-win for his team. The loss was his last NBA game.

Walton's was obviously not the only feel-good story in league history starring an NBA legend who was able to return to professional basketball because of the bench. Another as, if not even more, impressive career narrative is that of Alonzo Mourning, a 6'10" center, whose cold, physically imposing exterior at some point turned him into the most hated man in the NBA. And it was not without merit, as

> for much of his career he has worn the black hat with relish. Word has gotten around: Mourning refused autograph requests as a rookie with the Charlotte Hornets in 1992–93, brushing off kids like lint. He wanted a woman reporter to be kicked out of the Hornets' home locker room before a game. Last April, after being outplayed by Danny Schayes in Game 4 of a first-round playoff series between Miami and the Orlando Magic, Mourning snapped at reporters gathered around his locker, "Why don't y'all get the f--- out?" After hitting a victory-sealing three-pointer against the New York Knicks in Game 6 of last year's Eastern Conference semifinals, Mourning screamed nationally televised curses at the Madison Square Garden crowd.[19]

Mourning was always playing angry, with complete focus on the result, tensed to the point that the smallest affront would completely throw him off his game. The center would get into infamous fights with opponents like Larry Johnson and Dennis Rodman, and earn ejections in important games because of his highly visible frustration with his performance. His on-court persona did not make him a lot of friends on the opposing teams. Even his teammates would jokingly call Mourning "The Black Hole" because, once he got the ball in the post, his teammates would not see it again.[20] The consensus was that, although immensely talented, Mourning lacked the mental toughness to be a leader of a winning basketball team.

This was contradictory to Mourning's personal life, where he seemed utterly reasonable. When he was ten, his parents divorced. Because he could not bear their arguments, he decided all by himself to enter foster care:

"My entire life, I never wanted people making a big deal about me. ... I'm the most independent person in the world."[21] He honed his basketball skills at Georgetown, where he followed in the footsteps of former great NBA centers Patrick Ewing and Dikembe Mutombo. Mourning had to share the court with the latter until his third college year, playing the power forward position. It was only as a senior that he became the focal point of the team and ended his last year of college with averages of 21.3 points, 10.7 rebounds and five blocks per game. The 3.6 fouls per game though indicated that the player was not always able to contain his emotions on the court.

He entered the NBA as the league was undergoing a major generational change, with its biggest superstars so far retiring almost simultaneously. Bird and Johnson had just retired, while Jordan would finish his career a year later and move on to play baseball (as it turned out, just for a short time). The first three players selected in the 1992 NBA Draft were, respectively, Shaquille O'Neal (Orlando Magic), Alonzo Mourning (Charlotte Hornets) and Christian Laettner (Minnesota Timberwolves). Laettner was one of the best college basketball players at the time, especially remembered for the 15-foot buzzer beater that allowed Duke to take the win over Kentucky in the Elite 8 game of the 1992 NCAA Tournament. It was Laettner and not O'Neal or Mourning who would make the 1992 Olympic basketball team in Barcelona, yet the draft order was more than correct, as O'Neal became arguably the most dominant player in the league by the end of the decade, Mourning was a Hall of Fame–level defender, and Laettner would have a solid but rather unremarkable—especially considering the expectations imposed upon him when he entered the NBA—professional career, which he finished with averages of 12.8 points, 6.7 rebounds and 2.6 assists.

Mourning and O'Neal were at first linked together, as if theirs would be a new rivalry that would make headlines now that the main big-name superstars were gone. Mourning was presented as a hard worker, obsessed with keeping his body in the best shape and completely devoted to winning. Shaq on the other hand was a brash, young big man, who recorded rap albums and starred in movies. At least that was how they were perceived, fitting into the already successful narratives of the blue-collar Bird and the flamboyant, fun-loving Johnson. The two would never play against each other in the playoffs, as the Magic finally met Mourning's team—then the Miami Heat, who acquired him from the Hornets on the first day of the 1995–96 regular season—in the 1996–97 playoffs, a year after O'Neal signed with the Los Angeles Lakers. O'Neal led the Magic to the NBA Finals in 1995. He would win three NBA Championship titles on the Lakers and one on the Miami Heat, in 2006. The man backing him up was ... Mourning, making his sole finals appearance that year.

In Charlotte, Mourning was sharing the court with Larry Johnson, a power forward drafted a year before him, who had signed a 12-year $84 million contract with the Hornets, at the time the biggest in league history, on the same day Jordan announced his retirement (October 6, 1993). The two young superstars did not get along, as Mourning wanted the same recognition (and money) as Johnson, because he was as good a player if not better. He wanted to become the league's first $100 million man in Charlotte. Instead, unwilling to pay him that much money, the Hornets started shopping him around. Among of those interested were the Lakers, who would sign O'Neal a season later. Eventually Mourning was traded to the Heat. It was the first big move of Pat Riley, who infamously resigned from his job as head coach of the Knicks via a fax message, joining a rather unremarkable Miami team.

The Heat promised Riley more control, and he became head coach, president and part owner of the team. Mourning was the cornerstone on which he wanted to build the identity of his team. The player described his coach's attitude as follows: "What Riley taught his players was to compete with an intent to dominate and annihilate your competition, mentally and physically. When he coached the Knicks, he planted that seed. Then he coached the Heat and he planted that same seed. He literally built two monsters."[22] The monsters would clash four times in the playoffs, and each time the victor would emerge in the final game of the series, either Game Six (1998, 1999) or Game Seven (1997, 2000). The Heat won only the first postseason meeting of the two, while their most painful loss though came in the 1999 playoffs. In the lockout-shortened 50-game season, the Heat held the first seed in the East, and despite having home court advantage, the series was tied 2–2. In Game Five, with the Heat leading 77–76 with 4.5 seconds left, Allan Houston hit a floater which won the series for the Knicks. The Heat became the second conference leader in NBA history to be eliminated by the eighth seed in the playoffs. A year later they were swept by the Hornets in the First Round, and the loss began a full-on rebuild of the team.

The 1995–2001 Heat made the playoffs in each of their six seasons. Mourning and point guard Tim Hardaway, acquired in the middle of the 1995–96 season, formed the nucleus of a team that had high aspirations and enormous potential, yet never could deliver like it was expected to. A team that also featured Jamal Mashburn, P.J. Brown, Dan Majerle, and then Eddie Jones and Anthony Mason—Mashburn and Brown were members of the Hornets team that swept the Heat—for four years straight was on top of the Atlantic Division, yet made the Eastern Conference Finals just once, while losing four times in the First Round of the playoffs. However, in the 2000–01 season, the one after he was third in MVP voting and for a second straight season was named NBA Defensive Player of the Year, Mourning appeared in just 13 games due to a kidney disease.

The problems began when Mourning returned from the Olympics in Sydney. It turned out he was suffering from FSGS (focal segmental glomerulosclerosis), a kidney disease which is characterized, *inter alia*, by proteinuria, the excess of protein in one's urine. That was how Mourning found out he had the disease. He was not the first active NBA player suffering from it, as San Antonio small forward Sean Elliott had it as well. Not a month after he won his first NBA Championship as a member of the Spurs, on July 1999, Elliott made his disease public, even though he learned about it already during the 1992–93 season. Elliot even failed a physical that would send him from the Pistons to the Rockets in 1994 because of his kidney condition.[23] He needed to have a kidney transplant in the 1999 offseason, and even though there was no precedent of a professional athlete making a comeback following the procedure, he took the risk and was able to play for two more seasons, albeit not to his former level.

With no prior signs of illness, Mourning was shocked that he got so weak so suddenly: "I was the healthiest person I knew—thirty years old, six foot ten, 255 pounds with just six percent body fat. I benched over three hundred pounds with ease. I worked out with hundred-pound dumbbells."[24] Mourning, having looked like a prototypical basketball player, had no idea he was sick just by looking at his body. He had to completely change his eating habits, as well as take medication—up to 14 pills a day—and test his blood after every practice. His first game back was on the 27th of March 2001, against the Raptors. He went 3/11 from the floor and grabbed six rebounds. Throughout the season his play was uneven, just like his team's, but in the second-to-last game of the season it seemed that Mourning was back, as he was able to get 25 points, 16 rebounds and five blocks against the Bucks. But in the playoff series the Heat were utterly destroyed by the Hornets, who won the three games by a total of 67 points.

In the 2001–02 season the Heat failed to make the playoffs, even though Mourning played in 75 games. A year later he did not play at all, while the team won just 27 games, nine less than the season prior. Riley wanted to continue the rebuild and Mourning to mentor the younger players, but the center did not want to be a part of the process—he wanted to win an NBA Championship so that he could retire a winner. Plus, the Heat refused to offer him a long, lucrative deal, which was understandable, considering that the year prior he earned over $20 million even though he did not appear in a single game.

So Mourning, now a free agent, signed with the Nets for four years and $22 million. Him joining the team was part of the reason why the Nets' superstar, point guard Jason Kidd, decided to stay in New Jersey, despite a strong offer from the Spurs, the team that just beat the Nets 4–2 in the 2003 NBA Finals. With the Nets, Mourning was supposed to again share the locker room with his Georgetown teammate Dikembe Mutombo, but the team decided to waive the experienced center before the season started. Twelve games into it, Mourning, visibly tired and frustrated, retired from the NBA and underwent a kidney transplant. The team, somewhat miraculously, made the Eastern Conference Finals, but lost to the eventual champions, the Detroit Pistons.

A year later Mourning, following the successful transplant, returned. The public support for his fight with the disease was overwhelming, as a lot of different people, including his on-court nemesis and off-court friend Patrick Ewing, were willing to donate their kidneys to the player. The Nets were a different team though. Kenyon Martin, the promising young power forward, was gone. So was shooting guard Kerry Kittles. Displeased with the dismantling of the roster, Kidd also wanted to be traded. The Nets were interested in an exchange for power forward Shareef Abdur-Rahim from the Blazers, as their salaries matched, but the player from Portland would be a free agent the next season, while Kidd had a five-year deal, which would allow the Nets to rebuild. The deal did not go through, partially because Kidd was recovering from a knee surgery, and it was uncertain if he would be the same player following his return.

When Mourning returned, he said he hoped to play in all 82 games that season, but after appearing in just 18 he asked to be put on the injured list, as his body was breaking down. Instead of banging up under the baskets, he settled on jump shots; plus he could not take painkillers because of his disease.[25] In truth, Mourning also turned his back on a team that seemed to be going nowhere. He admitted as much after his first game back in New Jersey, albeit on a different team.[26] On the 17th of December 2004 Mourning was traded along with Aaron Williams, Eric Williams and two first-round draft picks to the Toronto Raptors for Vince Carter. Mourning did not want to play on a team that did not have championship aspirations, so he did not even travel to Toronto—after some negotiations the Raptors bought out his contract for $9 million, and he was free to return to Miami, for a mere $325,000. The Heat were also a totally different team. Riley stepped down as head coach and brought in Stan Van Gundy at the position, himself remaining team president. In the summer of 2003 he also traded for Shaquille O'Neal, whom Mourning would be now backing. The leader of that team was a second-year shooting guard, Dwyane Wade.

The Heat made the 2005 Eastern Conference Finals, where they lost to the Pistons in a seven-game series. Mourning played in 19 regular-season games for the Heat and 15 games in the playoffs, with five starts total. In Game Two of the First Round series against the Nets, coming off the bench and playing just 16 minutes, Mourning got 21 points and nine rebounds. He also fouled out, which shows that he still had a hard time keeping a cool head. The loss to the Pistons inspired big moves by the front office. In the summer Riley acquired veterans Jason Williams, James Posey, Antoine Walker and Gary Payton to make one last push for the finals. However, the team got off to a disappointing start, and after going 11–10, Van Gundy was fired. Riley replaced him with … himself, putting an end to the rumors about him taking over that began to circulate after the Heat's playoff exit in the 2005 Conference Finals. Riley took on a tougher approach toward his veterans than Van Gundy, and Mourning was presented as the embodiment of the attitude and work ethic that they needed to possess: "When they're coasting, when they're not playing hard or they're sitting out too long, I hope they look over at him and realize how they should be responding…. We need to get the whole team playing at the same level as Zo."[27]

The Heat were 41–20 following the coaching change and finished the season with 52 wins. Mourning played in 65 games, made 20 starts, and was averaging 7.8 points, 5.5 rebounds and 2.7 blocks per game. He finished sixth in voting for Sixth Man of the Year and eighth in voting for Defensive Player of the Year. More importantly, at 36 years old, he appeared in his first NBA Finals. Facing off against the Dallas Mavericks, led by Dirk Nowitzki and coached by Avery Johnson, who took the team over from a disgruntled Don Nelson in the middle of the previous season, the Heat had clearly more playoff experience, yet were down 0–2 after the first two road games. With Payton and Mourning determined to win their first NBA Championship, and O'Neal wanting to prove that he could win one outside of Los Angeles, without Kobe Bryant or Phil Jackson, it was the third-year Wade who turned the series around for his veteran teammates. In the next four games he averaged 39.3 points and 8.3 rebounds. Ferociously attacking the basket, he also shot 73 free throws. The Heat won their first NBA title, and it was Mourning, at least according to the Mavericks shooting guard Jason Terry, who was instrumental in their Game Six triumph:

> The guy that actually changed that game and really changed the series was Alonzo Mourning, and nobody ever talks about what Alonzo Mourning did for that team coming off the bench. He not only blocked shots…. Big rebounds. He had a huge impact on that game. Just his energy alone that he brought to his team, it helped them win that game.[28]

In 14 minutes Mourning had five blocks, six rebounds and eight points. With that championship title, playing limited minutes, he made the most of his second chance. An energetic, ruthless Mourning could not carry a team as its leader, but he worked perfectly as a spark off the bench for the 2006 Heat.

A year later almost the same roster, albeit depleted by injuries, was swept in the first round of the playoffs by the Chicago Bulls. On the 19th of December 2007, in a regular season game against the Hawks, after just four minutes of playtime, Mourning tore a tendon in his right knee. Refusing to leave the court on a stretcher, he left the court with the aid of his teammates, turning his response to the career-ending injury into his final statement: "That's not the way I envisioned myself walking off the court for the last time in my career. I've been through so much in my life. If I had to crawl off the court I would have. Nobody was going to push me off on a stretcher off the court. That wasn't going to happen."[29] Mourning did not retire on his own terms, but he left the floor exemplifying one characteristic that remained constant throughout his career—incredible, almost unmatched toughness.

Walton and Mourning remain two of the few players who were able to return to playing professional basketball following, respectively, a seeming career-ending injury and a very serious illness. Their comebacks were inspiring not only to fellow athletes, but to anybody who had to face adversity in their lives. These were possible thanks to the bench, as in the reserve role they were able to contribute on championship teams, despite physical limitations. While other players could have given up in frustration at the inability to remain as productive as they were prior to their misfortunes, both centers deserve a place in sports history for their career narratives, made possible thanks to their unbreakable spirits.

The Uneasy Transition from the Starting Lineup to the Bench

Isaiah Thomas
   Guard. In the NBA: 2011– . Seasons as a bench player: five.
Carmelo Anthony
   Forward. In the NBA: 2003– . Seasons as a bench player: one.
Allen Iverson
   Guard. In the NBA: 1996–2010. Seasons as a bench player: none.
Dion Waiters
   Guard. In the NBA: 2012– . Seasons as a bench player: five.
J.J. Hickson
   Forward/Center. In the NBA: 2008–2016. Seasons as a bench player: five.
Tyrus Thomas
   Forward. In the NBA: 2006–2015. Seasons as a bench player: six.
Michael Jordan
   Guard. In the NBA: 1984–2003. Seasons as a bench player: none.

Being a starter in the best basketball league in the world is a source of great pride and confidence. One needs to have both if wanting to perform at the highest level throughout the 82-game season, as well as the playoffs. While there are obvious contract incentives for starters, who usually get paid more than bench players, the issue has more to do with perception. Since someone is starting in the place of another player, he has to be better than him—at least that is how the fans view it. Billy Cunningham, the head coach of the Philadelphia 76ers and Bobby Jones, the first recipient of the Sixth Man of the Year Award in league history, described how "going from a starter to the sixth man is not an easy switchover. The biggest factor is mental preparedness, coming in and providing the team with what it needs at the time."[1] The transition from starting lineup to the bench becomes especially painful for players who used to be the alpha dogs on their teams, and almost unfathomable for those who were mentioned among the best in the league. The players described in this chapter highlight the complexity of the process of accepting a supposedly less-exposed role on the roster. Whether it had to do with marketability or pride, the players that I discuss here reacted badly to even a possibility of losing their starting role on an NBA roster.

A good example of said complexity was the case with Isaiah Thomas's move to the Lakers. No stranger to adversity, Thomas worked his way up from being the last pick in the 2011 NBA Draft to one of the best point guards in the league. When Kyrie Irving went to Boston in exchange for a first-round draft pick that the Celtics acquired from the Nets a couple of years previously in the blockbuster trade that sent Kevin Garnett and Paul Pierce to Brooklyn, Thomas, the 5'9" player, was coming off the best season of his career—he was fifth in the MVP voting, while averaging 28.9 points and 5.9 assists per game. The problem was that Thomas severely injured his hip during the playoffs, and it was uncertain whether he would remain the same explosive player as before. He was instrumental in the Celtics' deep playoff run that season, for example when he scored 53 points in Game Two of the Eastern Conference Semifinals against the Wizards. He left the court during Game Two of the Eastern Conference Finals against his future team, the Cavs, not to return during that postseason. The Celtics lost the series 1–4. It was later reported that he was playing with loss of cartilage and some arthritis in his hip for several years, which made his return to form all the more unlikely.

Thomas appeared in his first game for the Cavs on January 2, 2018. He came off the bench and scored 17 points, which was also the point difference by which his team has beaten the Portland Trail Blazers. However, after just 15 games, the Cavaliers traded Thomas to the Lakers. After the injury the player lost his explosiveness, with which he was able to make up for his lack of size. His scoring average dropped by almost half—14.7 from 28.9 the season before—while his field-goal accuracy dropped by over 10 percent to 36.1, as opposed to 46.3 as a member of the Celtics. With the Cavs hoping to return to the NBA Finals, Thomas became a liability. He did not help his case by criticizing his teammates.

Following his great season with the Celtics, Thomas said that his team would have to "bring the Brinks truck out"[2] to deliver all the money he was due as a free agent in the summer of 2018. Thomas believed that he was worthy of a max contract, as he sacrificed his health for team success. Less than a year later he was on his third team and about to lose the starting spot to rookie Lonzo Ball, who was also heavily criticized for his play. Before Thomas's move to the Lakers, his agent texted ESPN presenter

Rachel Nichols that his client would not be coming off the bench for the new team. However, Magic Johnson convinced Thomas that he would not start, yet would get "a lot of minutes,"[3] so the player changed his mind about the move. He started only once in the 17 games he played for the Lakers, before he underwent a season-ending surgery for his hip. The Lakers did not re-sign him in free agency. Instead of a max contract with the Celtics, Thomas signed a one-year, $2 million deal with the Nuggets. Before the 2019–20 season, he signed with the Washington Wizards in order to serve as backup to John Wall, but when the star point guard went down with a season-ending injury, Thomas became a starter. He played in 40 games and was traded to the Clippers, who simply waived him.

Before the start of the 2017–18 season the NBA Western Conference looked as stacked as ever. With Kyrie Irving leaving the Cavaliers and LeBron James' shadow to become the leader of the Celtics, it was pretty obvious that only one conference counted when it came to winning it all. The reigning champions, the Golden State Warriors, had four potential future Hall of Fame inductees in Steph Curry, Klay Thompson, Kevin Durant and Draymond Green. Chris Paul joined James Harden in Houston, to form what was expected to be the best backcourt in the league. Then there was the Oklahoma City Thunder, led by the reigning MVP, Russell Westbrook. Because during the previous season it seemed that he took the team to the playoffs single-handedly, general manager Sam Presti brought in Paul George and Carmelo Anthony to form a big three—or OK3, as they became known—that was supposed to challenge the supremacy of the Warriors. With the aid of George's all-round play and Anthony's shooting, Westbrook could make fans in Oklahoma City get over Durant's shocking departure to the Warriors just a year before.

The acquisitions of Anthony and George were also surprising, albeit for different reasons. The 6'8" player was with the Pacers for seven seasons and grew into one of the best guards/forwards in the league. In the 2016–2017 season he became very vocal about moving to Los Angeles during the next offseason, after his contract with the Pacers was up. The Thunder took a gamble on him, hoping he would fall in love with the culture and the city so much that he would end up staying in Oklahoma City. George was 27, about to enter the prime of his career.

Anthony, on the other hand, was 33 and already considered a player not only past his prime but more so better suited for a different era of basketball. He had an over-reliance on mid-range jumpers and unwillingness to play as a stretch four, even though he enjoyed the most success at that position (the 2013 scoring championship, 54 wins and Eastern Conference Semifinals on the Knicks). An established shooter who was never a solid defender, Anthony seemed really concerned with remaining a productive ballplayer, but he also had a certain reputation, that of a starter in the best league in the world. George Karl, who coached Anthony for six seasons in Denver, described him as "the best offensive player [he] ever coached. [Anthony] was also a user of people, addicted to the spotlight, and very unhappy when he had to share it."[4] In 2017 Anthony made his 10th All-Star Game appearance, he was still recognizable, and his website was viewed by around two million people per year. Yet very often when he spoke about his legacy, Anthony was referring to his various business endeavors. Instead of focusing on winning, he was making plans for his post-basketball career, which was an attitude that would never mesh with the competitiveness of Russell Westbrook.

Some recognized the project as doomed from the start. One journalist, during Melo's first press conference, asked the player if he would consider coming off the bench if that would help the team's chances of winning. Up to that point, for 13 seasons from 2004 to 2017, Anthony was always the starter for the Nuggets and the Knicks. He was selected with the third pick in the 2004 Draft, that also featured LeBron James, Dwyane Wade and Chris Bosh, and is considered among the best in league history. He scored at least 10,000 points as a member of both franchises he has played for so far, only the third player ever to do so. He was the 2013 scoring champion. After 976 consecutive starts, now he was asked whether he would consider coming off the bench. Anthony reacted to the question with astonishment, "Who? Me?" and laughed, before adding, "I don't know where that came from." He continued laughing for some time and with him some of the journalists gathered at the press conference.

Anthony started all 76 games he played in for the Thunder that season. The team finished fourth in the Western Conference with 48 wins and was eliminated in the first round of the playoffs by the quicker, more athletic Utah Jazz. In the six games (all starts) of the series, Anthony averaged 11.8 points on 37.5 percent shooting, including 21.4 percent for three. The Thunder outscored the Jazz by a total of 32 points when Anthony was on the bench. Anthony was dominated by a much more athletic rookie Donovan Mitchell, who averaged 28.5 points in the series, including 38 points in Game Six. After the series he said, "I'm not sacrificing no bench role. That's out of the question."[5]

In the summer Anthony (and the last season of his $28 million-a-year contract, from which he obviously did not want to opt-out) was traded to the Atlanta Hawks, who waived him. He joined the Rockets but was released after just ten games and two starts. Anthony admitted that, even though he was finally coming to terms with being a bench player, his contract was terminated before he was able to learn the team's style of play. After almost a year away from basketball, Anthony signed with the Portland Trail Blazers and started all 58 games he played in during the 2019–20 season. His biggest success came when he was named Western Conference Player of the Week for the last week of November and his team won all three of its games. Anthony himself said that the honor was "deeper than basketball."[6]

Anthony's situation was reminiscent of that of another great scorer, who was unable to come to terms with being the first player off the bench, Allen Iverson. For two years Iverson and Anthony were teammates on the Denver Nuggets. They were also coached by Karl, who considered Iverson past his prime when he left the Sixers at age 31. With Carmelo Anthony and Allen Iverson the team had two of the most offensively gifted players in the league at the time, but failed to make an impact in the postseason. After three games of the 2008–2009 season Iverson was traded to the Detroit Pistons, mostly because of his contract, which was up in the summer. The team gave up the player who was instrumental to their only championship in the 21st century, Chauncey Billups, as well as Antonio McDyess and Cheikh Samb, in order to get Iverson and his one-year, $20.8 million deal.

The trade was long overdue, as Iverson almost became a Piston in the summer of 2000, but the other Sixer who was also supposed to be included in the move, Matt Geiger, refused to waive his $1.2 million trade kicker. This meant that Iverson was forced to stay in Philadelphia, and the player responded with the best season of his career—not only did he win the MVP trophy, but A.I. also led the Sixers to the NBA Finals. Now, coming to the Pistons eight years later, he was not the same player as before. Mentally he still considered himself to be among the best in the league, but his signature quickness was gone, and his body was all bruised up after years of driving toward the basket took their toll on his small frame. Listed at 6'1", and weighing just 165 pounds, Iverson was reckless on the basketball court, taking constant damage from taller, much stronger opponents.

The Pistons already had a replacement for Billups, second-year point guard Rodney Stuckey, so the only thing they had to do was just wait out the season with Iverson on the roster and hope for another deep playoff run. Yet with Ben Wallace gone, Rasheed Wallace was feeling disposable, as his deal was also up in the summer with little chance of renewal, and Rip Hamilton arguing with rookie head coach, Michael Curry. The team finished the season 39–43. The Pistons lost 20 games more than the season before and ended a six-season streak of appearances in the Eastern Conference Finals. In the 2009 playoffs the Pistons did not make it out of the first round, getting swept by the Cleveland Cavaliers.

Iverson was no longer an active member of the team's roster at the time. The Pistons won just 22 of the 50 games Iverson started. He came off the bench during just one game, and the team won. After he went out with a back injury, the team immediately improved. When coach Curry announced that Hamilton, at whose expense Iverson was made the starter, would permanently regain his role as team's starting shooting guard, Iverson did not take the decision lightly and decided to leave for Georgetown, his alma mater, supposedly to further focus on his recovery. He played in only three more games for the Pistons, all three coming off the bench. With seven games left until the end of the season, Iverson was made inactive and his contract was not renewed.

Speaking about his time with the Pistons, Iverson described it as a bad fit. He said that he was promised that he would not be "disrespected" by coming off the bench: "You never heard of anybody before that in my whole career ever saying anything about Allen Iverson coming off the bench. You never heard anybody out of the blue say, 'Allen Iverson should come off the bench.'"[7] Actually, talks of Iverson coming off the bench appeared earlier, and he reacted to them even more furiously. In the 2003–2004 season Iverson clashed with interim head coach Chris Ford. While the player was already well known for missing practice, he also started to miss games. When he informed Ford an hour before one game that he was willing to play despite a minor injury, even though they agreed earlier that Iverson would sit this one out, the coach told his star player that he was going to come off the bench. The player responded by not dressing for the game and afterwards commented that he was insulted by the decision not to start him:

> Why wouldn't I start? I'm the franchise player here. I don't know any franchise players that come off the bench. I don't know any Olympian that comes off the bench. I don't know any All-Star that comes off the bench. I don't know any former MVP that comes off the bench. I don't know any three-time scoring champion that comes off the bench. I don't know any first team All-NBA (player) that comes off the bench. Why Allen Iverson? Why should I come off the bench? …
> I think it is an insult to me. Who I am as a player, who I am to this organization, who I've been to this organization, that's an insult to me to come off the bench if I'm a starter.[8]

Ford was fired after the end of the season as the Sixers did not make the playoffs for the first time in five years.

Since his contract was not renewed by the Pistons, Iverson signed with the Memphis Grizzlies. Due to an injury, he practiced with the team for only three days before the start of the 2009–10 season. He also missed the first three games of the season, as he was not yet in playing form. In the next three games he came off the bench behind the then-promising duo of guards Mike Conley and O.J. Mayo. The Grizzlies lost all three games, while Iverson noted career-low averages of 12.3 points and 3.7 assists. Following his third game with the team, Iverson again complained about his role: "I've never been a reserve all my life and I'm not going to start looking at myself as a reserve. If we're winning, I can play 10 minutes and I'm happy. When we're losing, that's when I trip out."[9] He did not play for the Grizzlies again and was given an indefinite leave of absence and released a week later. The Philadelphia Sixers signed him for the remainder of the 2009–10 season, but after 25 games, 24 of which Iverson started, team president Ed Stefanski declared that the player would not be returning to the team due to personal problems. Iverson officially retired in October 2013.

While Iverson is forever associated with Philadelphia due to the (mostly individual) success he enjoyed as a member of the Sixers, another player that was raised there, shooting guard Dion Waiters, was also adamant about becoming a reserve. Waiters, along with the two players mentioned next, is proof that not only superstars have problems losing a starting spot on a team—sometimes it is just a case of inflated egos. Waiters joined the NBA with the fourth pick in the 2012 draft and was supposed to form the backcourt of the future in Cleveland, alongside the reigning Rookie of the Year, Kyrie Irving.

After losing a starting role on the Cavs following his rookie season, Waiters' production actually improved as he was coming off the bench. However, his third season would turn out to be much worse, and he was traded to the Thunder in January of 2015. Following LeBron James' return and the acquisition of Kevin Love, Waiters' became the team's fourth offensive option, behind Irving, with whom he reportedly did not see eye to eye. It was only in the 2016–17 season, after becoming a member of the Heat, that he earned back the role in the starting lineup. While he appeared in just 46 games and his season was cut short due to an ankle injury, Waiters made such an impression on team president Pat Riley that he signed him to a four-year, $52 million contract.

Although during the previous season Waiters was one of the team leaders for the Heat that went on a 30–11 run and almost reached the eighth seed in the Eastern Conference, they started the next one 11–13, showing no signs of picking up where they left off. Waiters was making 39.3 percent of his shots and averaging 14.6 points per game during that period, which was worse than his previous season average of 15.8 points on 42.4 percent shooting. His streaky shooting would make him perfect for the role of sixth man on the Heat, as players like John Starks or J.R. Smith found considerable success in that role. When it was suggested that maybe it would be better for the team if Waiters came off the bench, he replied, "I'm a starter in this league man, that's who I am. We're going to nip that in the bud right now. I'm not coming off no bench."[10] Up to that point Waiters started 177 of the 359 games he played in the NBA. He got injured after just four more games of the season. On November 8, 2019, he had a panic attack caused by eating THC–infused gummies and was suspended for ten games by the team. He was traded to the Grizzlies, and waived and signed by the Lakers, where he once again met with LeBron James. He won his sole NBA Championship in 2020, playing just five games in the playoffs.

J.J. Hickson played with James for two seasons on the Cavaliers. Drafted in 2008 with the 19th pick, in his second year Hickson became a starter, even though he was playing just 20.8 minutes per game. James was entering the final year of his contract with the team and went to the NBA Finals only once, carrying one of the worst rosters in league history almost single-handed to a 2007 series against the Spurs, in which the team from San Antonio swept the Cavs. In the 2009–10 mid-season, Hickson was almost traded to the Suns for Amar'e Stoudemire in a package that would also include Cleveland-lifer Zydrunas Ilgauskas—then a reserve center, who lost his starting spot in favor of a 37-year-old Shaquille O'Neal, as well as a first-round draft pick. Stoudemire, just like James, was about to become a free agent after the season, but was averaging 23.1 points and 8.9 rebounds for the Suns. Hickson on the other hand was averaging 8.5 points and 4.9 rebounds, but was just 21 years old.

In the end, the deal fell through, although it is uncertain if the Cavaliers picked potential over current success or if the Suns hoped that they would be able to keep their star power forward. The Cavs finished the season 61–21, but lost to the Celtics in the Eastern Conference Semifinals. The Suns went on a surprisingly deep playoff run and ended up just two games from eliminating future champions the Los Angeles Lakers in the Western Conference Finals. In the summer the team lost Stoudemire, who signed with the Knicks in free agency, while the Cavs lost James to the Miami Heat, where in his four seasons there he would make the NBA Finals four times and win two championships. James' former team entered a rebuild, and Hickson was supposed to be one of its cornerstones, as he was the most talented of the young players the Cavaliers had on their roster.

Coach Mike Brown was replaced by Byron Scott, who had championship experience as a player with the Lakers and finals experience as a coach with the Nets. Hickson would have his best season yet under Scott—he improved his averages to 13.8 points and 8.7 rebounds per game—but due to inconsistency would find himself coming off the bench more often than he wanted to. Already in the preseason Scott became frustrated with the power forward, who was struggling while trying to learn the Princeton offense, which the coach preferred. Scott described that as "disappointing, especially as much as we go through it every day."[11] Still, he continued to play Hickson, with former starter Antawn Jamison relegated to the bench role. The 2003–04 Sixth Man of the Year was not fine with coming off the bench for one of the worst teams in the league and complained to the press,

"I don't know how many minutes I'll play. I'm up in the air, just like you."[12] He would eventually reclaim his role, as Scott's frustration with Hickson grew.

Hickson was also unhappy with his coach and his diminishing role on the team: "I'm not adjusting very good…. I don't think it's any secret. Coach [Byron Scott] knows I'm not happy. My teammates know I'm not happy. But as a professional basketball player, you deal with it as a pro."[13] Scott was eventually forced to put Hickson back into the starting lineup at center after starter Anderson Varejao went out with a season-ending injury. After the season Hickson was traded to the Kings for small forward Omri Casspi and a protected first-round pick. Hickson would be out of the NBA in 2016, and while he would have some solid seasons with the Nuggets and the Blazers, he was just never able to stay healthy long enough to make significant improvements.

Another power forward who did not handle the transition from starter to sixth man well was Tyrus Thomas of the Chicago Bulls. The team acquired him on 2006 draft night, as the Bulls traded their second pick, LaMarcus Aldridge, to Portland, for Thomas, Russian power forward Victor Khyrapa, who was averaging 5.8 points as a starter for the Blazers, and a second-round pick. Aldridge would become one of the best power forwards in the NBA, making the All-NBA Second Team two times and the All-NBA Third Team three times. Thomas became a starter during his third NBA season, which would turn out to be the best of his professional basketball career. He averaged 10.8 points and 6.4 rebounds per game on a team that went 41–41 and was eliminated by the Boston Celtics in one of the most evenly fought and entertaining first-round playoff series in recent league history. The second-seeded Celtics needed a combined seven overtimes to put away the Bulls.

Next season, coach Vinny Del Negro decided to put rookie Taj Gibson into the starting lineup, and Thomas said that he was "surprised" by the fact that he was not a starter, adding, "I don't even think it should be questionable, from what I've contributed to the team last season and what I did throughout camp. But like I said, he's the guy making the decisions. Whatever decision he makes, I still have to go out and play."[14] The athletic, but inconsistent, Thomas was traded in the middle of the season to the Charlotte Bobcats for Flip Murray, Acie Law and a future first-round draft pick. Thomas did not start for the Bobcats that season and on the whole started only 34 games during the next four seasons in the NBA. At age 29 he was out of the league.

Another former Bulls player is most representative of the hardships associated with turning from starter to sixth man. The most well-known player to ever come off the bench was also the most well-known (and probably best) player in basketball history, Michael Jordan. While he did come on as a reserve in his second season for 11 games, it was caused by the process of him returning to full health following the foot injury he sustained on the 29th of October 1985, during a game against the Golden State Warriors. After that, Jordan was never made to come off the bench, at least until he returned from his second retirement, as the member of Washington Wizards, in the 2001–2002 season. On the 19th of January 1999, he became the president of basketball operations and part-owner of the team from D.C. The Wizards had been to the playoffs only once in 11 seasons up to that point, despite having the talented duo of forwards Chris Webber and Juwan Howard for four of those seasons. The only time that they made the playoffs, in 1997, they were swept by Jordan's Bulls.

The first roster move of Jordan's front office career was to release Romanian center Gheorge Muresan, the tallest player in league history and 1996 Most Improved Player. In the last year of his three-season tenure as team president he also traded away Tracy Murray, Juwan Howard and Rod Strickland, clearing the team of four of the five starters he inherited when he took over the Wizards. The team won 18 (out of 50, due to the lockout-shortened 1998–99 season), 29 and 19 games respectively during said seasons. That last number was the second lowest in team history, placing only behind the 18 wins the Wizards noted in their first NBA season, 1961–62. While he was extraordinarily dominant on the court, off it, with his influence on the outcome of games limited, he was not able to build a winning organization. Feeling that he was not fulfilling the expectations of team owner Abe Pollin, Jordan decided to come out of retirement one more time. He continued to be responsible for team personnel decisions, even though his role was unofficial after he returned to actively playing professional basketball in September 2001.

Before the season Jordan not only hired coach Doug Collins, with whom he worked in the past in Chicago, before the team promoted assistant Phil Jackson, but also drafted with the first pick Kwame Brown, the first player ever to be selected straight out of high school with such a high pick. Apart from Jordan the team had three shooting guards: Rip Hamilton, Courtney Alexander and Hubert Davis. The team also had Laron Profit, who was traded away by Jordan, presumably because he told Jordan, "Yeah, you can't guard me with them old-ass knees" during a pickup game.[15] Originally a shooting guard, as a Wizard Jordan moved to the small forward position, and he was still great, averaging 22.9 points, 5.2 assists and 1.4 steals per game despite being 37 years old. However, the roster was not very good, and it won just 37 games. Jordan was openly frustrated with his teammates, as he criticized their lack of effort already in late November: "The way we'll be able to turn this around is to go out every night and have the effort. ... Sometimes, things may not go your way, but the effort should be there every single night."[16] Jordan missed the playoffs for the first time in his career playing.

His season ended after just 60 games due to a knee injury. In seven of those games Jordan came off the bench. Before the next season it was indicated that he would embrace the role of the sixth man. Such a high-profile player coming off the bench would be a rarity in NBA history, as Bill Walton, Magic Johnson and Bob McAdoo were the biggest names so far to accept their status as reserves. During the offseason Jordan traded Hamilton to the Detroit Pistons for fellow Tar Heel Jerry Stackhouse, and he signed a young combo guard Larry Hughes and power forward Charles Oakley, who was known as Jordan's on-court bodyguard during his early days in Chicago. The roster was improved, at least on paper, and the team looked ready to finally make a run for the playoffs. There were some concerns regarding team chemistry, predicted by one of the best basketball executives in history, Red Auerbach: "Has [Jordan] ever watched Stackhouse play? The guy needs the ball all the time. You can't have the ball all the time when you're playing with Jordan. Write this down: this is gonna be a disaster."[17]

One more thing was supposed to be important about that season— Jordan said that he would come off the bench. Journalist David Aldridge recalled:

> He was going to be the sixth man. He was going to let Stackhouse be the guy. And he would come in and clean up with the second-team guys, and I remember thinking, "That makes a lot of sense!" In fact, I picked him to be the sixth man of the year, just based on that. Because, I thought, a reduced Michael Jordan, going up against bench guys, is going to score 16 to 17 a game. It made all the sense in the world. And then, like, two weeks into the season, it ended. I don't know if it was his ego or if he just didn't think Stackhouse was good enough. He just put himself back in the starting lineup.[18]

In the first game of the season Jordan had just eight points, but in each of the next two he scored 21. On November 8, 2002, Jordan was instrumental in the Wizards winning at home against reigning champions the Los Angeles Lakers, who were coached by Phil Jackson, the man whom Jordan once proclaimed to be the only coach he wanted to play for. With 2.9 seconds left, after a Robert Horry three-pointer, the Lakers were leading 99–98. Jerry Stackhouse won that game for the Wizards with a last-second dunk. The way to the basket was open, as the Lakers were playing without Shaquille O'Neal, who was injured. In the post-game interview Jordan said that Stackhouse saved him—not the team, but him personally—as it was the missed free-throws by the 38 year old that made the score so close in the first place.

Stackhouse was unhappy about the move at the time, as he became a more team-oriented player in Detroit and was willing to sacrifice his minutes and his shots in order to make the Pistons better. In Washington the offense was supposed to go through him, at least at first, but after just 15 games Jordan decided to put himself back into the starting lineup. The Wizards were 6–9 at the time, so the move seemed somewhat justified. Stackhouse, who was compared to Jordan in the past, as he was also a shooting guard playing for North Carolina, did not enjoy his sole season in Washington, mostly due to Jordan's influence on Collins: "He wanted to get a little more isolations for him on the post, of course, so we had more isolations for him on the post. And it just kind of spiraled in a way that I didn't enjoy that season at all. The kind of picture I had in my mind of Michael Jordan and the reverence I had for him, I lost a little bit of it during the course of that year."[19]

The Wizards once again finished with 37 wins, once again finished fifth in the Atlantic Division and once again failed to make the playoffs. Jordan ended the season averaging 20 points, 6.1 rebounds and 1.5 steals while playing for 37 minutes in all 82 games of the regular season. After the season team owner Abe Polin fired Jordan for his inability to lead the team he has assembled to the postseason. Jordan took personal responsibility for the way the Wizards played. After it was certain that the team was going to miss the playoffs for the second year in a row, he said, "I didn't suit up just to create interest. I suited up to help these guys play with the passion that you need to play this game."[20]

While Jordan's competitive nature was almost unprecedented in the world of professional sports and was partially responsible for making him such a great player, it proved to be a double-edged sword, as he thought that the only way the team could win was because of or thanks to him. That meant Jordan being on the court as much as possible, despite bad knees and the inability to change his habits—he continued to drink, smoke cigars and stay up late, yet was able, at almost 40 years old, to play against much younger opponents. Because of his status, he was unable to allow himself to come off the bench. In this case, unlike some discussed in this chapter, that was fully understandable—after all, he was Michael Jordan—and he should be appreciated even for giving the experiment a try.

8

High-Volume Scorers

J.R. Smith
>   *Guard. In the NBA: 2004– . 2013 Sixth Man of the Year*

Jamal Crawford
>   *Guard. In the NBA: 2000– . 2010, 2014, 2016 Sixth Man of the Year*

Lou Williams
>   *Guard. In the NBA: 2005– . 2015, 2016, 2019 Sixth Man of the Year*

During the episode of his podcast devoted to the 2020 Sixth Man of the Year Award, Zach Lowe pretty much summarized the expectations regarding the sixth men in the modern NBA:

> The prototypical sixth man is someone who can score, is someone who can run the offense, that's why they're the sixth men, because putting them with the starters would be redundant and you take two of your starters out, two of your best starters or your best scorers … and you put this guy in to make up the difference … that naturally makes you gravitate away from guys who are like role-ish players no matter who's in the game around them.[1]

Lowe said that in reference to the 2020 award, fearing—for the lack of a proper word—that it would not go to Montrezl Harrell, the Los Angeles Clippers big man, but rather to his teammate, Lou Williams. Williams had another great season coming off the bench, but Harrell was said to be the better all-around player. In the end, Harrell won the award, and Williams was the one who delivered it to him, celebrating his teammate's success. That gesture epitomized what is expected of the sixth man—he needs to put team success ahead of his own. That means having a better understanding of the game, while also being a great locker-room presence, providing understanding and support to other players whenever needed. In some cases though that also means simply making a couple of shots and taking over games.

A good example of that type of player was Junior Bridgeman, the 6'5" swingman, who spent ten seasons on the Bucks (1975–1984) and got his number retired by the team. He averaged 13.9 points throughout that time.

113

Vinnie Johnson never won the Sixth Man of the Year Award, but his streaky shooting brought two championship titles to the city of Detroit and their Pistons (1990).

His coach, Don Nelson, expected his sixth man to be primarily a scorer: "The value of a sixth man is having someone who can immediately have a major impact on a game. Junior can do that. He can come in, hit three or four in a row and break a game wide open."[2] This is exactly what was expected of the three players described in this chapter, who have built their careers on their streaky shooting, which came, mostly, from the bench.

Before I begin though, there is one more player worthy of mentioning here. He could get "hot" in an instant, which earned him the nickname "The Microwave." Vinnie Johnson was the sixth man for the Detroit Pistons during their Bad Boys era in the mid- to late '80s and early '90s. Selected with the seventh pick in the 1979 draft, Johnson was traded to the Pistons by the Sonics just seven games into the 1981–82 season, after earning the starting role in Seattle the year before. He played in Detroit for almost a decade, before being released by the Pistons in 1991, despite having one more year left on his contract.

The team was rebuilding, following a sweep by the Chicago Bulls in the 1991 Eastern Conference Finals. Just a year earlier he signed with the team for wellbelow his market value, saying, "Sometimes you have to put dollar figures aside when you have this great an opportunity."[3] As a free agent Johnson signed with the Spurs, where he played one more season, before retiring in 1992.

Johnson earned his nickname after scoring a career-high 34 points (22 in the fourth quarter) against the Celtics in the 1985 Eastern Conference Semifinals. Pistons coach Chuck Daly said jokingly after the game, "What Vinnie did today, he does to Isiah every day in practice. I told Dick Harter, my assistant, 'Maybe if we put a red practice shirt on Vinnie, he'll do in a game what he does in practice.'"[4] In the next seasons Johnson would continue to play great off the bench. He never earned the NBA Sixth Man of the Year Award though. The closest he got to it was when he came up second in 1987. However, he won two NBA Championships as a member of the Pistons, in 1989 and 1990. It was Johnson's shot that sealed the Pistons' second championship—in Game Five, with two seconds left, he released an 18-footer in front of the Blazers' Jerome Kersey, making the score 92–90. Johnson was appreciated by the franchise, with his number 15 being retired by the Pistons in 1994.

I started this chapter with J.R. Smith, who is the least decorated of the three players when it comes to Sixth Man of the Year Awards—one to Crawford and three to Williams—yet, unlike them, can call himself an NBA Champion. While Crawford and Williams are both considered among the best sixth men of all time, Smith is also a quintessential sixth man. He is so comfortable with coming off the bench that, even during his sole season in the Chinese Basketball Association, he started just eight of the 32 games he played in, while earning the title of the league's highest scorer. He averaged 34.4 points and 7.4 rebounds, playing for 36.4 minutes per contest.

Smith was supposed to play for the University of North Carolina in the 2004–05 season. More than a year earlier he was a relatively unknown recruit from St. Benedict's Prep School, New Jersey, who made headlines after earning co-MVP honors (along with Dwight Howard) of the McDonald's All-American Boys Game, which took place on the last day of March 2004. Smith made 10 of 16 shots that night (5/11 from three) and had a game-high 35 points. Smith actually finished high school a year later than he was supposed to, in order to improve his ranking. As he himself put it, "When I re-classified, I went from not being in the top 100 to like top five within a day…. I wouldn't have been ready for this a year ago. Another year of prep school helped me a lot."[5] In the 2003 draft he would fall well beyond the first round, whereas a year later Smith was simply a better, more mature player at 19 years old, and his draft stock was higher, especially after the McDonald's game.

He was selected with the 18th pick in the 2004 NBA Draft by the New Orleans Hornets. Among the top 19 first round selections, eight players were taken directly out of high school. He was a starter on the Hornets during his rookie year and became Western Conference Rookie of the Month on three separate occasions. He averaged 10.3 points per game, shooting 39.4 percent from the floor. Bad shot selection and lack of defensive effort was what made coach Byron Scott relegate Smith to the bench during his second season there. Smith would regain a starting role only ten years later, after a mid-season trade between the Knicks and the Cavaliers on January 5, 2015.

In the summer of 2006 the Hornets traded Smith, along with veteran power forward P.J. Brown, to the Chicago Bulls for Tyson Chandler. Two things were interesting about the move: Chandler was traded in order to create cap space for the Bulls to sign Ben Wallace, the most dominant defensive player of the first decade of the 2000s, and Brown was garnering more attention than Smith as the focal part of the move.[6] The Bulls traded away Wallace in the middle of the 2007–08 season, after just one and a half seasons, while Chandler went on to become one of the best defenders in the NBA, even winning the NBA Defensive Player of the Year award in 2012. Brown left the Bulls after just one season and went on to win the NBA Championship in 2008 for the Celtics. Smith did not play a game for the Bulls, instead getting traded to the Nuggets for point guard Howard Eisley and two second-round picks. Smith would probably not see eye to eye with as big a disciplinarian as Scott Skiles—the Bulls coach even had a strict no-headband policy, making an exception only for Wallace because of his status.

Smith joined a Denver Nuggets team that already had two of the greatest scorers in the modern-day NBA in Carmelo Anthony and Allen

Iverson. With them in the starting lineup, a volume shooter like Smith was already surplus, so it made sense that Nuggets coach George Karl decided to move him to the bench. Then, there were also certain issues Karl had with Smith—just as with the Hornets, Smith was not willing to play defense and shot the ball whenever he had the opportunity. In the first round of the 2007 playoffs, against the San Antonio Spurs, Smith played a total of 47 minutes and went 0/12 from three in the first play-off series of his career. In Game Four, with eight seconds left and the Nuggets still in competition, Smith made a bad—to put things lightly— shooting decision. In a play drawn up for Anthony or Iverson, he caught the ball and shot from way over the three-point line. George Karl was so angry at Smith that he decided not to play him in Game Five, even though his team was 1–3 and facing elimination. The play also prompted Karl to say, "I just love the dignity of the game being insulted right in front of me."[7]

This was obviously not the last, nor the most infamous, on-court decision made by Smith. Later on, while on the Knicks, on January 13, 2014, in a regular season game against the Rockets, with the score tied 100–100 and 21 seconds left in the game, Smith got the ball, and instead of dribbling out the clock until the last seconds, and either giving it to an open teammate or going for an easy shot, he immediately shot from three. Smith missed, and Aaron Brooks of the Rockets got the rebound, was fouled and made the two free throws to seal his team's victory. After the game Smith said that he forgot the score.

The same thing happened on a much bigger stage and with much bigger consequences. In Game One of the 2018 NBA Finals and the score tied 107–107 with four seconds left, Smith, then on the Cleveland Cavaliers, got an offensive rebound and, instead of making a shot or a pass, ran with the ball to half-court. The game went to overtime, and the Warriors won it, on the way to just the ninth sweep in the finals history. LeBron James, who was standing next to Smith in the middle of the court, got really agitated by his teammate forgetting the score, and one can argue that the moment proved pivotal for the outcome of the series. Still, the Cavaliers did not have much of a chance of winning that series anyway, as the 2018 team was the weakest in the four consecutive seasons it faced the Warriors in the finals. Smith was the starting shooting guard during all four of them. Following the 2018 NBA Finals, the team got broken up, and Smith barely saw any playing time in the following year. The Cavs were the only team on which he was the undisputed starting shooting guard, coming off the bench in just 33 of the 255 games he played for them in the four and a half seasons in Cleveland.

The team on which Smith spent most time on was the Nuggets—in the five seasons there he played in 372 games, starting 48, all of them under George Karl. During that time Smith earned a couple of suspensions for on- and off-court altercations. His driver's license was suspended multiple times, and he spent almost a month in jail for reckless driving. Karl kept Smith on the bench as a means of disciplining the scorer. On his best nights Smith was capable of scoring in bunches, like on the 22nd of February 2008, when he had 43 points off the bench against the Bulls. Or, on the 13th of April 2009, he made 11 three-pointers in a game against the Kings. In the eyes of the coach the good did not outweigh the bad though, and when Smith returned from China, after a season spent with the Zhejiang Golden Bulls of the CBA, the Nuggets decided to pass on him.

In China, Smith had some incredible games like the one in which he had 52 points and 22 rebounds or a 60-point performance (14/18 from three). Instead of returning to the Nuggets, Smith went to the Knicks, where he would once again join forces with Carmelo Anthony, who was instrumental in bringing his former teammate to New York. Smith finished off the 2012 season on the Knicks and got re-signed to a new deal. Under coach Mike Woodson, Smith changed his attitude toward team play, as he stopped focusing solely on shooting. He would reach his career highs in scoring (18.1) and rebounding (5.3) in the 2012–13 season, but was now a different player, with an improved attitude. Before the season Woodson said: "I want his shorts pulled up. I want him to look presentable, be a professional."[8] That meant taking responsibility for his decisions, which up to that point were mostly bad—like settling on a long-range, step-back shot instead of finding an open teammate. Furthermore, instead of solely shooting jumpers, Smith started driving toward the basket more and noted career-high 3.9 free-throw attempts. He was named 2013 Sixth Man of the Year, earning 484 points (including 72 first-place votes) from the voters, 132 more than the runner-up, Jamal Crawford.

Already the winner of the award in 2010, Crawford won it again in 2014, and for the third time in 2016, in the process becoming the first NBA player in league history to do so. With that, he became synonymous with the sixth man in modern basketball—combining the roles of scorer and playmaker, which made him able to influence the outcomes of games either by shooting or distributing the ball. Not much of a defender, it was evident that Crawford was a plug-and-play player, providing a spark on the court when he was hot and shooting his teams out of games when he was not. Crawford was the eighth pick in the 2000 NBA Draft, arguably one of the worst in league history, which had only three All-Stars and actually made the NBA's on-court product worse off than it was before their arrival in the league.[9] Already on draft day Crawford was traded by the Cleveland Cavaliers to the Chicago Bulls for center Chris Mihm, selected with the seventh pick.

After a couple of seasons on the Bulls, Crawford was expected to become one of the cornerstones of the Chicago team, which was still trying to rebuild after the Michael Jordan era. In his third NBA season he finally became the first player to come off the bench, playing 24.9 minutes and finally averaging more than 10 points (10.7 points) per game. While these numbers may not look that impressive, in the last eight games of the 2002–03 season, he was making 23 points and 6.4 assists, showing great promise and giving a good enough reason to the coaching staff to insert him into the starting lineup. Indeed, next season Crawford improved to 17.3 points and 5.1 assists per game, while starting 73 of the 80 games he played in for the Bulls. In one game of that season, on April 11, 2004, he had 50 points, scored in an overtime victory against the Raptors. After three quarters Crawford had just 22 points, but got 24 in the fourth, plus four points in the overtime.

Still, general manager John Paxson made it imperative to move Crawford before the start of the 2004–05 season. Crawford went from working out with Michael Jordan and his trainer, Tim Grover, to being traded to one of the most dysfunctional teams in the league at the time, the New York Knicks. Earlier, Paxson believed in Crawford so much that he traded away Jalen Rose for being a bad influence on him. Bad shot selection and breaking plays were the reasons why the Bulls moved Rose,[10] but Crawford was already so concerned with being the top scorer on his team and making large sums of money that the Bulls decided to trade him despite his unquestionable talent. He carried that attitude over to New York, where he was paired up in the backcourt with Stephon Marbury, another shoot-first guard. The team also had veterans Allan Houston, Penny Hardaway and Vin Baker on the roster, who played 81 games combined during that season.

Crawford stayed in New York for four and a half seasons, until he was traded after 11 games of the 2008–09 season to the Golden State Warriors. Crawford and Marbury had developed some chemistry together, with the former being the primary scoring option, especially in crunch time. Crawford also worked on passing, his favorite target being his best friend, center Eddy Curry. After Crawford suffered a season-ending injury on the 26th of February 2007, in a game against the Miami Heat, coach and general manager Isiah Thomas gave him one of the greatest compliments a shooter can get, saying, "You're always a Jamal run away from winning a game or ending a game. And whenever you're out of the game, he's normally the guy that puts you back in the game."[11]

Even in the first games of that 2008–09 season, Mike D'Antoni's first with the Knicks, it was Crawford who was the Knicks best player, averaging 19.6 points and making 45.5 percent of his three-point shots. But the team was clearing cap space, rebuilding after atrocious contracts signed by Thomas. This included the six-year, $60 million contract with Eddy Curry, who had just one promising season as a Knick, after which heart issues, a string of injuries and off-court problems have turned his deal into one of the worst ever signed by the franchise.

The Warriors moved Crawford to the Hawks after the season concluded. In nine years in the league in the NBA up to then, Crawford had not made a single playoff appearance. He scored 50 or more points in one game as a member of the Bulls (as mentioned earlier), the Knicks and the Warriors, being one of only four players in league history to score that much during a game as a member of three different franchises—Wilt Chamberlain, Moses Malone and Bernard King, all Hall of Famers, were the other three. On the 9th of April 2019, Crawford became the only player ever to score 50+ points on four teams, getting 51 as a member of the Phoenix Suns against the Mavericks. He stole the show during Dirk Nowitzki's last game in front of the home crowd in Dallas. He also became the oldest player ever to get 50 points, surpassing Michael Jordan's 18-year-old record—Jordan scored 51 points on December 29, 2001, with the Wizards, playing the Hornets, just two days after his record streak of double-digit scoring games in a row stopped at 866,[12] when he scored just six points in a blowout loss to the Pacers. Jordan was 38 years and 315 days old at the time. When Crawford scored 51 for the Suns, he was 39 years and 20 days old.

The trade to the Hawks came after Crawford refused to opt-out of the last two years and $20 million remaining on his contract. It was however on the team from Atlanta that Crawford, age 29 and with nine seasons of NBA basketball under his belt, finally found his place in the league. Crawford played in 79 games in the 2009–10 season, not starting even one, coming off the bench behind the best player on the team, shooting guard Joe Johnson, and a more conventional point guard, Mike Bibby. Playing for 31.1 minutes per game, he was averaging 18 points and three assists per contest. For his contributions he won the 2010 Sixth Man of the Year Award. Crawford himself said that "No one grows up wanting to be a sixth man. That wasn't part of the deal,"[13] and yet he embraced the role, winning the award for the best reserve in the league two more times. That season Crawford also made his first playoff appearance.

After another season in Atlanta, the Hawks chose not to renew his contract, and Crawford signed a one-year deal with the Blazers. He joined the team after his protégé and friend, Brandon Roy, decided to retire due to the degenerative knee condition. A season later Crawford became the leader of one of the highest-producing benches in modern NBA history on the Clippers. He won the award for the best bench player as a member of the Clippers twice, in 2014 and 2016, starting a long tradition of "Bench Mob"—as the Clippers bench became known—remaining one of the best, most productive collections of bench players in the NBA. During the five seasons on the Clippers, Crawford averaged 15.3 points and 3.4 assists per game. In the summer of 2017 the team traded him to the Hawks, who bought out his contract. Despite an offer from the championship-hopeful Cleveland Cavaliers, he signed with the Minnesota Timberwolves. There he won the last individual award of his career, the Twyman-Stokes Teammate of the Year Award, proving that scoring can be a characteristic of a team player as well.

During the same offseason when they unloaded Crawford, the Clippers got a more-than-suitable replacement for him, Lou Williams. The two players were on the roster together for a couple of days, which made little sense, since they were so similar, but then Crawford was traded to the Hawks. Williams just had a great half-season with the Rockets, but the team traded him, along with six of his teammates and a first-round draft pick, in exchange for point guard Chris Paul. If Crawford set the blueprint for what being a modern bench player meant, Williams perfected it. On the 11th of March 2019, in a game against the Boston Celtics, Williams scored 34 points, going 14/20 from the floor, breaking the NBA record for most career points scored off the bench.

Thanks to that performance he passed Dell Curry, the father of Steph and Seth, but more importantly, one of the best bench players of the '90s. Curry appeared in 1,083 NBA games, but started only 99 of them. Drafted with the 15th pick in 1986, Curry played just 9.5 minutes per game for the Utah Jazz in his rookie year. He was picked up by the Cleveland Cavaliers, where he got more playing time thanks to an injury to starter Ron Harper, then good for 20 points per game. Despite a solid season (10 points per game, 49.1 field-goal percentage) Curry was given up in the expansion draft to the emerging Charlotte Hornets. There he embraced the sixth man role and continued to come off the bench for the next 14 seasons of his career. He was primarily known as a three-point shooter and led the league in three-point percentage (47.6) during the lockout-shortened 1998–99 season, his sole on the Milwaukee Bucks. When Curry retired, he was the all-time leading scorer on the Hornets with 9,839 points. He won the 1994 Sixth Man of the Year Award as a member of the team from North Carolina, and continued to contribute off the bench on the Bucks and the Raptors.

It was on the team from Toronto that Lou Williams would win his first Sixth Man of the Year Award 21 years later. While the league rules changed, giving more freedom to scorers, Williams won the award with the same means as Curry—scoring whenever called upon by his coach. Williams attributes that ability to his first one and a half seasons in the NBA, where he was mentored by Allen Iverson, until the latter was traded to the Nuggets. Even before he was drafted by the Sixers in the second round (45th pick overall) of the 2005 NBA Draft, Iverson was his role model, and Williams modeled his game after the superstar. It took the straight-out-of-high-school prospect some time to get adjusted to NBA basketball, but he picked up a lot from Iverson, the most important lesson being "Just stay ready. I played with A.I., whose favorite saying was, 'Stay ready so you don't have to get ready.' That is one of the mantras I took with me, the gems he gave me. That is always how I patterned myself and prepared for every situation."[14]

What he meant by that was exemplified by Williams on the 23rd of February 2017, when, in his first game on the Rockets, only three hours after joining the team, the shooting guard came off the bench during a game against the Pelicans, and had 27 points, including seven three-pointers. He described his debut on the Rockets as "a pretty decent introduction."[15] In his first two seasons on the Sixers Williams appeared in a total of 91 games and averaged just 3.5 points per contest. He had not started an NBA game until his fifth season on the Sixers, but by that time he was already averaging 12.8 points and three assists per game. As a starter, in the 2009–10 season, Williams was averaging 17.4 points and 5.1 assists, but he got injured, and later on the team signed Allen Iverson, to whom Williams willingly gave away the starting spot. Williams cited the acquisition of the Philadelphia great as the reason behind him embracing the sixth man role for the rest of his career.[16]

Williams' performances stem from his mentality—while the team remains his primary concern, he also wants to be the best player on the court. His motto is: "Always strive to be the best, always strive to be an All-Star, always strive to be a star player and everything, but if it doesn't work out, embrace whatever comes at you and be the best at that."[17] Another thing representative of Williams' play is the lightness of touch, and of movement, that he exhibits on the court. In order to feel as light as possible, he often does not eat for up to 12 hours before games. After them is a whole different story—it was Williams who had one of the most memorable meals in NBA postseason history, eating nachos after leading the Clippers to the largest playoff comeback ever. Losing by 31 points in the third quarter of Game Two of the first round of the 2019 playoffs to the Golden State Warriors, the team from Los Angeles was able to win 135–131, scoring 85 in the second half of the game alone. Williams had 36 points and 11 assists.

Williams has spent his career on the Sixers, the Hawks, the Raptors, the Lakers, the Rockets and the Clippers. He won his first Sixth Man of the Year Award during his sole season on the Raptors. He was the first player on the Raptors to win an individual award since 1999 and the first to win an award that was not given out to the best rookie in the league—won by Damon Stoudamire in 1996 and Vince Carter in 1999. Williams himself called the trophy his favorite.[18] The Raptors were the only team he left willingly, instead signing with the Los Angeles Lakers. All the other teams, except for the Clippers, his last one, included him in trade packages. It was a similar route for other sixth men, who too often bounce from team to team. Often though, these moves shape their character and turn them into better teammates, as was the case with Crawford or Smith.

Williams won the Sixth Man of the Year Award again in 2018 and 2019, his first two seasons on the Clippers, remaining dominant off the bench like no player before him—in the two seasons he was averaging 21.3 points and 5.3 assists per game. During the 2017–18 season, as a 31 year old, Williams notched his career-high, 50 points, against the Warriors in one of the 19 games he started that season. During the 2019–20 season he was averaging 18.2 points and 5.6 assists. In the voting he finished second to center Montrezl Harrell, who was his teammate on the Rockets and the Clippers. Actually, during the early stages of the season Williams predicted that the only player who could win the trophy instead of him in the 2019–20 season was Harrell,[19] and he was the one who presented him with the award.

Williams, Crawford and Smith all embody the most important characteristics of the sixth man, as they all meet the requirements of being shoot-first guards who can get hot whenever they are able to get a couple of shots in. All of them won games for their teams, as well as shot them out of competitions on their bad nights. Thanks to eventually embracing the sixth man role, they were able to remain longer in the league, oftentimes looking like the All-Stars they wanted to become, without earning the same recognition. With their play they were able to shed new light on the role, while being vital cogs in winning machines like the Nuggets, the Cavaliers or the Clippers.

9

Big Men Off the Bench

Clifford Robinson
> *Forward. In the NBA: 1989–2007. 1993 Sixth Man of the Year.*

Toni Kukoč
> *Forward. In the NBA: 1993–2006. 1996 Sixth Man of the Year. 1996, 1997, 1998 NBA Champion. Basketball Hall of Fame.*

Arvydas Sabonis
> *Center. In the NBA: 1995–2001, 2002–2003. Basketball Hall of Fame.*

Chris Andersen
> *Center/Power Forward. In the NBA: 2001–2017. 2013 NBA Champion.*

While the sixth man role is usually reserved for quick, explosive scorers, who can either drive to the basket or shoot from long distance, tall players, playing at the power forward or center positions, are equally worthy of consideration for the pantheon of great reserves. They may not be as flashy as the smaller players, but they do all the dirty work necessary to win. This was not the case with the players mentioned in this chapter, though, who were either ahead of their time or able to play unlike other big men. Their distinctive style made it especially complicated for coaches to fit them into the conventional offensive schemes. They served a different function on the court though, as they were not included in the starting lineups because of their uniqueness, making them somewhat unable to coexist in long stretches with the starters. The same uniqueness made them great as reserves, who could provide their teams with more than inside scoring, rebounds and blocks.

Sometimes, when delivered in spectacular fashion, these are enough to endear the player to the fans, while cementing his place in the pantheon of sixth men. That was what happened with Chris Andersen, whose career narrative made for quite a story, which was unlikely through and through: from going undrafted in 1999, to finding a spot on the Nuggets and the Hornets, then serving a two-year ban for violating the league's drug policy, only to coming back as a much better, more exciting player.

124

Toni Kukoc was supposed to be much more than just one of the best bench players of the 1990s (1995).

What is more important for this book, Andersen was efficient, a great role player who had his own *style*, which made him stand out among other, hard-working bigs. I am obviously referring here to his high-energy style of play and not the mohawk haircut or his colorful, rockstar-like tattoos.

Consider Sam Perkins, the 6'9" power forward/center, who was moved to the bench after turning 31 and joining the Seattle SuperSonics, by coach George Karl. Nicknamed "Big Smooth," Perkins would not be a good starter alongside the quick duo of Gary Payton and Shawn Kemp. Instead, coming off the bench, he was capable of spreading the offense with his long-range shooting ability, while leading the team's center away from the basket and opening the lane for smaller players. A career 36.2 percent three-point shooter, Perkins required a different pace than the two best players on the Sonics, and thanks to the move to the bench he was able to remain an important part of championship contenders, in Seattle and later in Indiana. During his last season, 2000–01, as a 40 year old, almost a decade after he became a sixth man, Perkins started 41 games for the Indiana Pacers.

In the '60s and '70s big men who had the speed, shooting touch and court vision that could rival the smaller ones were very rare. When the 6'9" Magic Johnson became the star in the USA and across the Atlantic Ocean the 7'3" Arvydas Sabonis and the 6'10" Toni Kukoč were making an impact as great dribblers and passers, they were inspiring the next generation of big men to focus on something beyond fundamentals. And the 6'10" Clifford Robinson proved that big men could also shoot from long distance. Without them, there would be no LeBron James, Lamar Odom, Kevin Durant or Giannis Antetokounmpo running the court and delivering an exciting pass or pulling up from three.

Another thing that connects these four players is that they all had to face some type of adversity in their careers. Sabonis, the eldest of the group, was in the toughest situation, as he had to face a superpower, which was the USSR. He was selected with the 77th pick in the 1985 NBA Draft by the Atlanta Hawks, but he was under 21 years old upon his selection, which was the reason for the league voiding the pick. The NBA's decision created some confusion at the time, as some of the general managers did not know that there were strict rules regarding player selection. After all, in the 1974 draft Moses Malone, a future Hall of Famer, was selected straight out of high school (albeit by an ABA team, Utah Stars), and in 1977 a female basketball player, Lusia Harris, was picked by the New Orleans Jazz, while just a year before Sabonis, in 1984, the Chicago Bulls selected track star and soon-to-be multiple Olympic gold medalist Carl Lewis. However, because Sabonis was such a big name player—by then regarded as one of the best in the world—and was from what can be dubbed "an enemy country"— the Lithuanian represented the USSR at the time, since his country would not free itself from Soviet occupation until 1991—the league decided to instill some rules. The Hawks then-GM Matt Kasten said years later, "I do not remember any question about his birthdate, which was less of an issue because it had already been certified through numerous international competitions."[1] The whole situation led to Sabonis being drafted a year later by the Portland Trail Blazers with the 24th pick.

He was courted by the Blazers for years, but could not leave the country, and once the Iron Curtain was lifted, had a valid contract in Europe. Sabonis joined the league in 1995, after Robinson and Kukoč—both younger than he, with Sabonis being born in 1964, Robinson in 1966, and Kukoč in 1968—were already established as vital parts of winning NBA franchises. Robinson was selected with the 36th pick in the 1989 draft by the Blazers. He was a successful college player, holding his own against the likes of Alonzo Mourning, Dikembe Mutombo, Derrick Coleman and other big men from the Big East conference. In his final year at UConn he averaged 20 points, 7.4 rebounds, 1.8 steals and 1.4 blocks per game. And yet, due to rumors surrounding his attitude, Robinson fell to the second round of the draft. While Robinson continued to smoke marijuana throughout his career, his off-court habits never affected his on-court performance. P.J. Carlesimo, his coach at Portland, said of Robinson, "He might go out and party at night, but he was a practice animal. I don't ever recall Cliff missing a practice or not playing 100 percent."[2] He was a beloved teammate and a durable player, appearing in every Blazers game during his first five seasons in the league. He also popularized wearing headbands and wristbands by NBA players, being one of the first players fully committed to the accessories.

On draft night Robinson was so angry at falling to the second round that he left Madison Square Garden where the draft took place, before his selection was even announced. Thanks to his declining stock he joined the Blazers, one of the best teams in the league. Furthermore, as pointed out by Kerry Eggers, "Robinson made an impact with the Blazers as a rookie, quickly earning Coach Rick Adelman's confidence with strong play at both ends and his versatility. He was long and could play all three front-line positions. He could score inside, had 3-point range."[3] He averaged 9.1 points and 3.8 rebounds per game for a team that made the NBA Finals that season. He also made his first career start during that postseason, serving a more conventional, defensive role, as exhibited by his increase in rebounds and blocks per game. In the 1989 Western Conference Semifinals he was able to hold his own on the defensive end against David Robinson, one of the best centers in the league.

As a rookie, Clifford Robinson was too anxious to show how much the skeptics were wrong when it came to his attitude and habits affecting his game. Years later he said about his first year, "I wanted to make something happen. I'd come off the bench, and I wouldn't go up and down the court twice before I'd shoot."[4] With the aid of his teammates and coach Robinson having come to terms with the bench role though understanding that by inserting him into the game for either center Kevin Duckworth, power forward Buck Williams, or small forward Jerome Kersey, Coach Rick Adelman was allowing him to exploit the weakest point in the opposing frontcourt. The Blazers once again made the finals in 1992, and for his performance during the 1992–93 season Robinson was named NBA Sixth Man of the Year. With 19.1 points per game he was the second-highest scorer on the team that season, behind Clyde Drexler. He was also averaging 6.6 rebounds and two blocks per game. But the team was eliminated in the first round of the playoffs and in need of a rebuild. Robinson was moved to the starting lineup and made his sole All-Star appearance in 1994.

Robinson wanted to spend the rest of his career in Portland and wanted to sign an extension, but the team was unwilling to prolong his original deal—a four-year $9 million contract, that he signed in 1992. Robinson was not with the team during the first 11 days of training camp, but eventually rejoined the Blazers. The 1994–95 season was the first under new management and a new coach, as Adelman was replaced with P.J. Carlesimo, and Geoff Petrie was replaced with Bob Whitsitt, who was fired by the Seattle SuperSonics. After a year-long break, Adelman returned to coaching for two unsuccessful seasons on the Warriors, where he was once again replaced with Carlesimo. The latter's aggressive, loud coaching style did not sit well with some of his players, and he was infamously choked by the Warriors' best player, Latrell Sprewell, during practice. The Warriors were already in a state of dysfunction, but Sprewell was the team's lone All-Star and would remain such until the 2013 All-Star Game. When he was traded, the Warriors would continue to struggle, making the playoffs only once between the years 1995 and 2012, thanks to a miracle run by the Don Nelson–led team of tough guys, outcasts and misfits like Baron Davis, Stephen Jackson and Matt Barnes.

In the 1994–95 season the Blazers entered full rebuild mode, after trading away the best player in franchise history, Clyde Drexler, to the Houston Rockets. Still, Carlesimo's team managed to make the playoffs, with Robinson as its primary offensive option. Just like Sprewell, he did not enjoy his coach's attitude and earned a suspension for calling him a "stupid motherfucker" when Carlesimo took him out of the game in a January 8, 1997, loss to the Heat.[5] It was a frustrating season, one in which even Robinson was booed by the home fans. After another first-round playoff exit by the Blazers—fifth in a row, next season would make it six—Robinson's deal was not renewed, and he signed as a free agent with the Phoenix Suns, who were coached by his former teammate Danny Ainge.

As a member of the Suns, Robinson would make All-NBA Defensive Second Team twice, in 2000 and 2001. After four seasons on the Suns, he was traded to the Pistons, where he played next to Ben Wallace. Robinson retired at age 40, following one season on the Warriors and three on the Nets. In his 18 seasons in the league, he missed the playoffs only once, in 2004, when playing in Golden State. One of the original stretch fours, Robinson ended his career with 35.6 percent accuracy from three, and averages of 14.2 points and 4.6 rebounds. Upon his retirement he was one of only three players to make at least 1,000 (actually 1,253) three-pointers and 1,000 (1,390) blocks in his career, the other two being Rasheed Wallace and Dirk Nowitzki.[6] He is also the oldest player to have his first 50-point game, as a member of the Suns on the 16th of January 2000. He was 33 years and two months old. Robinson missed the shoot-around that day and was sent home because of flu-like symptoms.

When one thinks of a player performing greatly despite similar problems, there is a different game that comes to mind though. I am of course referring here to The Flu Game—Game Five of the 1997 NBA Finals between the Chicago Bulls and the Utah Jazz. The Chicago won 90–88, making the series 3–2 thanks to Michael Jordan and his 38 points, seven rebounds, five assists and three steals. Profusely sweating, Jordan left the court with the aid of Scottie Pippen when the game was over, as he was too weak to walk on his own. Among the players who participated in that game was Toni Kukoč, the 6'11" forward, who arrived to the NBA a couple of years earlier. The hype surrounding him suggested that he would be much more than a mere participant in such games though. He was supposed to be the European Magic Johnson, Larry Bird or even Michael Jordan.[7] Before he joined the Chicago Bulls, Kukoč won four Yugoslav League championships and three EuroLeague championships and was the three-time Euro-League Final Four MVP and the Croatian Sportsman of the Year three times as well. He could dribble and pass like a guard, drive toward the basket and shoot from a long distance, all while being tall enough to play all five positions.

And yet, he could never adjust to the style of play in the NBA. Kukoč embodied the perception of European players as soft. He was a finesse player, unable to get physical. He tried lifting weights but that made him slower. Kukoč was not athletic or muscular, but that did not mean that he was not tough. He was capable of making big shots—like the one in Game Three of the 1994 Eastern Conference Semifinals, when with 1.8 seconds left in a tied game against the Knicks, Kukoč made a turnaround jumper to make the score 104–102. The 25 year old was just a rookie at the time, a sixth man who started only eight games his first year, averaging 10.9 points, four rebounds and 3.4 assists. Still, considering the expectations regarding Kukoč, these stats did not look all that impressive. Halberstam describes him as "immensely talented, a backcourt man who stood six foot eleven and had exceptional distance on his jump shot and great court vision. He could shoot and pass beautifully," yet constantly frustrated his coaches with his inconsistency, and his performance varied from game to game.[8]

Kukoč, unknowingly, alienated his future teammates even before he joined the Bulls. Having just signed a six-year deal with Benetton Treviso in 1991, he was encouraged to buy out of his contract and move overseas. The Bulls offered Kukoč $15.3 million for six years. In order to have the cap space if Kukoč changed his mind, the Bulls had one of the lowest payrolls in the league, yet managed to win NBA Championships. General manager Jerry Krause was so convinced of the impact Kukoč would have on the team and the league that he kept lavishing praise on the player, neglecting to acknowledge how special the players on the roster were. Sam Smith writes that "the team sent Jordan a half-dozen tapes of Kukoč so Jordan might see how talented Kukoč was. Jordan refused to watch them."[9] At one point Jordan even asked his agent to work out a trade if Kukoč got signed by the Bulls.[10]

It was then understandable why Kukoč did not want to enter hostile territory, especially since he was a truly dominant player in Europe. Joining the Bulls would force him to sacrifice his alpha-male position, which clearly belonged to Jordan. In the two years in Treviso he was averaging 19.8 points, six rebounds, 5.2 assists and 2.3 blocks per game. After three years of intensive talks, Kukoč eventually decided to enter the NBA in the 1993–94 season. Even before it started the team was dealt a major blow, as Michael Jordan announced his (first) retirement before they played a single game together. Krause declared after learning about Jordan's decision, "My dream was Toni with the ball on the break, with Michael on one side, Scottie on the other and Horace coming up from behind."[11] The unrealized dream actually proved to be a blessing in disguise, as Jordan was famously tough on his teammates, and Kukoč was used to a different attitude—having been so great at basketball, competing with professionals since he was 17 years old, Kukoč was coddled and responded badly to harsh criticism. Jordan could have negatively impacted his career, as he did by belittling teammates Brad Sellers or Kwame Brown.

Before he joined the Bulls, Coach Phil Jackson recognized the player's main deficiencies, which would remain the central cause of Jackson's frustration with the European superstar throughout his time in Chicago: "On defense, this is where Toni is a novice. He needs to work on his strength and stamina."[12] Even at Benetton, Kukoč's coach, Peter Skansi, was well aware of the main problem with his best player: "He doesn't always want to work hard. Usually he is playing 40 percent of the matches under his normal level."[13] What made things even worse was that "[Kukoč] hated coming off the bench. As far as he was concerned, it meant that he was not good enough to start on a great American team. So he fought Jackson's use of him, complaining openly and bitterly when he did not start."[14] And yet, he put up with the sixth man role for three seasons on the Bulls, finally earning a starting spot next to Jordan and Pippen in the 1997–98 season only because of Dennis Rodman's inability to stay focused on basketball, and his deteriorating health.

In the 1995–96 season Kukoč, the best bench player on the best team in the league (and one of the best in league history) won the Sixth Man of the Year Award. Starting 20 of the 81 games he played in, Kukoč was averaging 13.1 points, four rebounds and 3.5 assists per game. In the 1998–99 season, with the Bulls rebuilding, Kukoč became the primary offensive option on the team and had his best season statistically, noting career highs in points (18.8), rebounds (seven) and assists (5.3). However, his team won just 13 of the 50 games it played in the lockout-shortened season. Continuing the rebuilt, Krause, the man so infatuated with Kukoč before the player entered the league, traded him away in the middle of the 1999–2000 season for a conditional first-round pick in a three-team deal with the Sixers and the Warriors. Kukoč was supposed to be the second scoring option on a championship-hopeful team from Philadelphia, but he struggled in Larry Brown's system and was once again mostly coming off the bench. In the middle of the next season, Kukoč was traded to the Hawks as a part of a six-team deal that brought Dikembe Mutombo to Philadelphia. The Sixers made the NBA Finals that season, while the Hawks did not even enter the playoffs. Kukoč retired in 2006, after four seasons on the Bucks. He had not made the All-Star team once, yet entered the NBA Hall of Fame in 2021.

One of the first prominent European players to join the NBA, a Hall of Famer, and runner-up to the 1996 Sixth Man of the Year, was rookie Arvydas Sabonis of the Portland Trail Blazers, who entered the league as a 31 year old. Upon his move overseas he was 50 pounds heavier than when he got drafted. He was also much slower, due to two ruptured Achilles tendons, plus ankle, foot, and knee injuries. Before the injuries slowed him down he was a legendary player, a big man passer and shooter way ahead of his time, before Nicola Jokić or Dirk Nowitzki. Sean Elliott, who played against Sabonis in the 1986 FIBA World Championship, said that the 22-year-old Lithuanian "was David Robinson with a 3-point shot and a better passer.... He shot the three like Jack Sikma and passed the ball like Bill Walton."[15] Šarūnas Marčiulionis, Sabonis's teammate on Žalgiris Kaunas, as well as the USSR and the Lithuanian National Teams, attributed the big man's skills to his willingness to practice with smaller players: "He loved to shoot threes with us guards, to play horse, and not too many 7'4" guys love to shoot. He also wanted to play one-on-one, so he picked up pieces from guards, [like] shooting or to see the floor—his passing game. He learned his finesse skills by playing with the small guys."[16]

Sabonis had a great career in Europe, which somewhat explains why he found it so hard to join the NBA. Even in his last season in Europe, 1994–95, he was named Euroscar Player of the Year (best European player) for the fourth time—he would win the trophy two more times—and finished his third season at Real Madrid with averages of 22.9 points, 13.2 rebounds and 2.6 blocks. As his deal in Madrid was up, Sabonis would finally play in the NBA: "I decided I'm 30 years old, and Portland called me and said if you want, let's go, and I finished the contract with Real Madrid, and if I didn't come now, I didn't come ever; I don't get to feel what is NBA. It was the last bullet, you know?"[17] Despite being nagged by numerous injuries, the slower and less mobile Sabonis signed with the Blazers and, despite his legendary status, agreed to come off the bench during his first season in the NBA, behind Chris Dudley.

Dudley was a typical role player, who never averaged double figures in points or rebounds. Drafted with the 75th pick in the 1987 draft, he was a hard worker, who never shied away from physical play in order to give his team the best chance of winning games. He drew contact, fought for rebounds, set picks and often got in foul trouble. He never was the focal point of a team, yet P.J. Carlesimo decided that it was Dudley and not Sabonis who would fit in better with the starting lineup of Rod Strickland, Aaron McKie, Clifford Robinson and Harvey Grant. Interestingly, McKie would be later named 2001 Sixth Man of the Year for his play off the bench on the Philadelphia 76ers, who made the NBA Finals that year, improving after trading away Kukoč and center Theo Ratliff for Mutombo. The 1995–96 season would be his only time as a starter in the NBA. Dudley was a team's designated starter in only two seasons, both of them for the Blazers, 1994–95 and 1995–96. During that period he was averaging 5.3 points and 9.2 rebounds per game.

One year older than Dudley, Sabonis was obviously the better individual player, but he needed time to adjust to the more physical style of play in the NBA. He never complained about playing time, at least not openly, and Carlesimo, as well as Mike Dunleavy, who took over the Blazers in 1997, called him a great player to coach in Kerry Eggers's *Jail Blazers* book.[18] Sabonis was a professional, who did not develop strong relationships with his teammates due to the language barrier, as well as cultural and age differences. He was also almost always playing in great pain, which became evident whenever the staff members were looking at his X-rays. Jay Jensen, the Blazers' athletic trainer, would often wonder about how it was possible for Sabonis to still be able to run up and down the floor, despite all the pain that he felt.[19] Yet, Šarūnas Marčiulionis argues that the "Coming to America" Sabonis was the best version of himself, at least basketball-wise. In his earlier days he was a great fast break player and dunker, but he was also prone to committing "dumb turnovers." He could not jump or dunk, but was a much better shooter and passer than earlier in his career.[20] Johnny Davis, who played with Walton and coached Sabonis, said that "It was interesting to see how closely matched Arvydas was from an intellectual standpoint with Bill. They could dominate a game without just scoring. They're two of the best passing big men in the history of basketball. I can't think of anybody who passed the ball from the center position as well as Bill or Arvydas. Portland had perhaps the two best passing centers of all time."[21]

In his rookie year Sabonis was averaging 14.5 points and 8.1 rebounds. Next season he moved into the starting lineup, at the age of 32. For five seasons he was the man in the middle for the Blazers. He did not earn any individual honors, yet was known as one of only few players who could go toe-to-toe with the most dominant player of that era, Shaquille O'Neal. When Sabonis retired in 2001, at age 37, after just half a year he decided to return to professional basketball. The Lakers met with his agent, entertaining the thought of having both O'Neal and Sabonis on the same roster, but he decided to return to Portland instead. He was once again the reserve, limited to just 15.5 minutes per game in the 2002–03 season. He retired for good in 2003, with NBA career averages of 12 points and 7.3 rebounds.

The slow, heavy finesse of Sabonis was the opposite of the next player I want to characterize here, Chris Andersen. "The Birdman" became a fan favorite due to unparalleled enthusiasm and energy that he brought to the teams he played on. Unlike the three players analyzed earlier, Andersen was not a high-profile prospect. In fact, he quit Blinn College after just one season in order to become a professional basketball player. He first went to China, to Jiangsu Nangang, where he played against Yao Ming. The Hall of Fame Chinese center remembered Andersen and said that, even then, "He was different."[22] What made Andersen stand out even then was the way he played, the fun he had on the court, that would infect his teammates and the fans. George Karl, his coach on the Nuggets for four seasons, said of Andersen, "I've had good bench players before, but not like this, where [the fans] wait till he gets into the game to get involved. There's just a whole spirit about him."[23] It made perfect sense that, since his road to the NBA was so unlikely, Andersen wanted to enjoy every moment on the court. He did not possess any exceptional skills apart from a jumping ability, thanks to which he appeared in two Slam Dunk Contests. In the 2015 contest he needed 15 attempts to complete two dunks.

After playing in the Chinese Basketball Association, International Basketball League, International Basketball Association and Southwest Basketball League, Andersen was the first player ever selected in the NBA Developmental League draft, in front of 95 other players, that formed the rosters of eight teams playing in the newly created league. Andersen proved to be the right choice with this high of a pick, as he became the first player in NBDL history to earn a call-up to the NBA. After two games for the Fayetteville Patriots, in which he averaged six points, five rebounds and 2.5 blocks, he got picked up by the Denver Nuggets. He was a high-energy player and emphatic dunker for three seasons on the Nuggets, and one on the Hornets. During his second year with the team though Andersen hit a personal low—his fiancée broke off their engagement, and his house was destroyed by Hurricane Katrina. Andersen turned to alcohol and drugs, and he got suspended by the league for two years for violating its drug abuse policy.

Instead of heading the way of players permanently banned by the league, like Chris Washburn, Roy Tarpley or Richard Dumas, Andersen entered rehab and worked meticulously on his return to the NBA. On the 25th of March 2008, two years and two months after his last appearance in the league, he returned to the Hornets. He had just one block in five minutes of play, but he was back in the NBA. He played in five games for the Hornets and then was declared inactive for the rest of the season. In the offseason Andersen once again signed with the Nuggets. In his first full season back Andersen averaged 6.4 points, 6.2 rebounds and 2.5 blocks per contest. He was second in the league in blocks—both overall and per game—while playing just 20.6 minutes per contest. The 2009 Nuggets made the Western Conference Finals and took the eventual champions, the Los Angeles Lakers, to six games. Andersen averaged 5.8 points, 6.7 rebounds and 2.5 blocks in that series.

While he was still celebrated around the league for crafting such a great comeback story, his enthusiasm and image, in his fourth season on the Nuggets, with his numbers steadily declining, Andersen lost the place on the roster to rookie Kenneth Faried and was amnestied by the Nuggets in the summer of 2012. After almost a year of not playing professional basketball, he was picked up by the Miami Heat for a 10-day contract and after that period was signed until the end of the season. He played 15.2 minutes per game in the playoffs, averaging 6.4 points and 3.8 rebounds. The Heat won the 2013 championship and made the finals in 2014, with Andersen averaging 5.1 points and 5.9 rebounds in 20 games of that playoff run. The Heat traded him to the Memphis Grizzlies in the middle of next season. He was on the roster of the Cleveland Cavaliers in 2016 but suffered a season-ending injury in December of that year. He was traded to the Hornets for a conditional second-round pick and cash considerations and was waived immediately.

The big men analyzed in this chapter were very different from the rest of the league and one another, and their career arcs also played out very differently. Their uniqueness was the reason why they came off the bench in the beginning of or throughout their careers. While some coaches managed to adjust their play to them and executives were able to surround them with the right teammates, others relinquished their undeniable talent because of their inability to reach team or appreciate them for who they truly were. This especially applies to Robinson and Kukoč, who were both ahead of their time, yet required to play basketball conventionally, as it was played in the '90s and early 2000s, and hence were unable to fully show their potential, while still inspiring future generations of taller players to move away from the basket. Sabonis did the same thing with his flashy passing and long-distance shooting, only he had the luck of playing under coaches who believed in his undeniable abilities. And Andersen's career narrative proves that determination, energy and enthusiasm allow a player to not only carve a niche for himself in the league, but also earn cult status, when being unconventional is combined with the right work ethic.

10

Rotation Players

In this chapter I want to present some players who did not "make the cut"—were not included in the previous chapters—yet are important because of the way they influenced the perception of reserves or used the bench as a means of carving a particular niche for themselves in the league. While there were far more players worthy of inclusion, I have decided to limit my selection to a 12-man rotation, as is the case with every NBA team—a coach has to pick 12 players to dress for games, which is always a tough decision to make. The criteria for the selection were clearly subjective, but I hope that from these short biographies the reader can get an understanding of why such players have been included in the book.

Darrell Armstrong

The Orlando Magic is a team that does not retire player numbers. Instead, it includes them into its own Hall of Fame, which includes Shaquille O'Neal, Penny Hardaway and Tracy McGrady. On the 21st of February 2020 the Magic added its ninth member there—Darrell Armstrong, an undrafted point guard who played for nine seasons in Orlando. In his first season in the NBA he appeared in just three games. The 27 year old already played in the USBL, CBA, GBA, Cyprus and Spain, before getting a chance to finally appear in an NBA game. He entered the league as an athletic, shoot-first point guard, a player ahead of his time.

In his first three NBA seasons Armstrong averaged 5.6 points and 2.2 assists per game, playing 12.8 minutes per contest. In 1997–98 his minutes doubled, and he noted career highs in all statistical categories. It was however the lockout-shortened 1998–99 season that proved pivotal for Armstrong's career, as he won both Sixth Man of the Year and Most Improved Player Awards, averaging 13.8 points and 6.7 assists. A year later he was named the starter and team captain on a Magic team that was projected to be one of the worst in the league, yet almost made the playoffs, finishing

136

Anthony Mason was capable of guarding all five positions and bringing the ball upcourt as the team's point guard (1994).

41–41 under rookie coach Doc Rivers. Armstrong would remain the starter for the next two seasons, before once again moving to the bench. He retired in 2008, following stints at New Orleans, Dallas, Indiana, and New Jersey.

Earl Boykins

The 5'5" Boykins is the second-shortest player in NBA history, placing only behind the 5'3" Muggsy Bogues. His college coach inflated his height to 5'7" so that other coaches would not think that he recruited such a small, unimposing player. From a young age Boykins had to prove more than other players and work twice as hard.[1] In the league since 1998, the undrafted point guard has played for the Nets, the Cavs, the Magic, the Clippers and the Warriors, before finally landing in 2003 in Denver. While he already played 19.4 minutes per contest in the 68 games he appeared in for the Warriors, it was the Nuggets that offered him his first multi-year contract ($13.7 million for five years).

The three and a half seasons on the Nuggets were the best period of Boykins' NBA career. Teams were afraid of giving him a chance due to his height, even though Boykins was proving time and time again that he was more than capable of starting in the league. Instead, he started just 34 games throughout his career, 23 alone in the 2006–07 season, in which he was traded from the Nuggets to the Bucks. The year was the best in his career, as he finished it with averages of 14.6 points and 4.4 assists. During the next five seasons Boykins would play for five different teams, including a second stint on the Bucks, and a year away from the NBA, spent in La Forteza Bologna in Italy. He played just eight games in his last season as a member of the Houston Rockets, a team that prolonged his deal after initially signing him to a 10-day contract.

Bobby Jackson

Bobby Jackson was selected with the 23rd pick in the 1997 NBA Draft, but the team that drafted him, championship candidates Seattle Super-Sonics, traded him for the 32nd pick in that draft, James Cotton, and the second-round pick in the next year's draft, which turned out to be Rashard Lewis. The Nuggets were rebuilding, and they did not win the first 12 games. They finished the season with just 11 wins. Following his rookie year, Jackson was traded to the Timberwolves, where he was named the sixth man. His first year in the NBA would remain the only one in his professional career during which he was the starter.

After two seasons in Minnesota, the Kings acquired Jackson, and already in his first year there he was fourth in the Sixth Man of the Year voting. Next season he was the runner-up, behind Corliss Williamson of the Detroit Pistons. Jackson's team made the Western Conference Finals and lost in seven games to the eventual champions, the Lakers. In the 2002–03 season Jackson was finally named the best bench player in the league, with averages of 15.2 points, 3.7 rebounds, and 3.1 assists.

While his on-court production was great, and he remained a beloved teammate and fan favorite, Jackson was often nagged by injuries, and he appeared in 294 games of 410 possible in his five seasons in Sacramento. After he left the Kings, Jackson played for the Grizzlies, the Hornets, and the Rockets. Before his last season, 2008–09, he returned to the Kings. Throughout that time, he remained rather healthy, appearing in 71 games in three of the four seasons. He retired before the Kings last preseason game in 2009.

Eddie Johnson

Eddie Johnson was selected with the 29th pick in the 1981 NBA Draft. In his first season in the league he started 27 games for the Kansas City Kings. The team was not very good, as it won only 30 games that season, and Johnson was not averaging double figures in points (9.3 per game). In the next five seasons Johnson averaged 20.4 points per contest. This was even more impressive considering that after three seasons he was moved to the bench, which coincided with his team's relocation from Kansas City to Sacramento. Johnson was unhappy with being a reserve on a bad team— the Kings won over 50 percent of their regular season games while he was there only once—and before the 1987–88 season he was traded to the Phoenix Suns.

In his first season in Arizona he started 59 games and averaged 17.7 points per contest, while a season later, despite starting just seven games, he was averaging 21.5 points. More importantly, while the season prior the Suns won just 28 games, in the 1988–89 season they won 55 games and made the Western Conference Finals. Johnson was named NBA Sixth Man of the Year. Upon receiving the award he said, "That was definitely a goal. I believe whatever situation you're in, you should shoot for the highest goal. The highest honor for someone coming off the bench is to be named the best sixth man."[2] He continued to come off the bench for the rest of his NBA career, as a member of the Sonics, the Hornets, the Pacers, and the Rockets. He retired at age 39.

Bobby Jones

In 2019 Bobby Jones became the 17th player in Philadelphia Sixers history to be named to the Basketball Hall of Fame. Nicknamed "the Secretary of Defense" for his ability to block shots and steal the ball, the 6'9" power forward was known as a selfless, team-first player. After four seasons on the Denver Nuggets, two in the ABA, just before the merger, Jones joined the Sixers, where he continued to showcase his defensive play. He made the NBA All-Defensive First Team for eight years in a row, and with making the ABA All-Defensive First Team in his first two seasons in the league, Jones was the best defender at his position for a whole decade, starting from 1975. In 1985 he made the NBA All-Defensive Second Team. From 1974–75 up until the 1985–86 season Jones was sixth in steals (1,387) and 11th in blocks (1,319) for that time period.[3]

What is more impressive though is that he made those numbers playing limited minutes on the Sixers, for whom he was playing as a sixth man since the 1979–80 season. By moving Jones to the bench, Coach Billy Cunningham could insert him whenever the team was in need of strengthening its defensive performance, and he would help the team. Since he was not much of a scorer, as most of his points came from dunks and interior play, Jones focused on blocks and rebounds. Kings coach Cotton Fitzsimmons gave Jones as an example for his players to emulate, stating that "The biggest thing about Bobby Jones is that he knows his limitations and plays within them. He makes very few mistakes. He doesn't take bad shots and very seldom makes a bad pass."[4]

In 1983 Jones won the first Sixth Man of the Year Award despite career lows in points (9), rebounds (4.6) and steals (1.1) per game. The season, however, had immediately followed a four-year run that established him as one of the NBA's very best off the bench; might the voters have intended to reward his sustained excellence? The Sixers won the NBA Championship that year.

Dan Majerle

Nicknamed "Thunder Dan" for his dunking ability, Majerle is primarily remembered as a long-distance shooter—he made 1,360 three-pointers during his NBA career on 35.8 percent accuracy. He played in the league for 14 seasons, eight with the Phoenix Suns, which is also the number of seasons Majerle spent coming off the bench throughout his career; a lone season on the Cavs; and five with the Heat. The 14th pick of the 1988 NBA Draft, Majerle's selection by the Suns was welcomed by boos of the fans from Arizona.

He was gradually earning their trust and admiration with his scoring ability. The best season of his career, his fourth in Phoenix, came in 1991–92. Majerle averaged career highs in points (17.3) and rebounds (5.9) per game, for the first time appearing in 82 games and starting just 15 of them. His performance did not go unnoticed outside of Phoenix, as he became an All-Star for the first time in his career—a rare occasion when a bench player has earned such an honor.

Next season Majerle earned a starting spot, and while he never averaged more points than in the 1991–92 season, he led the league in three-point makes and attempts for two seasons in a row. In the 1992–93 season he increased the number of three-point shots per game from 2.8 to 5.3. In the 1994–95 season Majerle was losing playing time to rookie Wesley Person after the All-Star break, even though he earned his third (and last) selection to the All-Star team that season. After the season Majerle was traded to the Cleveland Cavaliers for center John Williams. He then joined the Heat, signing a three-year $8 million deal.

On the Heat Majerle was supposed to be the starter but injuries and great play by fellow three-point shooter Voshon Lenard allowed him to start 165 and appear in 225 games of the 328 possible in the four seasons the two were on the team. In 2000–01 the 35 year old played in 53 games, backing up either small forward Bruce Bowen or shooting guard Eddie Jones. For his final season Majerle rejoined the Suns, where he played a limited role on an underperforming Phoenix team.

Danny Manning

Manning was the surefire first pick in the 1988 NBA Draft. When the Clippers won the right to pick first, general manager Elgin Baylor was proudly presenting a Clippers jersey with Manning's name on it. He had lofty expectations for the player, praising him for being an "unselfish player, very coachable and an excellent scorer and passer."[5] The power forward/center led the Kansas team known as "Danny and the Miracles" to the 1988 NCAA Championship. After 26 NBA games, in which he averaged 16.7 points, 6.6 rebounds and 1.7 steals, he suffered a torn anterior cruciate ligament in his right knee and was forced to sit out the rest of his rookie season. When he came back, he was the best player on the team for the next four and a half seasons, making the All-Star team in 1993 and 1994.

However, the team was not very good, and Manning would play for five coaches in six seasons, as well as argue with management. His trade to the Heat in the 1993–94 season was vetoed at the last minute, as Baylor was hoping to re-sign him in the offseason. The disgruntled Manning was traded to the Hawks and after half a season joined the Suns. There he would undergo two more ACL surgeries. The season 1996–97 turned out to be his first full season in three years. Coming off the bench, he was averaging 13.5 points and 6.1 rebounds. A season later, for very similar averages, he was named the NBA Sixth Man of the Year.

His 1996 contract with the Suns forbade Manning from jet-skiing and other off-court activities that could have impacted his knees. Thanks to a limited role and carefully managed playing time, Manning was able to remain in the league until 2003, when he decided to end his career. He spent the last four seasons of his career on four different teams—the Bucks, the Jazz, the Mavericks, and the Pistons. He played a total of 883 games and 398 starts, and finished his career with averages of 14 points, 5.2 rebounds 2.3 assists and 1.1 steal per game.

Anthony Mason

Few players in NBA history personified toughness with their exteriors like Anthony Mason did. The 53rd pick in the 1988 draft had to fight for his place in the league. After rather brief episodes on the Nets and the Nuggets, intertwined with seasons spent in Turkey and Venezuela, as well as in lesser-known American leagues, Mason joined the Knicks. During the first day of training camp before the 1991–92 season, he got into a fight with teammate Xavier McDaniel, setting the tone for Pat Riley's tenure with the Knicks. At 6'7" Mason weighed 250 pounds and used his strength when facing other forwards. His fearless attitude turned him into a fan favorite among the New York fans.

On the Knicks he could bring the ball up court, as well as guard opposing power forwards. Not much of a scorer, he was a perfect role player on the Riley-coached New York Knicks. Mason had great confidence in his abilities, often complaining that the team's offense was not going through him. Ray Allen, who played with Mason on the Bucks between the years 2001 and 2003, wrote in his autobiography that the player completely disrupted team chemistry with his attitude—he did not listen to anyone, even the coaches, as everyone on the team was afraid of him.[6]

In the 1994–95 season, a year after the Knicks made the NBA Finals, Mason was named NBA Sixth Man of the Year, averaging 9.9 points, 8.4 rebounds, and 3.1 assists per game. A season later Mason would lead the league in minutes played, being on the court for an average of 42.2 minutes in the 82 games he played. In 2001 Mason made his only All-Star team, during his only season on the Miami Heat. He died of congestive heart failure on February 28, 2015.

Nate McMillan

Few players have been so ingrained in the fabric of the teams they played on and so beloved by the fans as Nate McMillan in Seattle. Known as

"Mr. Sonic," he was with the team for 19 seasons, 13 as a player, one as assistant coach, and five as head coach. He had such great authority that, when as a rookie coach he suspended former teammate Gary Payton for insubordination, the outspoken point guard, who would argue with coaches throughout his career, officially apologized. The 30th pick in the 1986 NBA Draft, McMillan was the starter for the first four seasons of his career, until he lost the starting spot to Payton.

McMillan was groomed to be a coach since his early days, as observed by his first head coach, Bernie Bickerstaff: "He knew where the ball was supposed to go and who it would go to and he never really compromised guys by getting them the ball in the wrong places. He was cognizant of all the things that go into being a good point guard, which means that he had that ability that you knew to become a good coach because of those things."[7] Just like Payton, McMillan was a great defender. He was selected to the All-NBA Defensive Second Team twice, in 1994 and 1995, both times off the bench. In 1994 Payton was on the first and McMillan made the second team, while also leading the league in steals, averaging three per game. McMillan retired with career averages of 5.9 points, four rebounds, 6.1 assists, and 1.9 steals. He averaged at least two steals per game for five seasons, two of them off the bench.

Ricky Pierce

Pierce won the Sixth Man of the Year Award twice, in 1987 and 1990, both times coming off the bench for the Milwaukee Bucks. Drafted with the 18th pick in the 1982 draft, Pierce was primarily a scorer. With his strong physique he could either drive toward the basket or shoot from mid- or long range. He was so confident in his shooting that, after his career was over, he developed a special ball with finger pads, teaching players about correctly holding the ball before releasing it for a shot. And while he did finish his college career at Rice with averages of 22.5 points and 7.6 rebounds per game, he did not get many chances to score in his first year in the league.

After playing just 39 games and one start as a rookie, Pierce was traded after the season to the San Diego Clippers for two second-round picks. He was once again traded after one season, this time to Milwaukee, along with power forward Terry Cummings, with whom he would become one of the more important parts on one of the best Eastern Conference teams of the 1980s. The Bucks had not missed the playoffs during the decade and made the conference finals twice, both times losing to the Celtics. Pierce would play 421 games for the Bucks, starting just 46, 31 coming in the 1986–87 season, his first as Sixth Man of the Year. While the team regressed from 57 wins to 50 in comparison to the previous season, Pierce improved his scoring average from 13.9 to 19.5 points per game.

In his second season as the best reserve in the league, Pierce was averaging 23 points per game, leading the Bucks in scoring. Next season he was traded to the Sonics for another great scorer, Dale Ellis. Pierce continued to score in double figures for five of the next seven seasons. At age 39 he retired from the league, once again playing for the Bucks, after stops in Golden State, Indiana, Denver and Charlotte. Pierce retired with career averages of 14.9 points, 2.4 rebounds and 1.9 assists.

Rodney Rogers

AT 6'7", 255 pounds, this physically imposing forward entered the NBA in the 1993 draft with the ninth pick. The 1993 Atlantic Conference Player of the Year joined a Denver Nuggets team that did not make the playoffs in three seasons. In his rookie year he was coming off the bench behind Reggie Williams, a journeyman who would finally find a home on the team from Colorado, playing for the Nuggets for six seasons. That 1994 Nuggets team shocked the Seattle SuperSonics, becoming the first eighth-seed in league history to eliminate the conference leaders. A season later Rogers became a starter, but in 1995 the team included him in the trade package for rookie Antonio McDyess with the Clippers.

After four seasons in L.A. Rogers signed a three-year $6.6 million deal with the Suns. During the 1998–99 lockout Rogers gained weight and reported out of shape for the training camp. Unable to get a contract extension, he lost focus on basketball and was no longer the rare kind of frontcourt player—at that time—who was capable of overpowering small forwards in the paint and shooting from a long distance. When playing on the Suns, he declared, "I'm in heaven, man,"[8] even though he was a bench player.

In his first season in Arizona, Rogers won the Sixth Man of the Year Award. In 1999–2000 he was making 13.8 points and 5.5 rebounds per game playing on the 53–29 Phoenix Suns. His coach Scott Skiles was confident that his sixth man would win the trophy, saying before the voting, "He has to win. He would be absolutely robbed if he doesn't."[9] After two and a half seasons on the Suns though, Rogers was traded to the Celtics as part of the package that brought in future All-Star Joe Johnson to Phoenix. The Celtics lost to the New Jersey Nets in the 2002 Eastern Conference Finals, and Rogers signed with the Nets in the offseason, playing in his first and only NBA Finals in 2003. He retired in 2005. In 2008 he suffered an accident while riding a dirt bike that left him paralyzed from the shoulders down.

Ricky Pierce won the Sixth Man of the Year Award twice while playing for the Bucks, in 1987 and 1990 (1989).

Corliss Williamson

Nicknamed "Big Nasty," Williamson was a 6'7" forward who dominated the post and mid-range by scoring on opposing frontcourt players, using either his strength or quickness, depending on the type of player he faced. While at Arkansas he was a power forward; in the NBA he was mostly a small forward, although he was equally effective playing at both positions. In his first two seasons on the Kings, Williamson was coming off the bench, but in his third year, 1997–98, he was named the starter and had the best season of his career, averaging personal bests in points (17.7), rebounds (5.6 rebounds) and assists (2.9). He was second in the voting for Most Improved Player, losing to the Hawks' Alan Henderson.

In the summer of 2000 he was traded to the Toronto Raptors for lockdown defender Doug Christie, but after 42 games the Raptors moved him to the Pistons. A season later, 2001–2002, Williamson won the Sixth Man of the Year Award. He led the league in points scored from the bench, averaging 13.6 points per game. Williamson was also the first Pistons player to win the award, but clearly not the first great reserve player from that franchise, which also had Vinnie Johnson and Dennis Rodman. Just like those two, Williamson won an NBA Championship for the team from Michigan, coming off the bench for the 2004 champions. After that season the Pistons traded him and his three-year $18 million contract to the Sixers for Derrick Coleman, a player the Sixers were eager to get rid of.

Stats

This part of the book is divided into three tables. The first one presents the stats of players who won the Sixth Man of the Year Award in that particular season when they have earned that honor. The second presents how other significant bench players, who have never won the award, fared statistically in the seasons when they had a good chance at winning it. The third shows the stats from exceptional postseason performances by bench players.

Michael Cooper was one of the best bench players in league history, yet he never won the Sixth Man of the Year Award (1985).

Winners of the NBA Sixth Man of the Year Award

Season	Player	Team	G	MPG	PPG	RPG	APG	SPG	BPG
1982–83	Bobby Jones	Philadelphia 76ers	74	23.6	9.0	4.6	1.9	1.1	1.2
1983–84	Kevin McHale	Boston Celtics	82	31.4	18.4	7.4	1.3	0.3	1.5
1984–85	Kevin McHale	Boston Celtics	79	33.6	19.8	9.0	1.8	0.4	1.5
1985–86	Bill Walton	Boston Celtics	80	19.3	7.6	6.8	2.1	0.5	1.3
1986–87	Ricky Pierce	Milwaukee Bucks	79	31.7	19.5	3.4	1.8	0.8	0.3
1987–88	Roy Tarpley	Dallas Mavericks	81	28.5	13.5	11.8	1.1	1.3	1.1
1988–89	Eddie Johnson	Phoenix Suns	70	29.2	21.5	4.4	2.3	0.7	0.1
1989–90	Ricky Pierce	Milwaukee Bucks	59	29.0	23.0	2.8	2.3	0.8	0.1
1990–91	Detlef Schrempf	Indiana Pacers	82	32.1	16.1	8.0	3.7	0.7	0.3
1991–92	Detlef Schrempf	Indiana Pacers	80	32.6	17.3	9.6	3.9	0.8	0.5
1992–93	Clifford Robinson	Portland Trail Blazers	82	31.4	19.1	6.6	2.2	1.2	2.0
1993–94	Dell Curry	Charlotte Hornets	82	26.5	16.3	3.2	2.7	1.2	0.3
1994–95	Anthony Mason	New York Knicks	77	32.4	9.9	8.4	3.1	0.9	0.3
1995–96	Toni Kukoč	Chicago Bulls	81	26.0	13.1	4.0	3.5	0.8	0.3
1996–97	John Starks	New York Knicks	77	26.5	13.8	2.7	2.8	1.2	0.1
1997–98	Danny Manning	Phoenix Suns	70	25.6	13.5	5.6	2.0	1.0	0.7
1998–99	Darrell Armstrong	Orlando Magic	50	30.0	13.8	3.6	6.7	2.2	0.1
1999–00	Rodney Rogers	Phoenix Suns	82	27.9	13.8	5.5	2.1	1.1	0.6

2000–01	Aaron McKie	Philadelphia 76ers	76	31.5	11.6	4.1	5.0	1.4	0.1
2001–02	Corliss Williamson	Detroit Pistons	78	21.8	13.6	4.1	1.2	0.6	0.3
2002–03	Bobby Jackson	Sacramento Kings	59	28.4	15.2	3.7	3.1	1.2	0.1
2003–04	Antawn Jamison	Dallas Mavericks	82	29.0	14.8	6.3	0.9	1.0	0.4
2004–05	Ben Gordon	Chicago Bulls	82	24.4	15.1	2.6	2.0	0.6	0.1
2005–06	Mike Miller	Memphis Grizzlies	74	30.6	13.7	5.4	2.7	0.7	0.4
2006–07	Leandro Barbosa	Phoenix Suns	80	32.7	18.1	2.7	4.0	1.2	0.2
2007–08	Manu Ginobili	San Antonio Spurs	74	31.1	19.5	4.8	4.5	1.5	0.4
2008–09	Jason Terry	Dallas Mavericks	74	33.7	19.6	2.4	3.4	1.3	0.3
2009–10	Jamal Crawford	Atlanta Hawks	79	31.1	18.0	2.5	3.0	0.8	0.2
2010–11	Lamar Odom	Los Angeles Lakers	82	32.2	14.4	8.7	3.0	0.6	0.7
2011–12	James Harden	Oklahoma City Thunder	62	31.4	16.8	4.1	3.7	1.0	0.2
2012–13	J.R. Smith	New York Knicks	80	33.5	18.1	5.3	2.7	1.3	0.3
2013–14	Jamal Crawford	Los Angeles Clippers	69	30.3	18.6	2.3	3.2	0.9	0.2
2014–15	Lou Williams	Toronto Raptors	80	25.2	15.5	1.9	2.1	1.1	0.1
2015–16	Jamal Crawford	Los Angeles Clippers	79	26.9	14.2	1.8	2.3	0.7	0.2
2016–17	Eric Gordon	Houston Rockets	75	31.0	16.2	2.7	2.5	0.6	0.5
2017–18	Lou Williams	Los Angeles Clippers	79	32.8	22.6	2.5	5.3	1.1	0.2
2018–19	Lou Williams	Los Angeles Clippers	75	26.6	20.0	3.0	5.4	0.8	0.1
2019–20	Montrezl Harrell	Los Angeles Clippers	63	27.8	18.6	7.1	1.7	0.6	1.1

Great Seasons by Reserve Players Who Have Never Won the Award
(But Were Eligible for It)

Season	Player	Team	G	MPG	PPG	RPG	APG	SPG	BPG
1982–83	Bob McAdoo	Los Angeles Lakers	47	21.7	15.0	5.3	0.8	0.9	0.9
	Tiny Archibald	Boston Celtics	66	27.4	10.5	1.4	6.2	0.6	0.1
	Mickey Johnson	New Jersey Nets	42	23.8	13.4	5.3	3.4	1.3	0.5
	Alton Lister	Milwaukee Bucks	80	23.6	8.4	7.1	1.4	0.6	2.2
1983–84	John Drew	Utah Jazz	81	22.2	17.7	4.2	1.7	1.1	0.0
	Kenny Carr	Portland Trail Blazers	82	29.9	15.6	7.8	1.9	0.8	0.4
1984–85	Clyde Drexler	Portland Trail Blazers	78	31.9	17.2	6.0	5.5	2.2	0.9
	Michael Cooper	Los Angeles Lakers	82	26.7	8.6	3.1	5.2	1.1	0.6
	Bob McAdoo	Los Angeles Lakers	66	19.0	10.5	4.5	1.0	0.3	0.8
	Mike Woodson	Kansas City Kings	78	25.6	17.0	2.5	1.8	1.5	0.4
	Jay Vincent	Dallas Mavericks	79	32.3	18.2	8.9	2.1	0.6	0.3
	Quintin Dailey	Chicago Bulls	79	26.6	16.0	2.6	2.4	0.9	0.1
	Vinnie Johnson	Detroit Pistons	82	25.5	12.8	3.1	4.0	0.9	0.2
1985–86	Michael Cooper	Los Angeles Lakers	82	27.7	9.2	3.0	5.7	1.1	0.5
1986–87	Vinnie Johnson	Detroit Pistons	78	27.8	15.7	3.3	3.8	1.2	0.2
	Michael Cooper	Los Angeles Lakers	82	27.5	10.5	3.1	4.5	1.0	0.5
1987–88	Thurl Bailey	Utah Jazz	82	34.2	19.6	6.5	1.9	0.6	1.5

Season	Player	Team							
	Dennis Rodman	Detroit Pistons	82	26.2	11.6	8.7	1.3	0.9	0.5
	Jay Vincent	Denver Nuggets	73	24.0	15.4	4.2	2.0	0.6	0.4
1988–89	Dennis Rodman	Detroit Pistons	82	26.9	9.0	9.4	1.2	0.7	0.9
	Vinnie Johnson	Detroit Pistons	82	25.3	13.8	3.1	3.0	0.9	0.2
	Xavier McDaniel	Seattle SuperSonics	82	29.1	20.5	5.3	1.6	1.0	0.5
	Thurl Bailey	Utah Jazz	82	33.9	19.5	5.5	1.7	0.6	1.1
	John Williams	Washington Bullets	82	29.4	13.7	7.0	4.3	1.7	0.9
	Ron Anderson	Philadelphia 76ers	82	31.9	16.2	5.0	1.7	0.9	0.3
	Manute Bol	Golden State Warriors	80	22.1	3.9	5.8	0.3	0.1	4.3
	Roy Hinson	New Jersey Nets	82	31.0	16.0	6.4	0.9	0.4	1.5
1989–90	Ron Anderson	Philadelphia 76ers	78	26.8	11.9	3.8	1.8	0.9	0.2
	Thurl Bailey	Utah Jazz	82	31.5	14.2	5.0	1.7	0.4	1.2
1990–91	Dan Majerle	Phoenix Suns	77	29.6	13.6	5.4	2.8	1.4	0.5
	Thurl Bailey	Utah Jazz	82	30.3	12.4	5.0	1.5	0.6	1.1
	Moses Malone	Atlanta Hawks	82	23.3	10.6	8.1	0.8	0.4	0.9
	Danny Ainge	Portland Trail Blazers	80	21.4	11.1	2.6	3.6	0.8	0.2
1991–92	Šarūnas Marčiulionis	Golden State Warriors	72	29.4	18.9	2.4	1.7	1.2	0.1
	Dan Majerle	Phoenix Suns	82	34.8	17.3	5.9	3.3	1.6	0.5
	John Williams[10]	Cleveland Cavaliers	80	30.4	11.9	7.6	2.5	0.8	2.3
1992–93	Danny Ainge	Phoenix Suns	80	27.0	11.8	2.7	3.3	0.9	0.1

Season	Player	Team	G	MPG	PPG	RPG	APG	SPG	BPG
	Tom Chambers	Phoenix Suns	73	23.6	12.2	4.7	1.4	0.6	0.3
	Nate McMillan	Seattle SuperSonics	73	27.1	7.5	4.2	5.3	2.4	0.5
	Todd Day	Milwaukee Bucks	71	27.2	13.8	4.1	1.6	1.1	0.7
1993–94	Nate McMillan	Seattle SuperSonics	73	25.8	6.0	3.9	5.3	3.0	6.0
	Craig Ehlo	Atlanta Hawks	82	26.2	10.0	3.4	3.3	1.7	0.3
	Armen Gilliam	New Jersey Nets	82	24.0	11.8	6.1	0.8	0.5	0.7
	Mario Elie	Houston Rockets	67	24.0	9.3	2.7	3.1	0.7	0.1
	Steve Kerr	Chicago Bulls	82	24.8	8.6	1.6	2.6	0.9	0.0
	Hubert Davis	New York Knicks	56	23.8	11.0	1.2	2.9	0.7	0.1
	Orlando Woolridge	Philadelphia 76ers	74	26.4	12.7	4.0	1.9	0.6	0.8
	Robert Pack	Denver Nuggets	66	20.9	9.6	1.9	5.4	1.2	0.1
1994–95	Nate McMillan	Seattle SuperSonics	80	25.9	3.2	3.8	5.3	2.1	0.7
	Chuck Person	San Antonio Spurs	81	25.1	10.8	3.2	1.3	0.6	0.1
	Dennis Scott	Orlando Magic	62	24.2	12.9	2.4	2.1	0.7	0.2
	Chris Gatling	Golden State Warriors	58	25.3	13.7	7.6	0.9	0.7	0.9
	Armen Gilliam	New Jersey Nets	82	30.1	14.8	7.5	1.2	0.8	1.1
	Dale Ellis	Denver Nuggets	81	24.6	11.3	2.7	0.7	0.5	0.1
1995–96	Arvydas Sabonis	Portland Trail Blazers	73	23.8	14.5	8.1	3.5	0.8	0.3
	Jayson Williams	New Jersey Nets	80	23.2	9.0	10.0	0.6	0.4	0.7

	Sam Cassell	Houston Rockets	61	27.6	14.5	3.1	4.6	0.9	0.1
	Chuck Person	San Antonio Spurs	80	26.6	10.9	5.2	1.3	0.6	0.3
	A.C. Green	Phoenix Suns	82	25.8	7.5	6.8	0.9	0.5	0.3
	Tracy Murray	Toronto Raptors	82	30.0	16.2	4.3	1.6	1.1	0.5
1996–97	Terry Mills	Detroit Pistons	79	25.3	10.8	4.8	1.3	0.4	0.3
	Sam Perkins	Seattle SuperSonics	81	24.4	11.0	3.7	1.3	0.9	0.6
	Dominique Wilkins	Atlanta Hawks	63	30.9	18.2	6.4	1.9	0.6	0.5
	Kevin Willis	Houston Rockets	75	26.2	11.2	7.5	0.9	0.6	0.4
	Gary Trent	Portland Trail Blazers	82	23.4	10.8	5.2	1.1	0.6	0.4
1997–98	Kobe Bryant	Los Angeles Lakers	79	26.0	15.4	3.1	2.5	0.9	0.5
	Dale Ellis	Seattle SuperSonics	79	24.5	11.8	2.3	1.1	0.8	0.1
	Tracy Murray	Washington Wizards	82	27.2	15.1	3.4	1.0	0.8	0.3
	Derek Anderson	Cleveland Cavaliers	66	27.9	11.7	2.8	3.4	1.3	0.2
	Alan Henderson	Atlanta Hawks	69	29.0	14.3	6.4	1.1	0.6	0.5
1998–99	Rasheed Wallace	Portland Trail Blazers	49	28.9	12.8	4.9	1.2	1.0	1.1
	Antonio Davis	Indiana Pacers	49	25.9	9.4	7.0	0.7	0.4	0.9
	Jalen Rose	Indiana Pacers	49	25.3	11.1	3.1	1.9	1.0	0.3
	Terry Poter	Portland Trail Blazers	50	27.3	10.5	2.8	2.9	1.0	0.2
	Tracy McGrady	Toronto Raptors	49	22.6	9.3	5.7	2.3	1.1	1.3
	Dee Brown	Toronto Raptors	49	28.1	11.2	2.1	2.9	1.1	0.2

Season	Player	Team	G	MPG	PPG	RPG	APG	SPG	BPG
1999–00	Cuttino Mobley	Houston Rockets	81	30.8	15.8	3.6	2.6	1.1	0.4
	Steve Nash	Dallas Mavericks	56	27.4	8.6	2.2	4.9	0.7	0.1
	Cedric Ceballos	Dallas Mavericks	69	29.9	16.6	6.7	1.3	0.8	0.3
	Tracy McGrady	Toronto Raptors	79	31.2	15.4	6.3	3.3	1.1	1.9
	Jerome Williams	Detroit Pistons	82	25.6	8.4	9.6	0.8	1.2	0.3
	Marcus Camby	New York Knicks	59	26.2	10.2	7.8	0.8	0.7	2.0
	Peja Stojaković	Sacramento Kings	74	23.6	11.9	3.7	1.4	0.7	0.1
	Andre Miller	Cleveland Cavaliers	82	25.5	11.1	3.4	5.8	1.0	0.2
	Austin Croshere	Indiana Pacers	81	23.3	10.3	6.4	1.1	0.5	0.7
2000–01	Tim Thomas	Milwaukee Bucks	76	27.4	12.6	4.1	1.8	1.0	0.6
	LaPhonso Ellis	Minnesota Timberwolves	82	23.8	9.4	6.0	1.1	0.8	0.9
	Travis Best	Indiana Pacers	77	31.9	11.9	2.9	6.1	1.4	0.1
	Ruben Patterson	Seattle SuperSonics	76	27.1	13.0	5.0	2.1	1.4	0.6
	Donyell Marshall	Utah Jazz	81	28.7	13.6	7.0	1.6	1.0	1.0
	Steve Smith	Portland Trail Blazers	81	31.4	13.6	3.4	2.6	0.6	0.3
	Tony Delk	Phoenix Suns	82	27.9	12.3	3.2	2.0	0.9	0.2
	Darius Miles	Los Angeles Clippers	81	26.3	9.4	5.9	1.2	0.6	1.5
2001–02	Quentin Richardson	Los Angeles Clippers	81	26.6	13.3	4.1	1.6	1.0	0.3
	Malik Rose	San Antonio Spurs	82	21.0	9.4	6.0	0.7	0.9	0.5

Season	Player	Team						
	Robert Horry	Los Angeles Lakers	81	26.4	6.8	5.9	2.9	1.0	1.1
	Troy Hudson	Orlando Magic	81	22.9	11.7	1.8	3.1	0.7	0.1
	Desmond Mason	Seattle SuperSonics	75	32.3	12.4	4.7	1.4	0.9	0.4
	Andrei Kirilenko	Utah Jazz	82	26.2	10.7	4.9	1.1	1.4	1.9
	Michael Redd	Milwaukee Bucks	67	21.1	11.4	3.3	1.4	0.6	0.1
2002–03	Michael Redd	Milwaukee Bucks	82	28.2	15.1	4.5	1.4	1.2	0.2
	Andrei Kirilenko	Utah Jazz	80	27.2	12.0	5.3	1.7	1.5	2.2
	Nick Van Exel	Dallas Mavericks	73	27.8	12.5	2.8	4.3	0.6	0.1
	Malik Rose	San Antonio Spurs	79	24.5	10.4	6.4	1.6	0.7	0.5
	Al Harrington	Indiana Pacers	82	30.1	12.2	6.2	1.5	0.9	0.4
	Adonal Foyle	Golden State Warriors	82	21.8	5.4	6.0	0.5	0.5	2.5
	Andrei Kirilenko	Utah Jazz	80	27.7	12.0	5.3	1.7	1.5	2.2
2003–04	Al Harrington	Indiana Pacers	79	30.9	13.3	6.4	1.7	1.0	0.3
	Earl Boykins	Denver Nuggets	82	22.5	10.2	1.7	3.6	0.6	0.0
	Shane Battier	Memphis Grizzlies	79	24.6	8.5	3.8	1.3	1.3	0.7
	Desmond Mason	Milwaukee Bucks	82	30.9	14.4	4.4	1.9	0.7	0.3
	Rafer Alston	Miami Heat	82	31.5	10.2	2.8	4.5	1.4	0.2
	Raja Bell	Utah Jazz	79	24.6	11.2	2.9	1.3	0.8	0.2
	Speedy Claxton	Golden State Warriors	60	26.6	10.6	2.6	4.5	1.6	0.2
2004–05	Ricky Davis	Boston Celtics	82	32.9	16.0	3.0	3.0	1.1	0.3

Season	Player	Team	G	MPG	PPG	RPG	APG	SPG	BPG
	Earl Boykins	Denver Nuggets	82	26.4	12.4	1.7	4.5	1.0	0.1
	Jerry Stackhouse	Dallas Mavericks	56	28.9	14.9	3.3	2.3	0.9	0.2
	Wally Szczerbiak	Minnesota Timberwolves	81	31.6	15.5	3.7	2.4	0.5	0.2
	Antonio Daniels	Seattle SuperSonics	75	27.0	11.2	2.3	4.1	0.7	0.0
	Kyle Korver	Philadelphia 76ers	82	32.5	11.5	4.6	2.2	1.3	0.4
	Mehmet Okur	Utah Jazz	82	28.1	12.9	7.5	2.0	0.4	0.8
	Hedo Türkoğlu	Orlando Magic	67	26.2	14.0	3.5	2.3	0.6	0.3
	Andres Nocioni	Chicago Bulls	81	23.4	8.4	4.8	1.5	0.5	0.4
2005–06	Speedy Claxton	New Orleans Hornets	71	28.4	12.3	2.7	4.8	1.5	0.1
	Jerry Stackhouse	Dallas Mavericks	55	27.7	13.0	2.8	2.9	0.7	0.2
	Antonio McDyess	Detroit Pistons	82	21.1	7.8	5.3	1.1	0.6	0.6
	Alonzo Mourning	Miami Heat	65	20.0	7.8	5.5	0.2	0.2	2.7
	Michael Finley	San Antonio Spurs	77	26.5	10.1	3.2	1.5	0.5	0.1
	Channing Frye	New York Knicks	65	24.2	12.3	5.8	0.8	0.5	0.7
	Derek Fisher	Golden State Warriors	82	31.6	13.3	2.6	4.3	1.5	0.1
	Charlie Villanueva	Toronto Raptors	81	29.1	13.0	6.4	1.1	0.7	0.8
2006–07	Jerry Stackhouse	Dallas Mavericks	67	24.1	12.0	2.2	2.8	0.8	0.1
	Alonzo Mourning	Miami Heat	77	20.4	8.6	4.5	0.2	0.2	2.3
	David Lee	New York Knicks	58	29.8	10.7	10.4	1.8	0.8	0.4

	Kyle Korver	Philadelphia 76ers	74	30.9	14.1	3.5	1.4	0.8	0.3
	Corey Maggette	Los Angeles Clippers	75	30.5	16.9	5.9	2.8	0.9	0.2
	Josh Childress	Atlanta Hawks	55	36.8	13.0	6.2	2.3	1.1	0.7
	Chucky Atkins	Memphis Grizzlies	75	27.5	13.2	1.9	4.6	0.7	0.1
	Matt Harpring	Utah Jazz	77	25.5	11.6	4.6	1.3	0.7	0.1
2007–08	Josh Childress	Atlanta Hawks	76	29.9	11.8	4.9	1.5	0.9	0.6
	Travis Outlaw	Portland Trail Blazers	82	26.7	13.3	4.6	1.3	0.7	0.8
	David Lee	New York Knicks	81	29.1	10.8	8.9	1.2	0.7	0.4
	John Salmons	Sacramento Kings	81	31.1	12.5	4.3	2.6	1.1	0.4
	Luis Scola	Houston Rockets	82	24.7	10.3	6.4	1.3	0.7	0.2
	Nate Robinson	New York Knicks	72	26.2	12.7	3.1	2.9	0.8	0.0
2008–09	Travis Outlaw	Portland Trail Blazers	81	27.7	12.8	4.1	1.0	0.6	0.7
	Chris Andersen	Denver Nuggets	71	20.6	6.4	6.2	0.4	0.6	2.5
	Nate Robinson	New York Knicks	74	29.9	17.2	3.9	4.1	1.3	0.1
	Andrei Kirilenko	Utah Jazz	67	27.3	11.6	4.8	2.6	1.2	1.1
	Corey Maggette	Golden State Warriors	51	31.1	18.6	5.5	1.8	0.9	0.2
	Kevin Love	Minnesota Timberwolves	81	25.3	11.1	9.1	1.0	0.4	0.6
	Paul Millsap	Utah Jazz	76	30.1	13.5	8.6	1.8	1.0	1.0
	Trevor Ariza	Los Angeles Lakers	82	24.4	8.9	4.3	1.8	1.7	0.3
2009–10	Udonis Haslem	Miami Heat	78	27.9	11.6	6.8	1.6	0.8	1.2

Season	Player	Team	G	MPG	PPG	RPG	APG	SPG	BPG
	Darren Collison	New Orleans Hornets	76	27.8	12.4	2.5	5.7	1.0	0.1
	Marcus Thornton	New Orleans Hornets	73	25.6	14.5	2.9	1.6	0.8	0.2
	Anderson Varejão	Cleveland Cavaliers	76	28.5	8.6	7.6	1.1	0.9	0.9
	Al Harrington	New York Knicks	72	30.5	17.7	5.6	1.5	0.9	0.4
	Kevin Love	Minnesota Timberwolves	60	28.6	14.0	11.0	2.3	0.7	0.4
	Chris Andersen	Denver Nuggets	76	22.3	5.9	6.4	0.4	0.6	1.9
2010–11	Thaddeus Young	Philadelphia 76ers	82	26.0	12.7	5.3	1.0	1.1	0.3
	Glen Davis	Boston Celtics	78	29.5	11.7	5.4	1.2	1.0	0.4
	George Hill	San Antonio Spurs	76	28.3	11.6	2.6	2.5	0.9	0.3
	Marcin Gortat	Magic/Suns	80	25.4	10.2	7.9	0.9	0.5	1.1
	Ty Lawson	Denver Nuggets	80	26.3	11.7	2.6	4.7	1.0	0.1
	Tony Allen	Memphis Grizzlies	72	20.8	8.9	2.7	1.4	1.8	0.6
	J.J. Redick	Orlando Magic	59	25.6	10.1	1.9	1.7	0.5	0.1
2011–12	Al Harrington	Denver Nuggets	64	27.5	14.2	6.1	1.4	0.9	0.2
	Taj Gibson	Chicago Bulls	63	20.4	7.7	5.3	0.7	0.4	1.3
	O.J. Mayo	Memphis Grizzlies	66	26.8	12.6	3.2	2.6	1.1	0.3
	Mo Williams	Los Angeles Clippers	52	28.3	13.2	1.9	3.1	1.0	0.1
	Thaddeus Young	Philadelphia 76ers	63	27.9	12.8	5.2	1.2	1.0	0.7
	Mike Dunleavy	Milwaukee Bucks	55	26.3	12.3	3.7	2.1	0.5	0.1

	Andre Miller	Denver Nuggets	66	27.4	9.7	3.3	6.7	1.0	0.1
	Klay Thompson	Golden State Warriors	66	24.4	12.5	2.4	2.0	0.7	0.3
	Nate Robinson	Golden State Warriors	51	23.4	11.2	2.0	4.5	1.2	0.0
2012–13	Jarrett Jack	Golden State Warriors	79	29.7	12.9	3.1	5.6	0.8	0.1
	Kevin Martin	Oklahoma City Thunder	77	27.7	14.0	2.3	1.4	0.9	0.1
	Ryan Anderson	New Orleans Hornets	81	30.9	16.2	6.4	1.2	0.5	0.4
	Andre Miller	Denver Nuggets	82	26.2	9.6	2.9	5.9	0.9	1.0
	Corey Brewer	Denver Nuggets	82	24.4	12.1	2.9	1.5	1.4	0.3
	Nate Robinson	Chicago Bulls	82	25.4	13.1	2.2	4.4	1.0	0.1
	Ramon Sessions	Charlotte Bobcats	61	27.1	14.4	2.8	3.8	0.8	0.1
	Vince Carter	Dallas Mavericks	81	25.8	13.4	4.1	2.4	0.9	0.5
	Amir Johnson	Toronto Raptors	81	28.7	10.0	7.5	1.5	1.0	1.4
2013–14	Taj Gibson	Chicago Bulls	82	28.7	13.0	6.8	1.1	0.5	1.4
	Markieff Morris	Phoenix Suns	81	26.6	13.8	6.0	1.8	0.8	0.6
	Reggie Jackson	Oklahoma City Thunder	80	28.5	13.1	3.9	4.1	1.1	0.1
	Vince Carter	Dallas Mavericks	81	24.4	11.9	3.5	2.6	0.8	0.4
	Dion Waiters	Cleveland Cavaliers	70	29.6	15.9	2.8	3.0	0.9	0.2
	Nick Young	Los Angeles Lakers	64	28.3	17.9	2.6	1.5	0.7	0.2
	Marco Belinelli	San Antonio Spurs	80	25.2	11.4	2.8	2.2	0.6	0.1
	Jeremy Lin	Houston Rockets	71	28.9	12.5	2.6	4.1	1.0	0.4

Season	Player	Team	G	MPG	PPG	RPG	APG	SPG	BPG
2014–15	Andre Iguodala	Golden State Warriors	77	26.9	7.8	3.3	3.0	1.2	0.3
	Isaiah Thomas	Suns/Celtics	67	25.8	16.4	2.3	4.2	0.9	0.1
	Tristan Thompson	Cleveland Cavaliers	82	26.8	8.5	8.0	0.5	0.4	0.7
	Marreese Speights	Golden State Warriors	76	15.9	10.4	4.3	0.9	0.3	0.4
	Nikola Mirotić	Chicago Bulls	82	20.2	10.2	4.9	1.2	0.7	0.7
	Taj Gibson	Chicago Bulls	62	27.3	10.3	6.4	1.1	0.6	1.2
2015–16	Andre Iguodala	Golden State Warriors	65	26.6	7.0	4.0	3.4	1.1	0.3
	Shaun Livingston	Golden State Warriors	78	19.5	6.3	2.2	3.0	0.7	0.3
	Enes Kanter	Oklahoma City Thunder	82	21.0	12.7	8.1	0.4	0.3	0.4
	J.J. Barea	Dallas Mavericks	74	22.5	10.9	2.1	4.1	0.4	0.0
	Will Barton	Denver Nuggets	82	28.7	14.4	5.8	2.5	0.9	0.5
	Zach LaVine	Minnesota Timberwolves	82	28.0	14.0	2.8	3.1	0.8	0.2
	Jeremy Lin	Charlotte Hornets	78	26.3	11.7	3.2	3.0	0.7	0.5
	Dennis Schröder	Atlanta Hawks	80	20.3	11.0	2.6	4.4	0.9	0.1
2016–17	Andre Iguodala	Golden State Warriors	81	26.3	7.6	4.0	3.4	1.0	0.5
	Zach Randolph	Memphis Grizzlies	73	24.5	14.1	8.2	1.7	0.5	0.1
	James Johnson	Miami Heat	76	27.4	12.8	4.9	3.6	1.0	1.1
	Enes Kanter	Oklahoma City Thunder	72	21.3	14.3	6.7	0.9	0.4	0.5
	Malcolm Brogdon	Milwaukee Bucks	75	26.4	10.2	2.8	4.2	1.1	0.21

	Tim Hardaway, Jr.	Atlanta Hawks	79	27.3	14.5	2.8	2.3	0.7	0.2
	Seth Curry	Dallas Mavericks	70	29.0	12.8	2.6	2.7	1.1	0.1
2017–18	Fred VanVleet	Toronto Raptors	76	20.0	8.6	2.4	3.2	0.9	0.3
	Will Barton	Denver Nuggets	81	33.1	15.7	5.0	4.1	1.0	0.6
	Kelly Olynyk	Miami Heat	76	23.4	11.5	5.7	2.7	0.8	0.5
	Wayne Ellington	Miami Heat	77	26.5	11.2	2.8	1.0	0.7	0.1
	Dwyane Wade	Cavaliers/Heat	67	22.9	11.4	3.8	3.4	0.9	0.7
	Kyle Kuzma	Los Angeles Lakers	77	31.2	16.1	6.3	1.8	0.6	0.4
	Terry Rozier	Boston Celtics	80	25.9	11.3	4.7	2.9	1.0	0.2
2018–19	Domantas Sabonis	Indiana Pacers	74	24.8	14.1	9.3	2.9	0.6	0.4
	Spencer Dinwiddie	Brooklyn Nets	68	28.1	16.8	2.4	4.6	0.6	0.3
	Terrence Ross	Orlando Magic	81	26.5	15.1	3.5	1.7	0.9	0.4
	Derrick Rose	Minnesota Timberwolves	51	27.3	18.0	2.7	4.3	0.6	0.2
	Dwyane Wade	Miami Heat	72	26.2	15.0	4.0	4.2	0.8	0.5
	Dennis Schröder	Oklahoma City Thunder	79	29.3	15.5	3.6	4.1	0.8	0.2
2019–20	Jordan Clarkson	Utah Jazz	42	24.7	15.6	2.8	1.6	0.7	0.2
	Norman Powell	Toronto Raptors	52	28.4	16.0	3.7	1.8	1.2	0.4
	Dennis Schröder	Oklahoma City Thunder	65	30.8	18.9	3.6	4.0	0.7	0.2
	Derrick Rose	Detroit Pistons	50	26.0	18.1	2.4	5.6	0.8	0.3
	Goran Dragić	Miami Heat	59	28.2	16.2	3.2	5.1	0.7	0.2

Great Playoffs by Bench Players[11]

Year	Player	Team	G	GS	MPG	PPG	RPG	APG	SPG	BPG
1985	Michael Cooper	Lakers	19	0	26.4	10.4	4.0	4.9	1.1	0.5
	Bob McAdoo	Lakers	19	0	20.9	11.4	4.5	0.8	0.5	1.4
	Charles Barkley	Sixers	13	2	31.4	14.9	11.1	2.0	1.8	1.2
	Vinnie Johnson	Pistons	9	0	26.1	14.2	3.0	3.2	0.7	0.1
1986	Bill Walton	Celtics	16	0	18.2	7.9	6.4	1.7	0.4	0.8
	Alton Lister	Bucks	14	1	23.9	11.9	6.9	0.9	0.5	1.6
	Michael Cooper	Lakers	14	0	30.1	9.7	3.3	4.9	1.3	0.3
	Dan Roundfield	Bullets	5	0	35.4	14.0	9.2	2.0	0.4	0.8
1987	Michael Cooper	Lakers	18	0	29.0	13.0	3.3	5.0	1.4	0.8
	Vinnie Johnson	Pistons	15	0	25.9	14.7	2.9	4.1	0.6	0.3
	Ricky Pierce	Bucks	12	2	26.4	15.9	2.3	1.3	0.8	0.4
1988	Roy Tarpley	Mavericks	17	0	33.1	17.9	12.9	1.8	1.2	1.5
	Thurl Bailey	Jazz	11	0	40.8	23.2	5.7	1.6	0.5	2.1
	Horace Grant	Bulls	10	0	29.9	10.1	7.0	1.6	1.4	0.2
	Jay Vincent	Jazz	8	0	25.0	17.5	4.6	0.8	0.6	0.5
1989	Vinnie Johnson	Pistons	17	0	21.9	14.1	2.6	2.5	0.2	0.2
	Mychal Thompson	Lakers	15	0	25.1	11.4	5.1	0.7	0.4	0.8
	Eddie Johnson	Suns	12	0	32.7	17.8	7.3	2.1	1.0	0.2

	Dan Majerle	Suns	12	0	29.3	14.3	4.8	1.2	1.1	0.3
	Ricky Pierce	Bucks	9	0	32.4	22.3	2.8	2.8	1.2	0.2
1990	Mark Aguirre	Pistons	20	3	22.0	11.0	4.6	1.4	0.5	0.2
	Dan Majerle	Suns	16	0	29.9	12.6	5.1	2.1	1.3	0.1
1991	Vinnie Johnson	Pistons	15	3	29.2	15.2	5.1	2.9	0.7	0.3
	Mark Aguirre	Pistons	15	2	26.5	15.6	4.1	1.9	0.8	0.1
	Kevin McHale	Celtics	11	1	34.2	20.7	6.5	1.8	0.5	1.3
	Šarūnas Marčiulionis	Warriors	9	0	22.9	13.2	2.6	3.0	1.2	0.1
1992	Clifford Robinson	Blazers	21	0	24.9	10.8	4.2	2.0	1.0	1.0
	Danny Ainge	Blazers	21	0	21.4	10.6	1.9	2.3	0.7	0.0
	John Williams	Cavaliers	17	0	33.4	15.0	7.6	2.5	1.4	1.0
	Tyrone Corbin	Jazz	16	0	27.9	11.3	5.5	1.1	0.8	0.2
	John Starks	Knicks	12	0	24.6	12.1	2.5	3.2	1.4	0.0
	Kevin McHale	Celtics	10	0	30.6	16.5	6.7	1.3	0.5	0.5
	Eddie Johnson	Sonics	9	0	27.4	18.4	3.0	0.9	0.3	0.3
	Nate McMillan	Sonics	9	2	27.3	9.6	3.7	7.0	1.8	0.3
	Dan Majerle	Suns	7	0	38.0	18.6	6.3	2.9	1.4	0.0
	Tom Chambers	Suns	7	0	27.7	15.6	4.4	2.7	0.3	0.7
1993	Anthony Mason	Knicks	15	0	34.0	12.5	7.3	2.7	0.7	0.4
	Dell Curry	Hornets	9	0	24.7	11.0	3.6	2.0	1.4	0.0

Year	Player	Team	G	GS	MPG	PPG	RPG	APG	SPG	BPG
	James Worthy	Lakers	5	0	29.6	13.8	3.4	2.6	1.0	0.0
	Tyrone Corbin	Jazz	5	0	32.2	11.8	7.6	1.8	0.6	0.2
1994	Sam Cassell	Rockets	22	0	21.7	9.4	2.7	4.2	1.0	0.2
	Brian Williams	Nuggets	12	0	24.1	9.3	7.4	0.9	0.3	0.9
	Robert Pack	Nuggets	12	0	27.7	11.8	2.3	4.3	1.5	0.5
	Toni Kukoč	Bulls	10	0	19.4	9.3	4.0	3.6	0.5	0.3
	A.C. Green	Suns	10	2	35.0	12.5	8.4	1.3	1.0	0.2
1995	Sam Cassell	Rockets	22	0	22.0	11.0	1.9	4.0	1.0	0.1
	Anthony Mason	Knicks	11	0	32.0	9.5	6.2	2.2	0.5	0.5
1996	Sam Perkins	Sonics	21	1	31.1	12.3	4.3	1.7	0.7	0.3
	Toni Kukoč	Bulls	15	5	29.3	10.8	4.2	3.9	0.9	0.3
	Sam Cassell	Rockets	8	0	25.8	10.4	2.1	4.3	0.8	0.1
	Chuck Person	Spurs	10	0	28.4	12.1	4.0	1.6	0.2	0.3
1997	Eddie Johnson[12]	Rockets	16	0	17.8	8.3	2.3	0.6	0.3	0.0
	John Starks	Knicks	9	1	28.1	14.0	3.4	2.8	1.1	0.0
	Danny Manning	Suns	5	0	23.2	13.2	6.0	1.4	0.8	1.4
1998	Dennis Rodman	Bulls	21	9	34.4	4.9	11.8	2.0	0.7	0.6
	Antonio Davis	Pacers	16	0	28.7	9.2	6.8	0.9	0.8	1.1
	Nick Van Exel	Lakers	13	0	28.2	11.6	2.5	4.2	0.6	0.1

	John Starks	Knicks	10	2	31.4	16.4	4.0	2.3	1.6	0.1
	Charles Barkley	Rockets	4	0	21.8	9.0	5.3	1.0	1.3	0.0
1999	Latrell Sprewell	Knicks	20	8	37.2	20.4	4.8	2.2	1.0	0.3
	Marcus Camby	Knicks	20	3	25.5	10.4	7.7	0.3	1.2	1.9
	Jalen Rose	Pacers	13	0	27.3	12.2	2.4	2.5	1.0	0.4
2000	Robert Horry	Lakers	23	0	26.9	7.6	5.3	2.5	0.9	0.8
	Anthony Carter	Heat	10	3	27.5	7.7	4.0	5.6	1.2	0.2
	Rodney Rogers	Suns	9	0	29.2	14.1	6.8	1.6	1.1	1.1
	Tim Thomas	Bucks	5	0	28.4	15.4	4.8	2.0	0.2	0.8
2001	Eric Snow	Sixers	23	9	31.2	9.3	3.7	4.5	1.2	0.1
	Tim Thomas	Bucks	18	0	26.6	11.3	4.5	1.6	0.5	0.6
	Glen Rice	Knicks	5	0	28.8	12.2	4.4	0.6	0.6	0.2
2002	Bobby Jackson	Kings	16	1	23.4	10.9	3.3	2.0	0.9	0.2
	Corliss Williamson	Pistons	10	0	26.9	13.3	5.3	1.0	0.9	0.2
	Malik Rose	Spurs	10	3	29.2	12.9	7.9	1.4	1.0	0.5
	Jamaal Magloire	Hornets	8	0	21.0	12.3	5.6	0.6	0.0	1.9
	Hakeem Olajuwon	Raptors	5	0	17.2	5.6	3.8	0.4	1.4	0.8
2003	Nick Van Exel	Mavericks	20	3	33.6	19.5	3.4	4.1	0.6	0.0
	Bobby Jackson	Kings	12	0	27.6	14.3	4.5	3.3	1.0	0.1
2004	Al Harrington	Pacers	16	2	26.7	9.5	6.4	0.8	1.4	0.6

Year	Player	Team	G	GS	MPG	PPG	RPG	APG	SPG	BPG
	Wally Szczerbiak	Timberwolves	12	0	24.8	11.8	3.3	1.7	0.5	0.2
	Brad Miller	Kings	12	0	30.5	10.5	8.7	3.2	0.8	0.9
	Manu Ginóbili	Spurs	10	0	28.0	13.0	5.3	3.1	1.7	0.1
2005	Jerry Stackhouse	Mavericks	13	0	31.0	16.1	4.1	2.3	0.6	0.2
	Antonio Daniels	Sonics	11	3	30.1	13.8	2.8	4.5	1.0	0.0
	Ricky Davis	Celtics	7	2	34.3	12.4	3.6	2.0	1.3	0.3
2006	Jerry Stackhouse	Mavericks	22	1	32.3	13.7	2.8	2.5	0.5	0.3
	Leandro Barbosa	Suns	20	3	31.6	14.2	1.6	2.7	0.8	0.2
	Donyell Marshall	Cavaliers	13	0	26.5	9.5	5.6	0.6	0.5	0.7
	Michael Finley	Spurs	13	4	31.6	10.5	3.8	1.4	0.6	0.2
	Corey Maggette	Clippers	12	2	24.3	15.3	7.3	1.4	0.6	0.4
	Antonio Daniels	Wizards	6	0	36.0	13.2	2.8	3.3	0.5	0.2
2007	Manu Ginóbili	Spurs	20	0	30.1	16.7	5.5	3.7	1.7	0.2
	Leandro Barbosa	Suns	11	1	31.7	15.8	3.5	2.2	1.1	0.2
	José Calderón	Raptors	6	1	24.3	13.0	1.7	5.3	0.8	0.0
2008	Manu Ginóbili	Spurs	17	6	32.9	17.8	3.8	3.9	0.6	0.3
	Reggie Evans	Sixers	6	0	24.7	6.8	7.8	0.5	0.8	0.0
2009	Lamar Odom	Lakers	23	5	32.0	12.3	9.1	1.8	0.7	1.3
	J.R. Smith	Hornets	16	0	27.2	14.9	3.3	2.8	1.1	0.3

	Jason Terry	Mavericks	10	1	32.5	14.3	2.8	1.9	0.6	0.3
	Kirk Hinrich	Bulls	7	0	30.0	12.6	2.7	2.9	1.7	0.4
2010	Jamal Crawford	Hawks	11	0	31.9	16.3	2.7	2.7	0.8	0.1
	Paul Millsap	Jazz	10	0	32.3	18.0	8.8	2.2	1.1	1.4
	Tony Parker	Spurs	10	2	33.5	17.3	3.8	5.4	0.6	0.0
	Jerryd Bayless	Blazers	6	2	27.7	13.5	2.7	3.8	0.3	0.0
	Jason Terry	Mavericks	6	0	29.0	12.7	2.5	2.0	0.7	0.2
2011	Jason Terry	Mavericks	21	0	32.6	17.5	1.9	3.2	1.2	0.1
	James Harden	Thunder	17	0	31.6	13.0	5.4	3.6	1.2	0.8
	Jamal Crawford	Hawks	12	0	29.8	15.4	1.3	2.5	0.8	0.3
	Lamar Odom	Lakers	10	1	28.6	12.1	6.5	2.1	0.2	0.4
	George Hill	Spurs	6	1	31.5	11.7	4.2	5.0	1.5	0.3
2012	James Harden	Thunder	20	0	31.5	16.3	5.1	3.4	1.6	0.1
	Manu Ginóbili	Spurs	14	2	27.9	14.4	3.5	4.0	0.7	0.3
	Andre Miller	Nuggets	7	0	28.6	11.3	5.6	6.0	1.3	0.1
	Taj Gibson	Bulls	6	0	22.8	9.5	6.5	0.7	0.7	1.7
2013	Ray Allen	Heat	23	0	24.9	10.2	2.8	1.3	0.5	0.1
	Manu Ginóbili	Spurs	21	3	26.7	11.5	3.7	5.0	1.1	0.3
	Jarrett Jack	Warriors	12	4	35.5	17.2	4.4	4.7	0.9	0.3
	Carl Landry	Warriors	12	3	20.5	11.8	5.2	1.4	0.6	0.2

Year	Player	Team	G	GS	MPG	PPG	RPG	APG	SPG	BPG
	Kevin Martin	Thunder	11	0	29.4	14.0	3.1	1.3	0.6	0.3
	Jason Terry	Celtics	6	1	31.5	12.0	2.2	2.0	0.7	0.3
	Andre Miller	Nuggets	6	0	25.7	14.0	3.3	3.8	0.3	0.0
2014	Manu Ginóbili	Spurs	23	0	25.5	14.3	3.3	4.1	1.6	0.1
	Jamal Crawford	Clippers	13	0	24.1	15.5	1.5	2.0	0.9	0.2
	Patrick Patterson	Raptors	7	0	28.4	10.4	6.7	1.3	0.4	0.4
	Tony Allen	Grizzlies	7	1	32.9	12.3	7.7	1.4	1.7	0.1
	Vince Carter	Mavericks	7	0	27.1	12.6	3.6	2.4	0.4	0.3
2015	Andre Iguodala	Warriors	21	3	30.2	10.4	4.5	3.6	1.2	0.3
	J.R. Smith	Cavaliers	18	4	31.1	12.8	4.7	1.2	0.9	0.6
	Otto Porter	Wizards	10	0	33.1	10.0	8.0	1.8	1.2	0.2
	Boris Diaw	Spurs	7	0	28.3	11.6	6.1	3.6	0.7	0.4
2016	Dennis Schröder	Hawks	10	0	19.1	11.7	1.9	3.6	0.4	0.1
	Jeremy Lin	Hornets	7	0	27.0	12.4	2.3	2.6	0.7	0.0
2017	Marcus Smart	Celtics	18	3	29.9	8.6	4.7	4.7	1.5	0.9
	Patty Mills	Spurs	16	6	26.0	10.3	2.1	2.7	0.8	0.1
	Pau Gasol	Spurs	16	7	22.8	7.7	7.1	1.9	0.4	0.9
	Joe Johnson	Jazz	11	2	29.6	12.9	3.2	3.9	2.5	0.5
	Eric Gordon	Rockets	11	2	32.5	12.9	3.5	3.9	2.0	0.7

	Lou Williams	Rockets	11	0	24.7	12.5	2.7	1.3	0.6	0.1
	Jamal Crawford	Clippers	7	0	28.0	12.6	1.3	1.9	0.6	0.1
2018	Marcus Morris	Celtics	19	4	29.6	12.4	5.4	1.1	0.4	0.3
	Eric Gordon	Rockets	17	2	32.3	15.4	2.6	1.6	0.6	0.5
	Marco Belinelli	Sixers	10	0	27.3	12.9	2.1	2.0	0.7	0.0
	Domantas Sabonis	Pacers	7	0	23.7	12.4	4.6	0.7	0.1	0.3
2019	Serge Ibaka	Raptors	24	0	20.8	9.4	6.0	0.9	0.5	1.0
	George Hill	Bucks	15	0	26.3	11.5	3.5	2.8	0.9	0.3
	Rudy Gay	Spurs	7	0	25.6	11.1	7.1	1.7	0.4	0.7
2020	Tyler Herro	Heat	21	5	33.6	16.0	5.1	3.7	0.4	0.1
	Rajon Rondo	Lakers	16	0	24.7	8.9	4.3	6.6	1.4	0.1
	Norman Powell	Raptors	11	0	24.8	13.4	2.4	1.0	0.5	0.3
	Serge Ibaka	Raptors	11	0	22.8	14.8	7.7	1.2	0.2	1.3
	Dennis Schröder	Thunder	7	0	32.4	17.3	3.7	3.6	0.6	0.1
	Jordan Clarkson	Jazz	7	0	28.6	16.7	3.4	2.1	0.9	0.0

Chapter Notes

Introduction

1. Alex Ward, "The Sixth Man," *New York Times*, March 4, 1984, section 6, 38.

2. The team's starting center, Marc Gasol, was acquired in the middle of the season and appeared in 26 games for the Raptors, playing 24.9 minutes per game.

3. You can find more on that in the Reddit post "[OC]: Toronto Had the Shortest Rotation of any Champion in 20+ Years" by u/0010001.

4. Terry Pluto, *Loose Balls: The Short, Wild Life of the American Basketball Association* (New York: Simon & Schuster, 2007), 367.

5. Kerry Eggers, *Jail Blazers: How the Portland Trail Blazers Became the Bad Boys of Basketball* (New York: Sports Publishing, 2018), 123.

6. David Halberstam, *The Breaks of the Game* (New York: Hyperion, 1981), 67.

7. Jackie MacMullan, Rafe Bartholomew, and Dan Klores, *Basketball: A Love Story* (New York: Broadway Books, 2018), 23.

8. MacMullan, et al., *Basketball: A Love Story*, 24.

9. Sam McManis, "Lakers Say Camp Riley Didn't Lead to Injuries," *Los Angeles Times*, June 13, 1989, Web.

10. Eggers, *Jail Blazers*, 265.

11. Andre Iguodala, *The Sixth Man* (New York: Blue Rider Press, 2019), 172.

12. Iguodala, *The Sixth Man*, 173–175.

13. Ralph Wiley, "And… it's Super Sub!" *Sports Illustrated*, May 11, 1987, 52.

Chapter 1

1. Sam Anderson, *Boom Town: The Fantastical Saga of Oklahoma City, Its Chaotic Founding… Its Purloined Basketball Team, and the Dream of Becoming a World-class Metropolis* (New York: Crown, 2018), 60–61.

2. Feinstein, John and Red Auerbach, *Let Me Tell You a Story: A Lifetime in the Game* (New York: Back Bay Books, 2004), 51.

3. Michael Schumacher, *Mr. Basketball: George Mikan, the Minneapolis Lakers, and the Birth of the NBA* (Minneapolis: University of Minnesota Press, 2007), 72.

4. UHP Staff, "The Trend of the Times: The Uline Arena," *The Ultimate History Project*, Web.

5. Feinstein and Auerbach, *Let Me Tell You a Story*, 46.

6. Charley Rosen, *The First Tip-Off: The Incredible Story of the Birth of the NBA* (New York: McGraw-Hill Education, 2008), 196.

7. Charley Rosen, *The Chosen Game: A Jewish Basketball History* (Lincoln: University of Nebraska Press, 2017), 62.

8. Rosen, *The First Tip-Off*, 87.

9. Not the original one established in 1898, because it ceased to exist in 1904. The one that merged with the BAA was established in 1935 as the Midwest Basketball Conference (MBC) but changed its name to the NBL two years later.

10. Gary M. Pomerantz, *The Last Pass: Cousy, Russell, the Celtics, and What Matters in the End* (New York: Penguin Press, 2018), 31.

11. Pomerantz, *The Last Pass*, 34–35.

12. William F. Reed, "Three Cheers!" *Sports Illustrated*, July 7, 1993, Web.

13. Pomerantz, *The Last Pass*, 105.

14. Frank Ramsey, "Smart Moves by a Master of Deception," *Sports Illustrated*, December 9, 1963, 57–63.

15. Pomerantz, *The Last Pass*, 146.

16. Pomerantz, *The Last Pass*, 243.

17. John Underwood, "The Green Running Machine," *Sports Illustrated*, October 28, 1974, 47.

18. Peter Carry, "They're Replaying the Sixth Man Theme," *Sports Illustrated*, November 13, 1972, 26.

19. Curry Kirkpatrick, "It's the End of a Long, Long Run," *Sports Illustrated*, April 10, 1978, 29.

Chapter 2

1. Bryant wore the number "8" in honor of his first basketball idol, Mike D'Antoni, which he later changed to "24" to underline his 24/7 work ethic.

2. Jonathan Abrams, *Boys Among Men: How the Prep-to-Pro Generation Redefined the NBA and Sparked a Basketball Revolution* (New York: Crown Archetype, 2016), 59–63.

3. Andrew van Buuren, *Between Dynasties: The Los Angeles Lakers in the years between Magic and Kobe* (Adelaide: Fletcher Thomas, 2018), 3.

4. Scott Davis, "Former NBA Coach Byron Scott Reveals the First Moment He Knew an 18-year-old Kobe Bryant Was Going to Take Over the League," *Business Insider*, December 19, 2017, Web.

5. Roland Lazenby, *Showboat: The Life of Kobe Bryant* (London: Orion Books, 2016), 251.

6. Lazenby. *Showboat*, 260.

7. Lazenby, *Showboat*, 268.

8. Paolo Uggetti, "Retracing the Histories of 'The Next Michael Jordan,'" *The Ringer*, May 4, 2020, Web.

9. Seth Davis, "Where Are They Now: Harold Miner," *Sports Illustrated*, July 7, 2014, 106.

10. Shaquille O'Neal, *Shaq Talks Back* (New York: St. Martin's Paperbacks, 2001), 95.

11. Phil Jackson, *The Last Season. A Team in Search of Its Soul* (New York: Penguin Press, 2004), 10.

12. Ian Thomsen, *The Soul of Basketball. The Epic Showdown Between LeBron, Kobe, Doc, and Dirk That Saved the NBA* (Boston: Houghton Mifflin Harcourt, 2018), 5.

13. Jack McCallum, *Seven Seconds or Less: My Season on the Bench with the Runnin' and Gunnin' Phoenix Suns* (New York: Touchstone, 2007), 23.

14. Dave McMenamin, "Unfounded Stigma Still Following Bryant," *ESPN*, May 17, 2010, Web.

15. Jack McCallum, "Chaos Theory," *Sports Illustrated*, February 25, 2013, 36.

16. Bill Plaschke, "This is Not the Steve Nash the Lakers Hoped For," *Los Angeles Times*, February 12, 2013, Web.

17. Back then the team that won three games in the first round progressed to the conference semifinals.

18. Dave Feschuk and Michael Grange, *Steve Nash: The Unlikely Ascent of a Superstar* (Toronto: Vintage Canada, 2014), 39.

19. Dan Woike, "Steve Nash Didn't Look Like a Hall of Famer When He Got to College," *Los Angeles Times*, September 7, 2018, Web.

20. Jack McCallum, *Seven Seconds or Less*, 160.

21. ESPN.com News Services, "Verbal Deal: Five Years, More Than $65M," *ESPN*, July 2, 2004, Web.

22. Monte Poole, "How Steve Nash Went from Traded After Two Seasons to Hall of Famer," *NBC Sports*, September 6, 2018, Web.

23. Lazenby, *Showboat*, 278.

24. Associated Press, "With $12-Million Deal, Prep Star is NBA Shoe-In," *Los Angeles Times*, June 19, 1997, Web.

25. Charlie Nobles, "A Hidden Agenda With the Magic," *New York Times*, February 9, 2003, Web.

26. Abrams, *Boys Among Men*, 83–85.

27. Franz Lidz, "Krause's Blocked-Buster Had Pippen Going Out, McGrady Coming In," *Chicago Sun-Times*, May 4, 2020, Web.

28. ESPN Archive, "Vince Carter and Tracy McGrady Interview (2016) / The Jump / ESPN Archive," *YouTube*, Uploaded: October 4, 2019.

29. Jackie MacMullan, "Friendly Rivals," *Sports Illustrated*, April 15, 1996, 64.

30. Abrams, *Boys Among Men*, 31.

31. Larry Bird, *Drive. The Story of My Life* (New York: Bantam Books, 1989), 174.

32. Feinstein and Auerbach, *Let Me Tell You a Story*, 155.

33. Years later another Celtics general manager, Danny Ainge, would also sell his first overall pick for the third selection in the 2017 NBA Draft and a future first-round pick, as he knew that he could take the

player that he wanted, Jayson Tatum, with that number. The team that made the trade, the Sixers, selected Markelle Fultz, who was traded one and a half seasons later to the Magic.

34. Irv Soonachan, "The Ballad of Joe Barry Carroll," *SLAM*, July 24, 2013, Web.

35. Peter May, *The Big Three. Larry Bird, Kevin McHale, and Robert Parish: The Best Frontcourt in the History of Basketball* (New York: Simon & Schuster, 1994), 139.

36. Alex Ward, "The Sixth Man," *New York Times*, March 4, 1984, section 6, 38.

37. Sam Goldaper, "McHale: Celtic Who Gives Rivals Fits," *New York Times*, May 27, 1985, section 1, 30.

38. David Halberstam, *Playing for Keeps: Michael Jordan and the World He Made* (New York: Broadway Books, 2000), 165.

39. Sam Smith, "The Bulls Sit at Picking Sixth in the Draft, But What Are the Odds at Moving Up?" *NBA.com*, May 2, 2018, Web.

40. Kelly Dwyer, "Sam Bowie Reveals That He Lied to Portland About Feeling Leg Pain Before the Infamous 1984 NBA Draft," *Yahoo! Sports*, December 11, 2012, Web.

41. Jack McCallum, "Ep1—Why I Had to Pull Out the Operation Card to Get Larry Bird," *The Dream Team Tapes* (podcast), May 18, 2020.

42. Curry Kirkpatrick, "The Big Brothers of Phi Slamma Jamma," *Sports Illustrated*, March 7, 1983, 33.

43. Jack McCallum, "Is Anybody Happy Here?" *Sports Illustrated*, January 16, 1989, 24.

44. Lowell Cohn, "Down Home Is Where Don Nelson Lives," *The Chicago Tribune*, May 27, 1990, Web.

45. Jonathan Warner, "Clyde Drexler Felt Trail Blazers Rebuilt Before His Trade Was Premature," *NBC Sports*, May 6, 2020, Web.

46. Eggers, *Jail Blazers*, 145.

47. Eggers, *Jail Blazers*, 240.

48. Actually that deal was a little bit more complicated, as the seven-year period takes into account the contract he already signed earlier, but there is no need to bore the reader with its details, as the deal ultimately amounted to $18 million for seven years.

49. Sam Smith, *The Jordan Rules: The Inside Story of a Turbulent Season with Michael Jordan and the Chicago Bulls* (New York: Simon & Schuster, 1992), 73.

50. Adrian Wojnarowski, "Jerry Krause joins Woj," *The Woj Pod* (podcast), February 1, 2017.

51. Halberstam, *Playing for Keeps*, 222.

52. Although Halberstam claims that he was rather skeptical (224).

53. Halberstam, *Playing for Keeps*, 227–228.

54. Smith, *The Jordan Rules*, 30.

Chapter 3

1. Eggers, *Jail Blazers*, 43.

2. Anderson, *Boom Town*, 27.

3. Jordan Ritter Conn, "How the Hornets and Hurricane Katrina Paved the Way for OKC Thunder," *The Ringer*, October 24, 2019, Web.

4. Anderson, *Boom Town*, 41.

5. Ray Allen, *From the Outside. My Journey Through Life and the Game I Love* (New York: Dey St., 2018), 176.

6. Kelly Dwyer, "Detlef Schrempf on the Former Seattle SuperSonics: 'We Gave [the Team] Away. We Screwed up,'" *Yahoo! Sports*, June 13, 2012, Web.

7. Anderson, *Boom Town*, 43–44.

8. Eggers, *Jail Blazers*, 145.

9. Eggers, *Jail Blazers*, 146.

10. Eggers, *Jail Blazers*, 215–216.

11. George Karl, *Furious George* (New York: Harper Collins, 2017), 173.

12. Alexander Wolff, "Two Bits, Four Bits, Six Bits, A Deutsche Mark!" *Sports Illustrated*, March 12, 1984, 47.

13. Wolff, "Two Bits…," 47.

14. Sam Goldaper, "N.B.A. 1985–86; Sizable Additions Promise a Higher Level of Play," *New York Times*, October 21, 1985, section c, 10.

15. Jack McCallum, "How Bad Can It Get?" *Sports Illustrated*, January 18, 1993, 87.

16. Hank Hersch, "Fast New Pace," *Sports Illustrated*, January 1, 1990, 36.

17. Phil Taylor, "Wide Awake in Seattle," *Sports Illustrated*, December 6, 1993, 30.

18. Jim Cour, "Shawn Kemp Upset About New NBA Millionaires," *AP News*, October 23, 1996, Web.

19. Karl, *Furious George*, 208.

20. Interestingly, team GM Wally Walker

said, "We didn't get McIlvaine to be a Shaq-stopper."

21. Karl, *Furious George*, 206–207.

22. Phil Taylor, "Spotlight: Jim McIlvaine," *Sports Illustrated*, November 11, 1996, 124.

23. Taylor, "Spotlight: Jim McIlvaine," 124.

24. Chris Baker, "Kemp Is Key Player in Three-Way Trade," *Los Angeles Times*, September 26, 1997, Web.

25. L. Jon Wetheim, "#5 Seattle Super-Sonics," *Sports Illustrated*, February 8, 1999, 94.

26. Anderson, *Boom Town*, 49.

27. Pete Thamel, "James Harden's Style at Guard Masks His Ability at Arizona State," *New York Times*, March 19, 2009, Web.

28. Jonathan Givony, "James Harden. College Road Report: Arizona State vs. UCLA & USC," *DraftExpress*, March 22, 2009, Web.

29. Anderson, *Boom Town*, 10.

30. Howard Beck, "Standing Out and Blending In," *New York Times*, May 26, 2012, Web.

31. Dan Feldman, "Failed Promise of the Thunder," *Yahoo! Sports*, July 12, 2019, Web.

32. Anderson, *Boom Town*, 73.

33. Andrew Sharp, "Let Us Step Back and Appreciate James Harden," *Sports Illustrated*, January 28, 2019, 69.

Chapter 4

1. Ethan Sherwood Strauss, *The Victory Machine: The Making & Unmaking of the Warriors Dynasty* (New York: Public Affairs, 2020), 105.

2. Associated Press, "Gary Payton Back with Celtics," *ESPN*, March 5, 2005, Web.

3. Marc Stein, "Finley Chooses Spurs over Heat, Suns," *ESPN*, August 31, 2005, Web.

4. Shawn Fury, *Rise and Fire* (New York: Flatiron Books, 2016), 211.

5. Fury, *Rise and Fire*, 201.

6. Halberstam, *Breaks of the Game*, 183.

7. Curry Kirkpatrick, "Shoot if You Must… I Must, Says McAdoo," *Sports Illustrated*, March 8, 1976, 26.

8. Pomerantz, *The Last Pass*, 227.

9. Bruce Newman, "Mac Has Been a Real Blast from the Past," *Sports Illustrated*, May 24, 1982, 43.

10. Sam McManis and Randy Harvey, "NBA Notebook: Jones, Auerbach Criticize McAdoo; Say He's 'Desperate for a Contract,'" *Los Angeles Times*, June 5, 1985, Web.

11. Michael Lee, "Former Wizard Mitch Richmond Elected to Basketball Hall of Fame," *Washington Post*, April 8, 2014, Web.

12. Associated Press, "Richmond Traded to Kings for the Rights to Billy Owens," *Los Angeles Times*, November 2, 1991, Web.

13. Jackie McMullan, "Inside the NBA," *Sports Illustrated*, March 9, 1998, 100.

14. James Ham, "Mitch Richmond Recalls Beating Kings with Lakers in 2002 NBA Finals," *NBC Sports*, April 30, 2020, Web.

Chapter 5

1. Jackson, *The Last Season*, 147.

2. Johnette Howard, "Sam I Am," *Sports Illustrated*, November 13, 1995, 84.

3. William C. Rhoden, "Forget the Centers, Study the Guards," *New York Times*, June 9, 1994, section b, 16.

4. Clifton Brown, "Knicks Take a Tumble, Right Back Into the Pressure Cooker," *New York Times*, June 13, 1994, section c, 1.

5. Chris Baker, "Mister Robinson Indeed!" *Los Angeles Times*, April 25, 1994, Web.

6. Jonathan Feigen, "'He Put on a Clinic': When Hakeem Olajuwon Upstaged David Robinson," *Houston Chronicle*, May 22, 2020, Web.

7. Phil Taylor, "Rocketing into History," *Sports Illustrated*, June 26, 1995, 48.

8. Mike Wise, "It Must Be June: The Lakers' Horry Comes Alive," *New York Times*, June 11, 2001, section d, 5.

9. Robert Horry, "How to Be a Big Shot." *The Players' Tribune*, June 12, 2015, Web.

10. Horry, "How to Be a Big Shot."

11. Howard Beck, "It's Horry, Yet Again, Who Hits the Big Shot," *New York Times*, June 20, 2005, Web.

12. Liz Robbins, "Thanks for Everything Mom (the Jumper, Too)," *New York Times*, May 13, 2007, Web.

13. McCallum, *Seven Seconds or Less*, 201.

14. McCallum, *Seven Seconds or Less*, 152.

15. Thayer Evans, "Diaw, the Second

Option, Saves the Suns in Game 1," *New York Times*, May 25, 2006, Web.

16. Marc Stein, "Suns get High-Scoring Richardson," *ESPN*, December 11, 2008, Web.

17. Andrew Sharp, "The Boris Experience," *Sports Illustrated*, May 9, 2016, 40.

18. Nate Robinson, *Heart over Height* (Morrisville: Lulu Publishing, 2014), 50.

19. Robinson, *Heart over Height*, 51.

20. Howard Beck, "Salvaging a Season, Whatever the Cost," *New York Times*, December 30, 2009, Web.

21. Robinson, *Heart over Height*, vii.

Chapter 6

1. Adrian Wojnarowski, "Grant Hill," *The Woj Pod* (podcast), August 23, 2018.

2. Scott Howard-Cooper, "Magic Reappears: It's 'Go Time': Magic Moment Finally Happens," *Los Angeles Times*, January 30, 1996, Web.

3. Jackie MacMullan, "Memo to Magic," *Sports Illustrated*, May 13, 1996, 80.

4. Brian Windhorst, "Three Days in July: The High-Stakes Maneuvers That Assembled LeBron, Wade and Bosh," *ESPN*, June 29, 2020, Web.

5. Scott Powers, "Bulls' Derrick Rose Tears ACL," *ESPN*, April 28, 2012, Web.

6. Walton was actually taller, but he made it a point to be perceived as not a seven-footer.

7. Halberstam, *Breaks of the Game*, 77.

8. Clay Skipper, "The Thing Bill Walton Still Can't Forgive Himself For," *GQ*, March 26, 2016, Web.

9. Sam Anderson, "Bill Walton's Long, Strange Tale of N.B.A. Survival," *New York Times*, March 25, 2016, Web.

10. Halberstam, *Breaks of the Game*, 65.

11. Halberstam, *Breaks of the Game*, 107.

12. With a short break for the "Jail Blazers" era in the early 2000s

13. Eric Neel, "Blaze of Glory," *ESPN*, 2007, Web.

14. John Papanek, "Climbing to the Top Again," *Sports Illustrated*, October 15, 1979, 110.

15. Arash Markazi, "Bill Walton Still Blames Self for Clippers' Departure from San Diego," *ESPN*, August 26, 2016, Web.

16. Frederick Waterman, "Walton Trade to Celtics Highlights NBA Wheeling and Dealing," *Los Angeles Times*, October 20, 1985, Web.

17. Ryan, Bob and Jeff Goodman, "Bill Walton Interview: Favorite John Wooden + Larry Bird Memories," *Bob Ryan & Jeff Goodman NBA Podcast* (podcast), May 11, 2020.

18. Halberstam, *Playing for Keeps*, 163.

19. S.L. Price, "The Man in the Iron Mask," *Sports Illustrated*, March 30, 1995, 74.

20. Phil Taylor, "Learning Center," *Sports Illustrated*, October 11, 1993, 76.

21. Alonzo Mourning, *Resilience* (New York: Ballantine Books, 2009), 13.

22. Harvey Aaraton, "A Mighty Tree Grows in Georgetown. It Belongs to Patrick Ewing and Alonzo Mourning," *New York Times*, January 3, 2019, Web.

23. Mike Wise, "Kidney Failure Imperils Career of Spurs' Elliott," *New York Times*, July 22, 1999, section d, 4.

24. Mourning, *Resilience*, 6.

25. Jason Diamos, "As His Body Breaks Down, Mourning Looks for Relief," *New York Times*, December 10, 2004, Web.

26. Liz Robbins, "Mourning Fires Shots at Nets in His Return to New Jersey," *New York Times*, March 4, 2005, Web.

27. Ian Thomsen, "The Strife of Riley," *Sports Illustrated*, December 19, 2005, 60.

28. MacMahon, Tim and Marc Stein, "Free Throws, Hotel Switches and the 'Phantom Call': An Oral History of the 2006 NBA Finals," *ESPN*, June 18, 2016, Web.

29. Associated Press, "Heat's Mourning Tears Knee Tendon While Playing Defense vs. Hawks," *ESPN*, December 20, 2007, Web.

Chapter 7

1. Sam Goldaper, "Bobby Jones: A First-Class Sixth Man," *New York Times*, February 1, 1981, section 5, 1.

2. A.J. Neuharth-Keusch, "Isaiah Thomas: Celtics Must 'Bring the Brinks Truck' to Re-sign Him Next Summer," *USA Today*, December 17, 2019, Web.

3. Ohm Youngmisuk, "Magic Johnson: Trade With Cavs Positions Lakers to Take Next Step," *ESPN*, February 8, 2018, Web.

4. Karl, *Furious George*, 283.

5. Harvey Aaraton, "Carmelo Anthony:

The Square Peg Superstar," *New York Times*, November 16, 2018, Web.

6. Baxter Holmes, "Carmelo Anthony Finally Feels Like He Belongs Again with the Blazers," *ESPN*, May 29, 2020, Web.

7. Scoop Jackson, "Allen Iverson Speaks out About the Pistons," *ESPN*, October 1, 2009, Web.

8. Paul Sancya, "Iverson 'Insulted' by Decision to Have Him Come off the Bench," *USA Today*, April 15, 2004, Web.

9. Marc J. Spears, "The Answer to 'The Answer,'" *The Undefeated*, September 8, 2016, Web.

10. Tom D'Angelo, "Heat's Dion Waiters Reacts to Fans Who Suggest He Comes off the Bench," *Palm Beach Post*, December 9, 2017, Web.

11. SLAM Staff, "Byron Scott Is Not Impressed with J.J. Hickson," *SLAM*, October 22, 2010, Web.

12. SLAM Staff, "Antawn Jamison Unhappy with Bench Role," *SLAM*, October 27, 2010, Web.

13. Bill Lubinger, "Rough Stretch Doesn't Have Cleveland Cavaliers GM Chris Grant Ready to Make Drastic Changes," *Cleveland.com*, December 11, 2010, Web.

14. SLAM Staff, "Tyrus Thomas Unhappy with Bench Role," *SLAM*, October 20, 2009, Web.

15. Sam Quinn, "Michael Jordan Traded Laron Profit from Wizards in 2001 Just for Trash-talking Him, Richard Hamilton Says," *CBS Sports*, May 29, 2020, Web.

16. Rob Maddi, "Collins Feels Jordan's Pain," *USA Today*, November 29, 2001, Web.

17. Feinstein and Auberbach, *Let Me Tell You a Story*, 215.

18. Roland Lazenby, *Michael Jordan: The Life* (Little, Brown and Company, 2015), Kindle Edition.

19. Ben Pickman, "Jerry Stackhouse Says He Wishes He Never Played With Wizards, Michael Jordan," *Sports Illustrated*, April 8, 2020, Web.

20. Associated Press, "MJ, They Hardly Knew You," *Los Angeles Times*, April 13, 2003, Web.

Chapter 8

1. Zach Lowe., "538's Chris Herring on Sixth Man of the Year," *The Lowe Post Show* (podcast), July 23, 2020.

2. Ward, "Sixth Man."

3. Sports People, "Pistons Reach Accord With Vinne Johnson," *New York Times*, October 20, 1990, section 1, 44.

4. Sam Goldaper, "Pistons Tie Series As Backup Hits 34," *New York Times*, May 6, 1985, section c, 3.

5. Andy Katz, "Smith Shining as Shooter," *ESPN*, June 16, 2004, Web.

6. Marc Stein, "Bulls to Deal Chandler to Hornets for Brown, Smith," *ESPN*, July 5, 2006, Web.

7. Mark Kiszla, "George the Ripper at it Again," *Denver Post*, May 1, 2007, Web.

8. Howard Beck, "A Changed Smith Gets Sixth Man Honor," *New York Times*, April 22, 2013, Web.

9. Kevin Pelton, "Is 2013–14 Worst Rookie Class Ever?" *ESPN*, April 2, 2014, Web.

10. Chris Ballard, "Bad Return on Investment," *Sports Illustrated*, December 22, 2003, 60.

11. Howard Beck, "Fracture for Crawford; Crisis for Thomas," *New York Times*, February 28, 2007, Web.

12. A record since beaten by LeBron James.

13. Chris Ballard, "Jamal Crawford: Last of the Ballers," *Sports Illustrated*, October 24, 2017, Web.

14. Marc J. Spears, "The Legend of Lou Williams Just Can't Stop—And It Won't Stop," *The Undefeated*, March 2, 2017, Web.

15. Spears, "The Legend...."

16. Marc J. Spears, "Why Lou Williams Embraced NBA Life as Bench Player," *The Undefeated*, March 12, 2019, Web.

17. Spears, "Why Lou Williams...."

18. Barnes, Matt and Stephen Jackson, "Lou Williams / Ep 5 / Clippers, Kawhi & PG, Undefeated GOAT & Iverson," *All the Smoke* (podcast), November 21, 2019.

19. Barnes and Jackson, *All the Smoke*.

Chapter 9

1. B. David Zarley, "'85 NBA Draft Revisited: The Strange Phantom Drafting of Arvydas Sabonis," *Vice*, June 24, 2015, Web.

2. Eggers, *Jail Blazers*, 11.

3. Eggers, *Jail Blazers*, 75.

4. Richard Hoffer, "A Cliffhanger," *Sports Illustrated*, February 22, 1993, 42.

5. Eggers, *Jail Blazers*, 50.

6. Casey Holdahl, "Clifford Robinson, A Player Before his Time, Passes Away Too Soon," *NBA.com*, August 29, 2020, Web.

7. Alexander Wolff, "The Toni Award," *Sports Illustrated*, June 22, 1992, 56.

8. Halberstam, *Playing for Keeps*, 285.

9. Smith, *The Jordan Rules*, 146.

10. Smith, *The Jordan Rules*, 147.

11. Harvey Araton, "A Fearless Kukoč Joins N.B.A," *New York Times*, October 10, 1993, section 8, 1.

12. Al Harvin, "After 3 Years, Bulls Finally Sign Kukoč," *New York Times*, July 20, 1993, section 8, 8.

13. Ian Thomsen, "American Dream," *New York Times*, December 12, 1992, Web.

14. Halberstam, *Playing for Keeps*, 287.

15. Eggers, *Jail Blazers*, 21.

16. MacMullan, et al., *Basketball*, 372.

17. Jonathan Abrams, "Arvydas Sabonis' Long, Strange Trip," *Grantland*, August 29, 2011, Web.

18. Eggers, *Jail Blazers*, 20–21.

19. Abrams, "Arvydas Sabonis' Long Strange Trip."

20. MacMullan, et al., *Basketball*, 373.

21. Eggers, *Jail Blazers*, 22.

22. L. Jon Wertheim, "Flight of the Birdman," *Sports Illustrated*, October 5, 2009, 62.

23. Wertheim, "Flight of the Birdman," 63.

Chapter 10

1. Bill Plaschke, "Boykins Is Tiny but Not Small," *New York Times*, November 20, 2001, Web.

2. Scott Howard-Cooper, "The Bench Mark," *Los Angeles Times*, May 25, 1989, Web.

3. Curtis Harris, "The Hall of Fame Case for Bobby Jones / Defensive Brilliance," *NBA.com*, March 13, 2019, Web.

4. Sam Goldaper, "Bobby Jones: A First-Class Sixth Man," *New York Times*, February 1, 1981, section 5, 1.

5. Sam Goldaper, "No. 1 Draft Pick Goes to Clippers," *New York Times*, May 22, 1988, section 8, 6.

6. Allen, *From the Outside*, 142–143.

7. Scott Agnes, "'He Was the Guy that Made the Machine Go': How Nate McMillan Was Molded into a Coach," *The Athletic*, April 30, 2020, Web.

8. Bob Baum, "Rogers Living Good Life in Phoenix," *Los Angeles Times*, April 16, 2000, Web.

9. Baum, "Rogers Living Good Lie in Phoenix."

10. This John Williams is a different player from the one mentioned above. The one playing for the Bullets was a small forward picked in 1986, while this one is the center who was drafted in 1985 and played mostly for the Cleveland Cavaliers. While the latter was nicknamed "Hot Rod," the former earned the nickname "Hot Plate" for his eating disorder and remains the only player in league history to be suspended by his team for being overweight.

11. The 1985 postseason is the first for which the data regarding playoff starts is available (at least on Basketball Reference, by far the best basketball website in the world), hence the reason why I start with that year.

12. While these stats may not look that impressive at first sight, it is important to note that Johnson was 37 years old at the time,

Bibliography

Books

Abrams, Jonathan. *Boys Among Men. How the Prep-to-Pro Generation Redefined the NBA and Sparked a Basketball Revolution.* New York: Crown Archetype, 2016.

Allen, Ray. *From the Outside. My Journey Through Life and the Game I Love.* New York: Dey St., 2018.

Anderson, Sam. *Boom Town: The Fantastical Saga of Oklahoma City, Its Chaotic Founding … Its Purloined Basketball Team, and the Dream of Becoming a World-class Metropolis.* New York: Crown, 2018.

Bird, Larry. *Drive. The Story of My Life.* London: Bantam Books, 1989.

Eggers, Kerry. *Jail Blazers: How the Portland Trail Blazers Became the Bad Boys of Basketball.* New York: Sports Publishing, 2018.

Feinstein, John and Red Auerbach. *Let Me Tell You a Story: A Lifetime in the Game.* New York: Back Bay Books, 2004.

Feschuk, Dave and Michael Grange. *Steve Nash: The Unlikely Ascent of a Superstar.* Toronto: Vintage Canada, 2013.

Fury, Shawn. *Rise and Fire.* New York: Flatiron Books, 2016.

Goldsberry, Kirk. *Sprawlball.* Boston and New York: Houghton Mifflin Harcourt, 2019.

Halberstam, David. *The Breaks of the Game.* New York: Hyperion, 1981.

______. *Playing for Keeps. Michael Jordan & the World He Made.* New York: Broadway Books, 1999.

Iguodala, Andre. *The Sixth Man.* New York: Blue Rider Press, 2019.

Jackson, Phil. *The Last Season: A Team in Search of Its Soul.* New York: Penguin Press, 2004.

Karl, George. *Furious George: My Forty Years Surviving NBA Divas, Clueless GMs, and Poor Shot Selection.* New York: HarperCollins, 2017.

Lazenby, Roland. *Michael Jordan: The Life.* Boston: Little, Brown and Company, 2015.

______. *Showboat. The Life of Kobe Bryant.* London: Orion Books, 2016.

MacMullan, Jackie, Rafe Bartholomew, and Dan Klores. *Basketball: A Love Story.* New York: Broadway Books, 2018.

May, Peter. *The Big Three: Larry Bird, Kevin McHale, and Robert Parish: The Best Frontcourt in the History of Basketball.* New York: Simon & Schuster, 1994.

McCallum, Jack. *Seven Seconds or Less: My Season on the Bench with the Runnin' and Gunnin' Phoenix Suns.* New York: Touchstone, 2007.

Mourning, Alonzo. *Resilience.* New York: Ballantine Books, 2009.

O'Neal, Shaquille. *Shaq Talks Back.* New York: St. Martin's Press, 2001.

Pluto, Terry. *Loose Balls: The Short Wild Life of the American Basketball Association.* New York: Simon & Schuster, 1990.

Pomerantz, Gary M. *The Last Pass: Cousy, Russell, the Celtics, and What Matters in the End.* New York: Penguin Press, 2018.

Robinson, Nate. *Heart over Height.* Morrisville: Lulu Publishing, 2014.

Rosen, Charley. *The Chosen Game: A Jewish Basketball History.* Lincoln and London: University of Nebraska Press, 2017.

______. *The First Tip-Off: The Incredible Story of the Birth of the NBA.* New York: McGraw-Hill Education, 2008.

Schumacher, Michael. *Mr. Basketball:*

George Mikan, the Minneapolis Lakers, and the Birth of the NBA. Minneapolis: University of Minnesota Press, 2007.

Smith, Sam. *The Jordan Rules: The Inside Story of a Turbulent Season with Michael Jordan and the Chicago Bulls*. New York: Simon & Schuster, 1992.

Strauss, Ethan Sherwood. *The Victory Machine: The Making & Unmaking of the Warriors Dynasty*. New York: Public Affairs, 2020.

Thomsen, Ian. *The Soul of Basketball: The Epic Showdown Between LeBron, Kobe, Doc and Dirk That Saved the NBA*. New York: Houghton Mifflin Harcourt, 2018.

van Buuren, Andrew. *Between Dynasties: The Los Angeles Lakers in the Years Between Magic and Kobe*. Adelaide: Fletcher Thomas, 2018.

Magazines and Websites

Associated Press ap.org
Business Insider businessinsider.com
Chicago Sun-Times chicago.suntimes.com
The Chicago Tribune chicagotribune.com
Cleveland.com
DraftExpress draftexpress.com
ESPN espn.com
Fox Sports foxsports.com
GQ gq.com
Grantland grantland.com
Houston Chronicle chron.com
Los Angeles Times latimes.com
NBA nba.com
NBC Sports nbcsports.com
The New York Times nytimes.com
Palm Beach Post palmbeachpost.com
The Players' Tribune theplayerstribune.com
The Ringer theringer.com
SB Nation sbnation.com
SLAM slamonline.com
Slate slate.com
Sports Illustrated si.com
The Ultimate History Project ultimatehistoryproject.com
The Undefeated theundefeated.com
UPI upi.com
USA Today usatoday.com
Vice vice.com
The Washington Post washingtonpost.com
Yahoo! Sports sports.yahoo.com

Podcasts

Barnes, Matt, and Stephen Jackson. *All the Smoke.*
Lowe, Zack. *The Lowe Post.*
McCallum, Jack. *The Dream Team Tapes.*
Ryan, Bob, and Jeff Goodman. *Bob Ryan & Jeff Goodman NBA Podcast.*
Wojnarowski, Adrian. *The Woj Pod.*

Index